Curry, Chaos and Love

The Story Of An Irish Girl's
Life-Changing Journey To India

Elizabeth O'Brien

ORLA
KELLY
PUBLISHING

Orla Kelly Publishing
27 Kilbrody,
Mount Oval,
Rochestown,
Cork,
Ireland.

To Alex, my rock and my love...
if it wasn't for you, I might actually
have done some yoga in India!

TABLE OF CONTENTS

Chapter 1

Why India?

September 2007

'Ma'am, would you like some tea or coffee? MA'AM!'
Fumbling with my eye-mask, I peered up at the demanding stewardess.

'Coffee, please,' I replied, pulling down my table top and rubbing my eyes. I hadn't slept well and, whether from nerves or the horrendous plane food, my stomach was in bits. Great stuff, I hadn't even landed yet and already some kind of gut-wrenching disease seemed imminent.

Why oh why had I decided to take off halfway across the globe, to a place that, quite literally, seemed to scare the crap out of me? With a yawn I considered, for about the hundredth time, the question that had plagued me this past year: why India?

Why India, when organising the visa, buying a mosquito net and booking accommodation nearly made me cry? Why India, when the thought of arriving there and coping on my own created a blank expanse of terror before my eyes? Why India, when the only (impossibly vague) reason I could ever give was 'I just have to go'?

I mean sure, I was a wanderer, the lure of new lands was as exciting to me as those initial heady stages of falling in love; the thrill of arriving to a country where everything is curious and different; reinventing yourself in order to navigate incomprehensible languages and unfamiliar streets; discovering the world anew through exotic sights and sounds and smells ... Travel brought me alive in a way little else could and I had spent the first few years of my early twenties indulging in my passion for it with au-pair jobs in Paris and northern Italy. I then spent a year as a nanny/bartender in the South of France where my brother also lived before finally venturing off completely alone to Spain, settling in the beautiful coastal city of Valencia for a year.

The years I spent exploring the Mediterranean were a joy, filled with croissants, Irish pubs, romantic languages and great memories. But staying in Europe always felt like the safe, easy option. The notion of travelling to India, on the other hand, filled me with excited dread. It was as big and daunting a challenge as I could possibly think to undertake by myself, something I wasn't actually even sure I could do. And that was, perhaps, one of the reasons I eventually decided I had to do it: just to prove to myself I could.

I still remember the exact moment the idea entered my mind.

Fifteen months earlier ...

'What's got you in a tizzy then, Lizzy?' Alan, a burly teacher from Liverpool, was on his usual stool at the bar, cracking open a packet of crisps while I poured his pint of Guinness.

'I'm bored,' I declared, topping up the creamy stout and handing it to him before leaning against the counter and resting my chin on my hands. 'I think I've outgrown my time in Spain – maybe it's time to move on again.'

'Well! Lizzy's bored. What are we gonna do about that, eh, chief?' He elbowed his mate, Noel, sitting beside him. The two English lads were expats living in the Spanish coastal city of Valencia. They were also long-time regulars at St Pat's Irish Pub, where I'd been working for the past eight months.

'If you feel like moving on then I say do it.' Noel winked at me with a grin. 'What are you hanging around here for, dealing with drunken brutes like us all the time? Pack your bags and start your next adventure.'

'Yeah, bugger off!' Alan agreed, taking a sup of his drink. The corners of his mouth twitched.

'Alright then, where exactly should I *bugger off* to?'

Noel paused with his drink mid-air, looking at me thoughtfully.

'Go to India!' he said suddenly, before taking a swig of his beer. He lowered the glass and wiped the cream from his moustache with a smile. 'Yeah, you'd love it. Sorted me right out.'

'Don't know if I'd go that far, chief. You're still bloody mental.'

'Alright, mate, I was only there a few months,' Noel said defensively and Alan sniggered into his pint. 'Still reckon you should go, Liz. It's the best thing I've ever done.'

Before I could respond, new customers arrived and work became too busy for chit-chat. The seed of my trip to India had been planted and it instantly took root.

At first I innocently assumed it would be much the same as country-hopping around the EU and so, when it turned out that travelling to India solo was in fact a lot more complicated and daunting than anticipated (vaccines? visas?

malaria?), I chickened out and returned to Ireland instead. Trying to ignore the idea, however, left me distinctly and unfathomably dissatisfied: quite simply, India was calling me and she wouldn't stop until I'd answered her, respectfully and in person. It took a full year for my courage to catch up with my wanderlust but when at last it did, I bit the bullet and booked my flights to Mumbai.

It was time. I was ready. Sort of.

I shared an emotional goodbye with my parents at the airport – I think all three of us feared for my life in one way or another.

'Mind yourself!' my dad said gruffly, giving me one of his characteristic hugs. If trees could hug, they'd feel like his, rough and awkward but full of love.

'Thanks, Dad, don't worry,' I said, resisting a strong urge to head back home with them in the car and forget the whole crazy idea. 'It'll be fine. I'll be fine,' I tried to reassure us all. A second later I was engulfed by my tearful mum.

'Call us when you get there. Have a great time!' she wept.

'I will, Mum,' I mumbled into her shoulder. 'I'll be fine,' I repeated pointlessly.

I untangled myself from her embrace and headed off to security, butterflies doing a samba in my stomach. The journey had begun.

I may have been twenty-four years old but as I set off to London Heathrow to catch my connecting flight to Mumbai, I felt small and fearful, like a lost child. The woman at the check-in desk was very reassuring. 'You're going to India by yourself? Aren't you scared?'

Cheers, darling. Collecting my boarding pass, I managed a weak smile. The butterflies in my stomach had switched to doing somersaults, like gymnasts on speed. Was that vomit at the back of my throat? Oh, help!

* * *

Sipping the bitter coffee, I gazed out of the plane's window at the rugged, arid terrain below and realised that this was the farthest I'd ever been from home and arrival time to Mumbai's Chhatrapati Shivaji airport was fast approaching. My stomach did an excited little flip and now I really felt like I might poop my pants. The plane began its descent and suddenly I could make out buildings and trees and, to one side, the ocean.

'Oh crap,' I thought, as the plane finally landed and taxied down the runway. 'There's no going back now.'

Unbeknownst to me, however, the universe was looking down kindly on my utter terror. As we disembarked the plane and wandered towards passport control, a tall guy with milky white skin and long, grungy hair glanced over at me and smiled hello.

'Hey, you been here before?'

An Irishman, I knew it before he spoke. There was something about his overall demeanour that felt deeply familiar, to say nothing of his pale skin.

'No, first time,' I replied with a nervous laugh.

The guy shrugged. 'Me too, but I've already been around Thailand, Laos and Cambodia,' he said, in a tone that I interpreted was meant to be off-hand and show what a well-seasoned traveller he was. Yet I sensed an endearing innocence as he fidgeted with his *Lonely Planet* guide. (Remember, we were travelling in 2007 in the days before smartphones and free Wi-Fi, when the world wasn't always accessible at the press of a button. A golden era, I do believe, aside from having to carry that brick of a guidebook in my backpack. But I digress. Back to Mumbai airport and this friendly, *Lonely Planet*-carrying lad.) He looked to be in his late twenties or early thirties and had a reassuringly soft Irish accent and open smile. I found myself drawn to this potential travel buddy, like a drowning swimmer to a buoy.

We shuffled along through a terminal that looked much like the ones I'd left back home but I was only too aware that on the other side of those big dusty windows was a completely different world. The first hints of it so far were dark-skinned men in regal turbans, older stern-faced women dressed in elegant saris, and a subtle hint of incense or musky perfume. My excitement and terror grew steadily.

'Have you sorted out where you're staying?' the guy asked as we turned a corner and joined hordes of other people waiting to go through passport control.

'Yeah, I reserved a room online. Couldn't arrange airport pick-up, but it's meant to be really close to the airport.'

'Aw man, why are you staying so far away from Colaba? That's where I'm headed, it's like Mumbai central.'

'Oh yes, Colaba …'

A vague memory of someone suggesting it as the back-packer hub of Mumbai flitted through my mind and I cursed myself for not having paid more attention.

'Well, I only paid a deposit – four euros, I think,' I said as we inched our way to the front of the queue.

'Sure, that's nothing. Forget about it and share a cab with me into the city. I haven't booked anywhere to stay, we can look for something together.'

It took less than a second for me to decide: negotiate a taxi on my own to some random hotel miles away from the city centre, or share a cab with a fellow Irish backpacker into the renowned tourist hub of Mumbai.

'Alright, cool. I'm Liz, by the way,' I said, holding out my hand.

'Paul,' he answered, with a firm handshake.

Without a second thought, I accepted him as my trustworthy travel partner, a silent prayer of thanks sent heavenwards; now, at last, I felt ready for my introduction to the vast subcontinent.

Passport stamped – check. Luggage not detoured to Kuala Lumpur as feared – check. Euros changed to Indian rupees – check. Ticket for prepaid taxi – check. Overwhelmed by touts, noise, heat and chaos – check. Welcome to India, Liz!

The drive to Colaba lasted around an hour in our 'AC' cab (which apparently just meant windows open). Interestingly, in India the rules of the road appear to be like those of a car-racing game I used to play on my phone – take the fastest route to your destination, earning bonus points for overtaking and shortcuts, and don't forget to beep, loudly, incessantly and quite aggressively. You get extra lives for that (and I'm not just talking about the game here).

Eventually, I surrendered to the wild and reckless driving and turned my attention to observing India as she whizzed past us. After all the books, pictures and documentaries, it was mind-blowing to finally be here in person.

Entire communities living in flimsy, tumble-down shacks lined the busy, dirty main road. Taking in this unfamiliar vista, we sped past a mum and her cute toddler who was lathered in suds, bathing in a large bucket. The image of that kid, well, that was when India first got me. It may seem strange, certainly I've seen more shocking things over the years, but you must understand that as a privileged, pampered young Westerner, I had simply never seen such a thing before in person. Coming face to face for the first time with the reality of people conducting their entire day-to-day life on the side of the road (everything from sleeping to cooking to bathing their children) shifted something inside me and expanded my whole perspective on life.

'Oh cool, those crows are eating a dead rat!' Paul laughed, pulling out his camera to take a photo while we were stopped. Ah yes, he was going to be a good travel buddy.

India is renowned for being a backpacker haven of super-cheap accommodation, but Mumbai? Not so much. Land in this overpopulated city comes at a premium and as such, most of its hotels come at a price close to those back home. Our first night in India cost us eighty euros for a shared room with AC. Not quite what I'd anticipated but it was cool and spotless and we were too hot and overwhelmed to keep looking. At least this time, AC actually meant real air conditioning.

We dumped our bags and I took a few deep breaths, like a boxer about to head into the ring against a formidable opponent. It was time to venture out into the madness of Mumbai.

People say that arriving into India is a total assault on the senses. People say it because arriving into India is a total assault on the senses.

There's the erratic, demented roar of diesel engines and odours and aromas so pungent they almost paralyse your lungs. There are the dazzlingly vibrant colours that make home seem like a grey, foggy dream; the cloying, humid heat that leaves your clothes clinging to your skin. Then, pervading the entire scene like a magical spirit that holds it all together, there's the wonderful sense of complete and utter chaos.

On top of this sensory overload, my virginal European mind had never before experienced being vastly outnumbered by humans of a totally different colour and I found it unnerving. It probably didn't help that the entirety of Mumbai seemed focused on me and Paul, appearing to stare at us with a mild aggression and intimidation as though we were moving targets.

This was the one thing nobody had ever warned me about before coming to India and it floored me. Every face I looked at was staring intently at me. I couldn't figure it out: did they consider me dangerous? Was I in danger? Was I an unwelcome intruder in their world?

It turns out that there were three main reasons why they were staring at us (and obviously I'm generalising here, so bear with me):

1. Many Indians envy our exotic white skin, considering it more beautiful than their own. Ironic given the amount of time and effort we Irish spend trying to get a tan.

2. The shrewd ones see us as walking dollar signs, certainly in the big cities; they know that they can often make a few easy bucks out of an unsuspecting tourist like myself.

3. It's just what they do when they're curious. No intimidation or threat intended, Liz!

I would gradually learn all of this, but in the meantime, I continued my psychotic imaginings of abduction and possible murder. It felt as if I'd arrived in another world, an alien land with absolutely no bearing on the one I'd left behind in Ireland. My poor frazzled brain was frantically rewiring its whole system in order to accommodate a spectacularly different angle on the world as I knew it. It's safe to say India was already changing me and I hadn't even been there two hours.

Colaba, right in the heart of Mumbai, was full of wide streets and restaurants, shops and cafés. As we left our hotel and walked along the busy footpaths, we passed both modern swanky stores selling Levi's jeans and tiny makeshift stalls. Everywhere you looked there was noise, movement and vibrant energy and while the general scene wasn't as picture-perfect as a city in Europe, nor was it filled with squalor and poverty.

We had been walking just ten minutes when Paul stopped suddenly. 'Here, this is it,' he told me, excitement in his voice. 'Leopold's Café. Oh man, I can't wait to see this.'

We entered a buzzing, bright café, easily finding a table for two. There was a fifty–fifty mix of locals and tourists and a host of tired, churlish-looking waiters in shabby uniforms.

'Man, this is *nothing* like I imagined it to be.' Paul's face fell, as he took in the reality of a place he'd previously created in his imagination. 'That dude talked it up so much … I mean he practically lived here. Weird.'

Paul's 'dude' was the main character from the novel *Shantaram*, based on the true story of an Australian convict on the run who came to Mumbai and adopted the city as his own. He was a tough gangster who worked for the city's mafia but kept his values and principles, who fought with his fists, who drove a Royal Enfield, who, basically, was Paul's hero. A part of the story's magic was now crumpling as we sat in the unremarkable, somewhat westernised café that had been in so many of the book's pivotal scenes.

While Paul struggled with his disappointment, I fretted and worried over what might be safe to eat before nervously ordering vegetarian noodle soup. It's amazing just how convinced I was in those early days that anything I consumed in India was going to poison me.

'I can't believe this place,' I said to Paul later, sitting back as the waiter cleared the table.

'I know, what a let-down,' Paul complained. 'Though at least the beer's alright.'

'I meant Mumbai – India – in general,' I clarified, watching the people around us eating and chatting, relaxed and carefree, which I was not.

'Oh that, yeah, it's pretty wild, isn't it? You know, I'd love to get hold of some weed but you've got to be so careful here,' he added in a lower voice, leaning towards me conspiratorially. 'Guys will offer you drugs on the street. If you give them money for it, then they call the cops and you're busted and, man, you do not want to spend time in an Indian prison cell, believe me.'

I suppressed a smile as Paul leaned back in his chair and took a swig of his beer.

'Are they pretty bad, yeah?'

'A hellhole!' Paul affirmed, missing the sarcasm in my voice. 'Though maybe not as bad as the ones in Thailand.'

'Did you spend a lot of time in those, too?'

He looked at me, finally catching on.

'OK look, I've never been to these places but you hear plenty stories, you know what I mean?'

'Sure.' I smiled. He was clearly fascinated by the murky gangster world but I already had him down as a big softie. 'So you want to head out and explore this wild metropolis then?'

We spent a few more hours wandering around Colaba, not straying too far from the general area of our hotel as we tried to adjust our shell-shocked brains to the new surroundings, including being trailed by a beggar and her scruffy toddler for nearly twenty minutes. In the end we sprinted across a busy main road to escape them and narrowly missed being run over by a speeding bus. Somewhat ashamed, and with a racing heart, we carried on more sedately, having managed to shake off the woman but quite possibly a few years of my life too.

That evening, after a jet-lagged nap, we splurged on dinner, eating in the fancy, plush surroundings of the Khyber Restaurant. While it used up nearly a full day's budget, it was totally worth it. The meal was some of the best Indian cuisine I've ever had and it finally satisfied my disturbed stomach, which was still churning from both anxiety and the awful plane food.

As we left the restaurant late in the night, stepping out into the humid heat, a bizarre sight greeted us: everywhere we looked were bodies, endless bundles of families, all sleeping on the pavements. We had to keep to the now empty road just to avoid tripping over the numerous human mounds that spilled across the footpath. It was another demonstration of the divide between the wealthy and the poor and, as I later locked our hotel room door, turned on the AC and climbed into my clean, comfortable bed, a reminder of how undeniably blessed I was. Ignorance may be bliss, but sometimes awareness can pave the way for immense gratitude.

Chapter 2

And then there were three ...

The first thing we did the next day was to change hotels; my budget for four and a half months in India had not factored in forty euros a night on accommodation. Luckily, we managed to get ourselves a twin-bed, AC room in the nearby Salvation Army hostel for just ten euros each. It was relatively clean, if a little shabby; we had our own bathroom and the cockroaches gave us glowing reviews. Perfect.

Once settled, we did some quick emailing in an internet café. I wrote a group message to let everyone know I was still alive and then I sent one to Jack.

Jack was an American guy I'd met a year before. We had both participated as volunteer organisers on a Vipassana meditation retreat in Ireland and got along really well, despite him being a lot older. We'd kept in touch sporadically since, with him hinting at something more than friendship and me intentionally ignoring said hints. A few weeks before leaving for India, I received an email from Jack saying that he was in fact already in India himself, pursuing spiritual nirvana in a yoga ashram down south in Kerala.

At that moment, all uncertain feelings or confusion were completely brushed aside in place of a crude subconscious survival instinct: get through travel in India at any cost. Unbeknownst to him, I now saw Jack as my lifeline and intended to use him as such. It was a dumb-ass plan if ever there was one, but fear will make idiots of the best of us.

Hi Jack,

So guess who made it to Mumbai?! I'm freaking out, I think I might have actually landed on another planet. Met Paul, an Irish guy, on the same flight. He's cool and it means I don't have to manage this insanity on my own, cause I wouldn't know where to start. Anyway, not sure how long I'll stay in Mumbai, maybe a couple days and then head down to Goa. You still in Kerala doing yoga? How's it going? Can't wait to meet up, it'll be nice to see a familiar face in this strange land.

Liz

* * *

Our first real excursion in Mumbai was a trip to Elephanta Island. Paul and I strolled to the iconic Gateway of India, from where we caught an ancient passenger ferry across to the nearby isle. The ride lasted half an hour and our boat was full of chubby, wealthy Indian tourists snacking on biscuits and crisps. I watched in horrified disbelief as they casually tossed the plastic wrappers and food scraps into the sea without a second's thought, as though the ocean itself were a rubbish bin.

To clarify something, I'm pretty sure that's not how those Indians would have seen it. Prior to the recent arrival of man-made packaging and plastic, food in India usually came wrapped in banana leaves or other such natural materials which, when thrown away, would soon decompose and turn to mulch, blending harmlessly back into the earth. Still today, the tradition of naturally biodegradable utensils exists in the form of the many side-of-the-road chai stalls that serve their brew in tiny clay pots, which disintegrate after one use; piles of these crumbling miniature pots appear each day next to the stalls as people discard them after drinking their chai and it's completely harmless. You can see why the concept of recycling or disposing appropriately of rubbish, at least back in 2007, was a little-known concept.

At any rate, that day in Mumbai I was too shy to say anything to the people tossing their rubbish into the water and simply watched them in mute shock. Our decrepit ferry managed to get us safely across to the island and Paul and I spent the afternoon exploring it. The name is a bit misleading if, like me at first, you thought we were going to find herds of elephants. Therefore you can imagine my disappointment when I discovered that, instead of the island being full of the magnificent mammals, it's actually full of caves with carvings of various Hindu gods and goddesses. But then it clearly helps if you do a little research. Manoj, a politely persistent tour guide, persuaded us to let him explain the history and stories behind the different religious figures (for a small fee, of course). The sculptures date back to around the fifth century AD and they are impressive in size and beauty and full of intricate detail. But my heart had been set on finding giant, tusked creatures lumbering around the island and in my disappointment I missed out on appreciating the full splendour of the caves.

At any rate, I was soon distracted by the island's brazen monkey population. They'd long since decided that this land was their turf and no feeble human effort to shoo them away was going to change that. Sitting outside a ramshackle, touristy café, Paul was forced to relinquish half his lunch to an intimidating young brute who simply hopped up on our table and began taking chunks of rice in his tiny hands, stuffing his face, crumbs flying. You know there's no point arguing when local Indians are fleeing the scene.

Ironically, dear Paul got the bright idea of buying some bananas to feed the poor, helpless creatures. He successfully peeled two and handed them over to the gathering troupe, but the rest were swiftly snatched from under his arm by a sneaky opportunist. As you might have guessed, I'm a real softie when it comes to animals, but these monkeys seemed more like a violent mob from the dodgy end of town and so I felt it might be time to beat a hasty retreat back to mainland Mumbai. The people of India suddenly seemed so friendly and welcoming!

The approaching Gateway of India was a sight for sore eyes as our ferry gradually brought us back to the city. The comforting, rhythmic splashes of the water against the boat along with the cool sea breeze soothed my nerves and allowed me some downtime to process the sensory overload of this new world. I had come so far out of my comfort zone that I was actually starting to enjoy myself. India was slowly working her magic on me. It also didn't hurt that one of the dudes working on the boat was a delicious bit of eye candy. I tried not to stare. Then again, it wouldn't have mattered if I did.

On our second night in Mumbai, Paul and I headed up to the hang-out area of our hostel, hoping to meet up with some other travellers. Entering the cafeteria we spotted a guy around our age at a table, writing in his journal. Paul walked straight over to him.

'Hey man, do you know where there's a party tonight?' he asked hopefully.

'I don't know, but I can come with you and see,' the guy answered with a smile, quickly packing away his things and looking pleased to have company.

With his blue eyes, short blond hair, peachy skin and chiselled features, I took a moment to admire this fine hunk of a man. Then he stood up and I found myself eye-level with his stomach. That was our Rob, six feet four inches tall, with an incredible Austrian gym body and legs the size of tree trunks. Glancing skywards I could just make out those clear baby-blue eyes smiling down at us. He sure was handsome ... and two metres too tall for me.

We chatted with several other travellers staying in the hostel but in the end, it was just Paul, Rob and I who headed out for drinks, back to Leopold's Café where Paul was valiantly trying to recapture some of the gangster cool of *Shantaram*.

'*Ja*, this country is crazy, *oder*?' Rob asked us, as we ordered three Kingfisher beers. I liked how he threw in the odd German word when he spoke. Then again, I was starting to like most things about this lad.

'I feel like I've left planet Earth,' I said.

'Aww man, it's so hot!' Paul complained. 'I've never sweated so much in my life.'

'And it's so difficult to get clean drinking water, I thought I was going to die today,' Rob added in his cute, clipped accent.

'What do you mean?' I asked, puzzled. 'They sell it at every second stall.'

Rob looked from me to Paul.

'I walked past so many stalls selling bottled water, but I didn't think they were safe for us to drink. Are you kidding me?' He grinned, slapping his forehead. 'I can't believe it! I walked the entire day in the boiling heat, looking for a supermarket but I couldn't find a single one. In the end, when I was almost ready to collapse, I bought one in this posh hotel.' He was laughing as he poured beer into his glass.

'And when I called my mum to let her know I'd arrived, I was so lonely and homesick, I actually started crying,' he groaned, shaking his head at the memory. 'So I just told her the line was really bad and I'd call back tomorrow.'

'That's a rough first day.' I giggled, taking a sip of my own beer, and inwardly swooning. If he just wasn't so damn tall.

'So what are all your travel plans?' Rob asked us.

'I've got four and a half months to explore India, then it's back home to Ireland,' I answered.

'Man, I've got the most amazing few months planned. Two months here then I'm flying to Thailand, gonna explore it properly this time, cos I partied way too hard on the last trip. I'll probably visit Laos or Cambodia too, then I'm flying to New Zealand for two weeks and then San Francisco. Five months in total. It's gonna be amazing!'

'Oh cool, *ja*, so you also have the round-the-world ticket?' Rob asked.

'Yeah, man. You?'

'*Ja*, so I have two months in India, then like you also, I fly to Thailand and South-East Asia. Then I fly to South America, it is one full year of travel, my first time leaving Europe. But *ja*, I've been saving a long time for this trip.'

We remained in Leopold's for several hours and Paul finally got to quench his thirst with more rounds of Kingfishers as we chatted and laughed, bonding over our mutual love of travel. When we finally left the café late in the evening, we stopped by a phone booth (simply a side-of-the-road stall with several telephones, run by a young man) and called our families. Besides a quick email the previous day, it was my first time speaking with my parents since leaving Cork and they sounded relieved that I was a) still alive and b) had already found two fellow backpackers for company. I was feeling pretty relieved myself. After a while I realised the boys were finished and were waiting patiently for me, so I said my goodbyes, paid up and we walked back to the hostel together.

It's a funny thing, how quickly one tends to connect with other travellers in Asia; not even twenty-four hours after meeting him I had shared a hotel room with Paul, while here I was in a foreign city late at night, trusting two men I barely knew. It could have been a gut feeling, or because I'd grown up with two older brothers, or maybe because they were just such good, kind humans, but hanging out with Paul and Rob felt as normal and natural as if my own two brothers were there in India with me. Which, given the circumstances, was incredibly reassuring.

* * *

'Come on, Liz, come up north with us. We're gonna go to Goa anyway in a few weeks,' Rob said for the third time, as they patiently waited for me to make up my mind.

It was the following morning and the boys and I were at the train station, booking our onward journeys out of Mumbai. Rob and Paul had decided to travel together to

Jodhpur, a city in the state of Rajasthan, as they both wanted to explore some of northern India.

My original idea, however, had been to head straight
down to Goa and I was torn now between sticking to this
plan and the brand new possibility of travelling to Rajasthan
with the two boys. There were several other tourists from
our hostel who had tickets to Goa for that very evening, so
company for that journey was readily available, and Jack was
just a little further on in Kerala. So, go south?

I hadn't counted on finding myself two fine lads for
company, hadn't even considered the option of travelling up
north and exploring a totally different side of India or visiting the Taj Mahal. I might not get the chance to do it again.
Kerala – and Jack – would still be there a couple weeks from
now. So, go north?

Hmmm.

Sometimes you are given moments in life when you just
know that the choice you make could have far-reaching implications. I find them terrifying given the immense respon-
sibility involved – what if I choose wrong? This was one of
those moments and I floated in a bubble of indecisiveness
for almost twenty minutes.

North or South, Rajasthan or Goa …

So far, it seemed that making travel plans in India was a
sure-fire way to ensure I did the total opposite. In a moment
of sudden courage I chose: Rajasthan with the boys it was.

As we explored Mumbai later on that day, I came to
realise just what a pampered little princess I really was, as
lean-muscled men well into their sixties pulled cart-loads
that most young lads back home would struggle with. They
did it in the intense heat, with very few breaks, for less

than an hour's wage of our money, all the while negotiating crowds of people, cows, traffic and the occasional dumb tourist getting in the way. One more layer of ignorance peeled away, thank you India.

As the day wore on, I began to notice something odd about the streets and the bazillions (honestly) of Indians in them: around 90 per cent of all the people we'd seen so far were male. Where were all the women? For a country that has had such a powerful female prime minister and that worships an infinite number of divine goddesses, India really seems to be a man's world.

Just when we were starting to get hungry, we chanced upon a random vegetarian restaurant and we entered the gloomy diner. A barefoot waiter came and motioned for us to follow him upstairs. There he handed us A4-sized menu cards and left us to it. None of us knew what anything was and we laughed at our ignorance, finally opting for the first three items in the list. As we chatted and awaited our mystery dishes, I noticed, across the room, a young boy who looked to be only about thirteen. Squatting in a dingy uniform and absentmindedly sweeping the floor, he seemed utterly enthralled with us. I imagine our lives couldn't have been more different from his.

When the food arrived, it turned out to be light, fluffy lentil pancakes, filled with different spiced curries. Alas, I was still fully convinced that local Indian food would induce some kind of horrific illness and so I tentatively picked at the filling inside and left the rest for muscle-hungry Rob to polish off. Total costs for all our food: less than two euros. Even despite our half-full bellies, I knew a bargain when I saw one.

After our pit stop we ambled on, coming across some cricket fields and viewing, for the first time, one of India's many 'religions'. The game followed us out onto the busy main road where some young men were having a full-blown match in the middle of the street, ducking and dodging cars and taxis. It made me laugh in delight. Only in India!

Hi Jack,

I know I was meant to be coming straight down to Goa but I've decided to visit Rajasthan with Paul and Rob (another backpacker, from Vienna). Hope you don't mind my change in plans, just thought I should grab the chance to see some more of India with the boys. We should be travelling back down south in a week or so. How's the yoga – you able to levitate yet? See you soon.

Liz

Paul poked his head around the door of the internet café.

'You nearly done, Liz? We've a taxi waiting to take us to Chowpatti.'

'Coming!' I replied and hit send.

Taxis in Mumbai were generally ancient battered cabs in black and yellow with dusty interiors, a complete lack of seat-belts, and bored drivers who only agreed to reasonable fares after much persuasive haggling. Being budget backpackers, every rupee counted, of course, but compared to prices back home, even the 'expensive' fares were ridiculously low. As we careered along the wide promenade towards the beach, Paul leaned out of the window and hollered enthusiastically at a couple of passing cars, to which Rob laughed and the driver glanced back a little nervously.

'Yeah, man! We love you, Mumbai!'

'*Na ja*, you Irish are so crazy,' Rob said, turning around to look at us.

'Nope, just him,' I said emphatically. Rob shared a grin with me before turning away again as we whizzed past the wide open ocean to our left.

Chowpatti beach, Mumbai's popular hang-out scene, was bustling with food vendors and locals, all of them staring at the three white tourists who had just arrived. As beaches go, it wasn't exactly golden sands and turquoise waters – this is littered, overcrowded Mumbai we're talking about. But there was a light atmosphere with the hopeful feeling that, at least in this moment, anything was possible (including bats the size of small cows flying overhead). Our last day in Mumbai had been an enriching one. Slowly and subtly, India was unravelling some of my assumed beliefs, biased judgements and illogical fears; she was gently rousing me from my one-dimensional world perspective and helping to open my mind to a vastly different way of life. She was working her magic.

Chapter 3

It's a dirty, smelly world out there

The next day it was time to begin our travelling for real. The three of us crammed ourselves into a rusty, clanging cab and, with our backpacks precariously stashed on the roof, we belched and spluttered our way through the manic Mumbai traffic to Victoria Terminus. I was so excited I thought I might poop in my pants (at least, I hoped that was due to excitement).

At the station, the challenge of travelling in India began in earnest. For a start, we could find no mention of our train on any of the board listings. Paul decided to check at the enquiry desk while Rob and I settled ourselves on a bench and waited, absorbing the hustle and bustle of the busy station, with its shoe polishers, beggars, cleaners and droves of regular commuters.

Moments later, an agitated Paul came sprinting over to us.

'Guys, we're at the wrong station!' Rob and I stared up at him in puzzlement. 'We're supposed to be in Bandra; it's thirty minutes on a local train from here, come on!'

We scrambled to get our cumbersome backpacks on and chase after Paul. Buying three tickets for Bandra, we made our way to the correct platform and luckily, a couple minutes later, a local commuter train pulled up. Paul checked his watch as we spluttered out of the station – we had fifty minutes until our train to Jodhpur left. There was nothing we could do but sit and wait.

As the train trundled along frustratingly slowly, a well-dressed man next to Rob started up a conversation with him. Meanwhile I glanced around to find a sea of big brown eyes all fixed on me. I was oblivious, on that occasion, to the fact that local commuter trains hold separate carriages for females only, a way to make travel for women more comfortable and hassle-free, particularly during rush hour. Hence I was the only female and, as such, quite the novelty for the local men sharing our carriage. Feeling like a deer in headlights, I turned around towards the boys and began listening to Rob's conversation.

'So, once we are arriving in Bandra, it is the rickshaw you will be taking, yes?'

'Rickshaw?' Rob repeated blankly. Uh-oh.

'Yes, yes, rickshaw.' The knowledgeable man wobbled his head self-assuredly. 'It is to Bandra Junction you must be going.'

Rob turned to look at us with an 'oh crap' expression on his face. Catching our train was becoming decidedly complicated.

We finally arrived into Bandra station and in the midst of awkward backpacks, throngs of people, grateful thank-yous and the urgency to catch our soon-departing train, there was little space left in my brain to absorb and process what lay right alongside the station. Hurrying across the overhead bridge, we got a view of immense heaps of rubbish and whole groups of people living among them. This was my first glimpse of the slums of India. For a second, I caught sight of a stooped old man, in rags soiled beyond words, rummaging through some loathsome pile of waste. That solitary image imprinted itself on my brain.

Emerging from the station we found a small cluster of rickshaws, India's top-notch, three-wheeled, cheap and cheerful taxis.

'Can you take us to Bandra Junction?'

We were met with blank incomprehension from the drivers.

'BAN-DRA. JUNC-TION,' I enunciated loudly, assuming that shouting the words would make them understand.

Again, vacant stares and zero response.

I looked at the boys in exasperation. Time was ticking by and not one driver could work out where we wanted to go. Not a single one of them was able to work out that Bandra Terminus was what we actually meant, though we didn't realise it yet. Around us car horns blared incessantly, dust and filth clung to our perspiring faces and adrenaline pumped through our bodies as the train's departure time rapidly approached.

'Bandra Terminus? Oh, madam!' One driver suddenly lit up with understanding. 'You want Bandra Terminus, yes?' Realising our error with the name, we nodded and yessed enthusiastically. Finally!

Wired with excitement, Paul and I threw ourselves and our bags into the tiny tuk-tuk and had nearly taken off before we suddenly remembered Rob. For a split second, as the adrenaline pumped crazily through my veins, a wild voice screamed in my head to forget him and just GO!

Instead, I leaped back out of the tiny taxi and helped him find another cab. With seconds ticking by and a sour look on our driver's face at being made to wait, Rob finally got lucky and launched himself into another taxi. The roaring diesel engines had us careering over wicked potholes, dodging cows and other erratic drivers and, frankly, if I hadn't been about to poop in my pants earlier, I certainly was now.

It took less than ten minutes until Bandra Terminus was finally in sight. We flung rupees at our surly drivers, rushed into the station and found our train at last. There she was, about two miles long, and our carriage was at the opposite end. My shoulders ached as my backpack slapped up and down but there was no stopping me now. As the train let rip a deafening blast of her horn, I ran like a woman demented, hair plastered to my sweaty face while Paul sprinted with his head down, a man on a mission. As we pelted down the platform, Rob glanced at his watch and slowed his gait.

'Guys, I don't think we need to keep running,' he gasped, sweat dripping into his eyes and streaming down his bright pink cheeks. 'We still have ten minutes till it leaves!'

I grinned back at him but couldn't stop – it was as if my legs were somewhat disconnected from my brain and I was pretty sure that if I tried to walk at this stage I'd fall flat on my face.

And then it was all over as we finally reached our carriage and clambered on, laughing and panting and utterly exhilarated. Travel in India, stage one, was complete.

* * *

On the eighteen-hour journey to Jodhpur we shared our cabin with a sweet Indian family of three. Mohita, the mum, was a friendly, generous woman with the most fantastically stained buck teeth. She was so incredibly kind, she insisted on feeding us nearly half of the home-cooked food and snacks she'd brought along for her family but, despite her best efforts, by the time evening came we were starving, so we accepted the vendors' offers of cheap train food. Eating anything in India was still a nerve-wracking experience for me, but I had realised it was time to stop being such a scaredy-cat or I'd starve to death over the next four months.

The hot food was surprisingly good, but we were left with a small dilemma when we'd finished. What to do with the dirty packaging? Seeing our confusion, the family confidently indicated where to put it: out of the window. We smiled at them, assuming they were joking. Realising we didn't get it, Mohita grabbed Paul's tray and lobbed it outside the moving train with a big smile and a head wobble, as if to say, 'You see? That's how you do it!'

It feels like a vile, dirty confession admitting to it, but I ended up following her example, Rob too. It seemed that, like the Indians on the ferry across to Elephanta Island, this was just how you disposed of rubbish in India. It felt weird and inherently wrong, but it was either that or use it as a pillow. I sighed as I realised that some of India's cultural practices were going to be hard to get used to.

As the night drew on and we lay down on our bunk beds to sleep, India didn't change very much. She continued her hub of activity around us right through till morning. I dozed fitfully, strange sounds and the jolting of the train frequently disturbing me. Each time I awoke I was shivering in the chill night and wrapped my thin cotton sheet tighter around me in a futile effort to warm up.

Sunrise woke me, stuffed with a rotten, snotty head cold. It was mostly due to smoggy pollution and an excess of freezing air conditioning in Mumbai but the cold, sleepless night on the train was the final straw. Staring glumly out of the window, I noticed the stark contrast in the landscape since leaving Mumbai's state of Maharashtra: less green and a lot more sand. We'd arrived into the desert terrain of Rajasthan.

Disembarking the train, our sweet little family guided us through the chaos of Jodhpur's station, giving a tuk-tuk driver the name of a hotel for us, arranging the fare in advance and sending us on our way with big smiles and waves, like benevolent angels (the first of many that I would encounter). The short taxi ride revealed a very different vista to the comparatively clean, smart streets of Mumbai. Jodhpur was full of old crumbling walls, open sewage and skinny cows. It also oozed history and character, particularly the old town area with its ancient flat-roofed blue buildings, a quirk that earned Jodhpur the name 'blue city'. There are numerous theories as to why blue was the choice of colour, from it being closely associated with the Brahmins (the priestly caste of Hinduism in India) and the blue buildings belonging to them, to keeping the houses cool, to preventing termites with the paint's mixture of copper sulphate and limestone. Whatever the reason for the colour, it made for a beautiful and fascinating view as I started to feel like I'd finally arrived in the India of my imaginings back in Ireland. There was something raw and authentic about the city, something I'd had a sense of in Mumbai but felt even more strongly here in Rajasthan. Perhaps it was the history within the land or the cultural vibes of the people who lived there, or perhaps because it was so completely different to anything I was used to in Europe. Whatever it was, I loved it and, in hindsight, that was probably the moment I really fell for India.

It didn't fully register there and then, however, thanks to my headache and blocked sinuses. India's magical qualities were way down the list of my concerns, as all I wanted was a decent breakfast and a snooze. Thankfully, after navigating a few more quirky, narrow streets, the taxi entered a quieter area and we arrived at our hotel, where we were greeted by an extremely polite and well-spoken owner. The hotel was clean and pretty with some of the typical features of the region – decorative arches over the doorways and whitewashed walls – and our request to share the one room was willingly obliged, with an extra camp bed supplied. A shower washed off a lot of the weariness and grime of the journey and breakfast on the terrace provided the most incredible view: Jodhpur's Mehrangarh Fort towered above, a majestic and regal creation by the Mughals. It couldn't be left unexplored so, feeling rested and recharged, we joined the uphill tourist path to check it out.

The fort itself was spectacular, a vast ancient structure, sprawling over the hilltop to keep watch over its azure city below. The sandy-hued architecture was typically Mughal in design, with incredibly ornate arches and endless chambers and corridors. The awesomeness of the great structure, however, simply couldn't compete with the cuteness of its resident chipmunks and squirrels, and it's quite possible I took more photos of the furry vermin than the fort. After such a disastrous encounter with the monkeys on Elephanta Island, I was thrilled to find these lovable little creatures, but still, I'm an idiot. The fort truly is an awe-inspiring creation yet I only have vague memories of it, thanks to running around after chipmunks. After a few hours of sightseeing my energy levels were rapidly fading, so I passed on exploring the town with the boys, instead going straight back to the hotel for a much-needed siesta. They arrived back a couple hours later.

'This place is so polluted!' Paul exclaimed as he took off his sunhat and glasses and leaned back on the bed, kicking off his sturdy hiking boots.

'*Ja*, it was like I could feel all the dust inside my nose and throat. When we came back here, the hotel-owner asked us how we liked Jodhpur, and we both told him 'it's so dirty',' Rob said, while washing his face in the bathroom. 'I think he was offended we didn't like his city. I feel bad because *ja*, I didn't want to be rude, but look,' he said coming out of the bathroom and indicating his white towel; there was a dark, dirty patch where he'd dried his face on it.

'You were right not to come with us,' he told me with a grin. 'It's a dirty, smelly world out there!'

Chapter 4

'Just buy me chai!'

Thanks to its hectic streets and dusty pollution, Jodhpur didn't entice us to spend long within its blue walls, so next morning we organised the next leg of our trip. We hadn't discussed it much, but it seemed only natural that we would continue travelling together as a trio, and we quickly agreed on the city of Jaisalmer as our next port of call. Walking to the nearby train station, we tried to book a ticket but were vaguely told to go back outside 'near the post office'. As we left in confusion, a man with two thick facial scars and a bandage on his flip-flopped foot limped up to us, smiling.

'You are looking something, my friends?' he asked us curiously.

'We're trying to buy a bus ticket,' Rob told him.

'Where you are going?'

'Jaisalmer.'

'Ah, so you come, I show you place to buy ticket. You come!' He waved his hand to get us to follow. 'My name is Sharma. I see you enter train station so I follow you. Then I see you *leave* train station, so I think you are needing the something and that,' he paused with a hearty chuckle, 'maybe I can help, yes?'

He certainly was very friendly and, despite his odd English, full of confidence. So we followed him down the crowded, dirty main street until we reached a stall at the side of the footpath. The booth was covered in Hindi script and was run by two sour-faced young men who looked at us, seemingly with aversion. A barrage of shouting in Hindi ensued between Sharma and these young guys, until a little ticket book was thrust towards us, the total price for our three bus tickets scribbled in the corner. Oblivious to the tidy commission dear Sharma had just brokered, as much as we were to the correct price for our tickets, we were full of gratitude.

Throwing his hands up in surrender with a smile, he graciously assured us of his motives.

'I am not looking money for thanks,' he said solemnly, an air of saintliness floating around him. 'Just buy me chai, I am happy.'

In our innocent minds, buying him tea was the very least we could do and so we gladly walked with him to a nearby busy chai stall. This side-of-the-road business consisted of little more than a gas stove and some battered utensils.

'*Bhai-saab, char chai!*' he ordered the local *chai wallah* (tea-maker) and we all perched together on broken, battered stools around an equally shabby little table, just feet away from the racket and incessant traffic that never dimmed and the many passers-by who stopped to stare at us in fascination.

The ritual of making and drinking chai is an integral part of the subcontinent's culture, from the most southerly tip right up to the Himalayas. Loose tea, spices and a copious amount of sugar are boiled together in milk and cooked until you have a deliciously sweet cup of Indian tea.

'So, you are all three in India, how long?' Sharma asked us, his good foot propped on the leg of his stool, an elbow slung casually over his knee.

'I have two months, Paul also,' Rob replied. 'And Liz has over four months. We just arrived a few days ago in Mumbai.'

'Ah yes, new for India, all new,' Sharma commented, nodding his head in a manner that indicated he'd already figured as much. 'So how you are liking it? Jodhpur is great city, yes?'

We glanced at each other a little awkwardly, giggling.

'Umm ...' I trailed off, not wanting to offend yet another Jodhpurian.

Sharma looked at us in exaggerated astonishment.

'You are not liking Jodhpur? How is this possible? Is very beautiful city, you see the fort?'

We nodded.

'It's not that we don't like Jodhpur, it's a fascinating place and the fort is truly amazing. I think we're just not used to so much chaos,' I explained politely.

'Man, your city's so dirty and polluted,' Paul interjected, while I cringed at his rather blunt honesty. 'There's rubbish everywhere and the pollution is crazy.'

Sharma nodded soberly in agreement. 'Yes, traffic too much. Too much dirt also, the people they take plastic, they throw everywhere.' He gave a flick of his hand in emphasis.

'I have the idea,' he said after a moment, rubbing his chin thoughtfully before he leaned forward on his stool. 'Today, you come with me, we visit small Jodhpur village in countryside. You see real India and leave crowded city.'

Our four little cups of chai had since arrived and he sat back to take a loud slurp of the hot brew, allowing us a moment to consider.

'I arrange car, not expensive,' he quickly added as reassurance. 'We are visiting real, local village. Something special, no tourist India.'

Burning my tongue as I sipped my tea, I looked questioningly at the boys.

'Do you want to go? It sounds interesting.'

They were both nodding.

'I would like to see how it is outside the city,' Rob said.

'Yeah, man, why not,' Paul agreed. 'Let's do it!'

And so just twenty minutes and a couple of loud phone calls later, a hired car arrived and we piled into it, beeping our way out of the chaotic city centre. Helpful fun fact for you, dear reader: not all friendly Indians are necessarily acting out of the goodness of their hearts. Of course, not all friendly Indians are necessarily out to rip you off either, as evidenced by the sweet family we met on the train. There's a fine line between those out to make a few bucks off you and those who are genuinely kind and helpful. Unfortunately, at this early stage in our travels, we weren't yet able to differentiate between the two and so we unwittingly went along with Sharma's open offer of a visit to the 'real India'.

Driving to a village twenty minutes away, we arrived into a calmer, quieter India than what we'd previously experienced (although that didn't stop our driver from blaring the car horn repeatedly the whole way there). Here the rough roads were wider and emptier and, although we were now in the countryside, the sparse trees and prickly shrubs dotted among the small concrete houses reminded me that this was very much Rajasthan and not lush, green Ireland.

The clean air no longer choked my nose and throat but, given the arid climate, everything was coloured by a light layer of sandy dust. The village lay in a flat landscape filled with traditional whitewashed houses (no more blue!) that sat alongside small local factories and the air was peppered with the sound of goats bleating occasionally from the shelter of mud huts.

The novelty of it all made us want to take photos but it felt a little uncomfortable, as though we were parading our wealth in the faces of locals who worked long and hard for little in return; they stared at us with cryptic expressions, which transformed into instant shy smiles if we acknowledged them. I had to wonder what on earth they thought of us white tourists, grinning awkwardly and snapping endless pictures.

We didn't have too much time to ponder it all, though, as Sharma got us busy dabbling in pottery with the local potter, who squatted outside his home with a manual wheel and was sculpting the most beautiful, shapely pots and bowls. Our creations were a far cry from his skilled work yet he seemed entertained by our feeble attempts. Having enjoyed a mini pottery masterclass, we all felt obliged to purchase some of the numerous items on display in the open barn, little figurines and ornaments and knick-knacks. Sharma then walked us around the town and a trail of fascinated kids began to follow behind. We offered to buy them sweets from the local shop, which they shyly accepted before scurrying away giggling. Sharma was so willing to oblige our every wish that he even organised a cold beer for Paul (I'm still not sure how, as it's not like there was a local pub in the area) and we hung out in a large barn, with an audience of local men forming around us while Paul sipped on a Kingfisher. It was all quite bizarre.

Our last stop in the village was a small textile factory with endless colourful rugs piled up in the showroom. I decided that purchasing one of these small pretty tapestries would make a great gift for my parents and set about selecting one, which Sharma then suggested they could post for me at a very reasonable fee. I happily agreed.

As the afternoon wore on, we began to wonder about Sharma's infinite 'generosity and friendliness'. We finally drove back to the city and he brought us into a jewellery shop, an unappealing premises off the main street run by two young men. I'm not sure what finally pulled the blinkers off but as Sharma suggested we drink chai yet again, the boys started fidgeting and making excuses to head back to the hotel. Sharma tried persuading us to stay a little longer but we had all decided that it was time to go. Relaxing in the courtyard later on, we proceeded to dissect the day's events.

'I think he was just out to scam us from the start,' Paul commented, lying back on the dry grass, his head resting on crossed arms. 'That guy was a hustler. When we were in the last shop, all I could think of were those stories of how they put drugs in the chai and then they rob you while you're passed out.'

I groaned, sitting cross-legged on a chair, combing my hair.

'I never got a receipt or anything for that rug, you know, and I was warned about this kind of thing before I left. Guess I can kiss that money goodbye,' I lamented, realising now that the pretty mat would probably never leave Jodhpur.

'How much did you spend – 1,000 rupees?' Rob asked.

'1,400,' I answered glumly.

'So that's what, not even thirty euros. You could easily spend that at home going to a club, even a lot more than that. It's not so much,' he smiled reassuringly at me. 'And now we've learned our lesson.'

He took out a pack of beedies and lit one of the tiny Indian cigarettes, made with minimal tobacco and dried banana leaves.

'Aw, those beedies are shit, man!' Paul stated categorically. 'They're like smoking air, totally pointless.'

'They're not great, *ja*,' Rob conceded, relighting his several times. 'But at five rupees a pack, what do you expect?'

Later that evening our hotel-owner sat with us and it turned out we were not the first and probably not the last to fall prey to Sharma's clutches; he knew exactly who we meant as we described the scars on Sharma's face and his limp. He apologised profusely but also warned us to be more careful in future. I may have imagined it, but he seemed to be looking at me in particular as he said this. I wondered if I had the words 'naive and gullible' written all over my face.

We were up at dawn next day to catch our bus on towards the desert town of Jaisalmer. It was a relief to be leaving Jodhpur. Sharma's sneaky tricks had left a sour feeling in me for this city, but we were older and wiser now. Travel in India stage two completed – and I have to say, it wasn't quite as much fun as the first one had been.

Chapter 5

Camels, whiskey and stars

Rajasthan, which translates as 'land of kings', is laden with Mughal palaces and forts, incredible ancient creations many of which are several hundred years old. It is a land rich in history and culture, with several of its incredible monuments listed on the World Unesco Heritage site, including Jaisalmer Fort. Not that I knew much of this back when I was there; in fact, a lot of the 'educational/historical' stuff I'm including in this book (which isn't much, let's be honest) I learned after my travels. I think I was so scared before going to India that the only way I could summon up the courage to get my ass over there at all was to go blind. Once I arrived, everything was so fascinating and different and mind-blowing, I got too busy soaking it all up to do any real research. But there is such a wealth of history to the subcontinent that it's well worth reading up on it before you go, if only to make sure you don't miss out on somewhere as vibrant and beautiful as Rajasthan (a place I'd barely even heard of before the two boys decided to travel there).

But back to our travels: Jaisalmer's golden fort, with its yellow sandstone walls, rose like a massive sandcastle in the desert as our taxi neared the great structure. Unlike the fort in Jodhpur, it was busy and sprawling inside, a miniature town filled with hotels, restaurants and shops. We stayed in simple and ridiculously cheap accommodation just outside the fort, costing not even three euros total for a three-bed room. The suave and confident Mr J welcomed us into his hotel and wasted no time in persuading us to choose his own package tour for a camel safari. With promises of authentic, experienced camel drivers, visits to remote rural villages and even whiskey with our dinner, we were sold. Lawrence of Arabia here we come!

Camel safaris are as synonymous with Jaisalmer as Guinness is with Dublin and, sure enough, everywhere we walked that afternoon we saw signs promising the best and most authentic camel safaris with either this hotel or that travel agent. We began to wonder if we should have shopped around but, given we'd already paid upfront, we let it go and made the most of exploring the fort. After the hectic buzz and mayhem of the past few days, here was a much gentler, laid-back atmosphere. We wandered down narrow stone walkways, a maze of paths weaving around quirky little souvenir shops and restaurants, tourists and cows. Finding an internet café, I checked my mail and saw a new one from Jack.

Hi Liz,

I would have loved to see you in the throes of culture shock, the entertainment value would have been priceless. So you've jetted off to Rajasthan and left me pining down in Kerala. Nice. I've a few more days here in the ashram before leaving. Been getting headaches, I figure I'm just burning off bad karma as I do my 'selfless service'. It could also be the chemicals in the incense they burn here

all day. I've found my mind a bit distracted when trying to meditate, so I started using your name as a silent mantra in my head and it worked very well. Imagining you there as a visual meditation, however, let's just say I don't think it was fully in keeping with the discipline of ashram life. Parental discretion advised and all that. Enjoy Rajasthan. Get your lovely culture-shocked self down this way soon.
Jack

I rolled my eyes as I read it through – always with the jokes and the innuendos. I'd figured he had a thing for me yet it was never explicitly spoken; it was the big elephant in the room and it annoyed me. I wanted him to be straight up. (The problem with this, however, is that you shouldn't ask it of someone if you won't do it yourself … even if you're unaware of the discrepancy.)

Hi Jack,
made it to Jodhpur. Incredible city but really polluted and I think I got scammed. Came to Jaisalmer for a camel trek, might be bit longer than a week before we head down south, the boys have been talking about seeing the Taj Mahal and a couple other cities. I reckon it would be mad to miss out on that while we're so close. You and your jokes are hilarious, not annoying at all. Will write once we're back from our big safari, day after tomorrow. Namaste!
Liz

p.s. stop thinking about me when you're supposed to be meditating, that's weird.

Once done in the internet café, I went shopping for a hat and shawl with the boys, looking forward to our safari adventure. My sleep that night was broken by a mixture of excited anticipation and a pack of howling, snarling street dogs who sounded like they were trying to eat each other.

* * *

'Guys, wake up!' I was roused from my dreams by Rob's frantic voice. 'It's 6 am, my alarm never went off!'

Remembering that our jeep was supposed to leave at 6 am, we scrambled out of bed. There was an ensuing frenzy of bag-packing and general blind scurrying as we hurried to the jeep downstairs, dumping our backpacks in the locker room to be collected after the trek. Then, feeling like idiots, we hung around rubbing our eyes and yawning for another half hour. We hadn't yet learned we were on Indian time.

Two Australian girls, Bea and Alma, were booked on the trek with us and finally, when our driver was ready to leave, we travelled on the road for nearly forty minutes, leaving the city far behind us. The empty arid countryside of Rajasthan was beautiful bathed in the gentle light of sunrise. Eventually we pulled off the highway and soon approached a small herd of camels and their drivers. A short, portly man who reminded me of an Indian Teletubby was introduced to us as Baba Sham, our head camel driver. Several other young Indians were there, tending to camels or squatting beside a camp stove preparing a breakfast of jam on toast and some bruised bananas. Oh, and of course, some Indian sugary chai. With the smoky flavours and the al fresco dining experience in the Thar Desert of Rajasthan, it was one of the nicest breakfasts I have ever had.

Breakfast over, I was shown to my camel. Raja was a beautiful animal with huge, liquid brown eyes framed by exquisite eyelashes, and the aloof, snooty disdain of a creature that knows it's far superior to everyone else. My soppy attempts to pat and cuddle him were met with a bored yawn. Not in the slightest bit deterred, I hopped up onto my four-legged desert companion and nearly went flying straight off as he did a lumbering, rolling action to hoist himself up onto all fours. Let the safari adventure begin!

If you're picturing the golden sands and rolling dunes of the Sahara, it's a far cry from Rajasthan's Thar landscape. This is a vast expanse of flat arid soil, dotted all over with tough prickly shrubs and, never far away, a long line of electric pylons. Lawrence of Arabia was nowhere to be seen. Our pace was unhurried, the gentle plodding of the camels rhythmically slow and steady. Along the route we stopped off at a couple of villages, comprised mostly of rustic mud huts and the odd concrete house with a smattering of goats dotted throughout. These visits always produced a flurry of kids whose brazenness bordered on aggression. They had an obsession with our water bottles, some grabbing them roughly out of our hands (I had a funny sense of déjà vu, recalling a certain island full of monkeys, though these little rascals were far cuter). One of our guides eventually had to tame the rowdy youngsters, yelling at them in Hindi to give Paul back his camera, while I retreated hastily to the protective presence of Raja.

Our trekking continued, the gentle monotony coloured by one of the guides training in an adolescent camel. With sand and dust adding dramatics to the scene, the guide clung on expertly (no saddle or stirrups, by the way) as his unruly young mount hurtled off across the plains like the devil himself was in hot pursuit, only to come careering back towards us moments later in a cloud of galloping madness, his rider somehow still glued to his back. Raja barely flicked his Maybelline-esque eyelashes at the youngster's rebellious antics. He plodded steadily on and raised his nose high in disdain, or perhaps in response to the loud farts erupting out of another camel's bum that was just inches from his face.

We took a few hours to relax over lunch and avoid the most intense heat, but the rest of the time we were in the saddle, ambling slowly onwards. A snail could have overtaken us. Eventually, just as the sun started setting, we reached one distinctly Sahara-like dune devoid of any plants. This was to be our campsite for the night. Our guides set about preparing a dinner of smoked dhal (lentil curry) with smoked *chapatti* bread. It went down well and was followed by dessert – a massage from Baba Sham. Bea sat there obediently while our tubby little camel driver kneaded and worked on her shoulders. After Alma politely declined his offers of 'relaxation', he came to me. It moved rather oddly, from me sitting in front of him having the kinks in my shoulders worked out, to suddenly lying on my side, his stumpy leg wrapped around my torso as he lovingly rubbed my arms and hands.

Unsure as to how exactly I had ended up in this bizarre situation, my confused brain eventually cleared enough to get me to disentangle my hands from his firm clasp, thank him for his kind efforts and firmly refuse any further physical contact. Poor Paul, trying his luck with Baba's skills on his stiff, sore shoulders, was rendered the briefest treatment as Baba Sham mindlessly pummelled them for all of thirty seconds. It seemed that this 'relaxation' treat was for females only. Unsurprisingly, I felt a little out of sorts after the experience so I started to indulge in the whiskey. There's a delightfully detached-from-reality wooziness that begins to fill your head, some point between sober and total inebriation, and I decided to drive full steam towards it. A little while later, as I giggled and spurted off some random comment about the need for more vegetarian world leaders, in between swigs of the fiery golden liquid and several beedies, Rob started to look at me like he'd suddenly noticed a big boil growing on the side of my head.

'Everything is OK, Liz?' he quizzed.

'Super fantastic, Rob-a-doodle!' I replied, sputtering whiskey out of my mouth as I laughed.

Rob frowned at me, wearing a look of concerned parenting.

'You're acting funny, you weren't like this before. What's going on?'

'Yeah, Liz, spill the beans,' Paul chimed in. 'You're acting weird and drunk.'

Ensconced snugly between my two buddies and confident the guides were well out of earshot, I related the strange event of being wrapped up in Baba Sham's arms and legs during the massage. Rob and Paul had been sitting in front of me at the time, so they hadn't seen any of it, and their response was typically male: they found it hilarious.

'Baba just wanted some girl-time,' Rob said. 'He's a man of the desert, he must get lonely, *oder*? Why didn't you let him have a little cuddle?'

'Nah, Rob, I'd say Liz would rather snuggle up to something furry with four legs.'

I glared at the two boys who were laughing at my expense. 'You think it's funny?'

'Yeah, it's pretty hilarious!' Paul blurted. 'Liz getting some downtime with the wild camel herders of Rajasthan.'

'There wasn't any 'downtime', as you put it,' I muttered between clenched teeth, now ready to smack the whiskey bottle off the boys' heads.

'Aww, Lizzy, we are teasing you,' Rob assured me, still laughing. 'Here,' he added, handing me the rest of his bottle. 'Go for it, how do you say, knock yourself out, *oder*?'

'Yeah and we'll bring one of the camels to snuggle next to you, once you've passed out,' Paul added.

The whiskey flowed freely and we chatted and joked with each other until at last it was time to sleep, wrapped up in our smelly camel blankets. As I snuggled up in Raja's comforting earthy odour, I stumbled through the dregs of my school-level German with Rob and gazed at the vast expanse of space up above, sprinkled with trillions of tiny sparkles. Drifting across the middle of it all, a faint, swirly haze of magic, was our very own Milky Way.

'Ich habe noch nie so viele Sterne gesehen,' I repeated after Rob. (I've never seen so many stars.)

It was the kind of immensely astounding beauty that dazzles your eyes and makes your brain hurt, especially when drunk and trying to speak German.

'Dude, do you think there are any snakes around here?' Paul asked at one point, just as I was about to doze off.

'Oh, thanks a lot, Paul, *ja*, now I will not be getting any sleep,' Rob complained, sitting up anxiously.

'Or scorpions, because I heard there are some deadly scorpions in India, the size of–'

'Oh, *mein Gott,* excuse me!'

I peered over groggily and saw Rob leaping out of his bed and hurrying over to the guides, inquiring about exactly how safe it was for us to be camping out in the wilderness. He returned just a moment later, looking slightly relieved.

'They say it is fine here, no snakes or scorpions.'

'Really? Oh cool, man, cause I don't fancy getting stung in the face several hundred miles from the nearest hospital,' Paul replied.

'No snakes,' Rob told him firmly. 'No snakes,' he repeated as he lay back down. My inebriated little brain had no fear of snakes in the night or anything else as, moments later, I conked out completely.

I awoke once in the middle of the night and rolled over onto my back, blinking sleepily up at one of the universe's most spectacular works of art. It is no exaggeration to say that right there, in that moment, was one of the highlights of the entire trip. Or even my life. To awaken from the depths of slumber to the sight of such a vast otherworldly beauty reminded me that my life was but an insignificant blip on the bigger scale of things. I didn't contemplate it quite so profoundly right then, instead turning over onto my side and falling straight back asleep, but it has stayed with me ever since.

The brightening sky woke me at dawn. Poking my head out from under my blankets, I looked over at the boys. Rob was still in the land of dreams, a divine sleeping angel, but Paul was already sitting up. He looked over at me.

'How's the head?'

'Fine, actually.'

And I was fine, no small feat considering the quantities of cheap Indian whiskey I'd consumed.

Rustling and a few grumbles told us Rob was stirring. Leaning up on my elbows, I greeted him cheerily.

'Morning, sunshine! No snakes biting in the night then?'

'No, no snakes. But I would nearly prefer a snake over those fucking dogs.' He yawned tiredly, trying to rub away the grogginess.

'What dogs?' I asked curiously.

'What do you mean "what dogs"? Didn't you hear them during the night?' He looked at me with an expression of disbelief on his face.

'I didn't hear anything,' I said truthfully.

'They were howling and fighting each other about three feet away from you. You must have heard something?' His face now wore an expression of exasperation.

'Nope,' I replied. I was surprised myself. Where did the dogs come from in the first place?

'I knew you were drunk, but that whiskey must have knocked you out cold,' Paul chipped in. 'Explains why you were snoring anyway.'

I rolled my eyes at him and yawned. With a big stretch, I sat up properly, surveying the morning scene. Our trusty steeds were standing nearby, placidly chewing cud, the utter image of peace/boredom. The guides were setting up the gas stove for morning chai, chatting softly to each other and wrapped up in shawls against the cool morning air – one of them was cleaning the dirty cups and plates with sand (I skimmed over that image).

The early hours always hold a special stillness but most especially when out in such a remote area; the gentle clinking of pots and pans, the hissing of the little stove and the intermittent babble of human voices like delicate music –

feeling a sensation in the depths of my body, I stared around the landscape in concern. Where the hell was I gonna do my poo?

* * *

As we continued our second day's trekking, we became ever more grateful to have opted for just the one night, unlike poor Bea and Alma. Now that the novelty had worn off, we realised we were probably just being led round in circles, plus our butts were bruised and tender and there was a slightly dissatisfied atmosphere, mostly due to the guides' total incompetence. We had obviously camped close to a village given the appearance of the dogs and, thanks to not cleaning up properly after dinner, the leftover food had attracted the brawling hounds, keeping everyone (bar Liz) awake half the night. To make matters worse, while we were stopped for lunch, the group of guides started shouting and roaring at each other.

It turned out they were drunk. The only one still sober, a young lad named Aanan, was taking me and the boys back to the jeep – the two girls were not impressed. We wished them luck as he led us away. Aanan was a funny mix of male-Indian surliness interspersed with splashes of unguarded softness, rare moments that popped up when he sang to the camels while saddling them up, or as he rode sideways behind Paul, listening to Bollywood music on a tinny portable radio and swinging his legs like a little kid. He showed no pleasure when we left him a tip before saying goodbye. Maybe we didn't give him enough. Or maybe he just preferred the sweet camels to us Westerners.

Sitting in the jeep later as we sped back to civilization, all I could think about was washing out the wildlife that had taken up residence in my hair and changing out of my grubby clothes. I had the feeling that the camel safari was going to be one of those things that I enjoyed talking about more than I'd enjoyed actually doing, though I had loved the gorgeous camels (I'd hugged Raja fondly before leaving – he ignored me completely) and, of course, sleeping under the epic Rajasthan sky.

* * *

'Can I read your palm, Miss Liz?'

It was the evening after our safari and, washed and fresh, for once we three musketeers had split up: Paul was drinking beer with a bohemian American tourist downstairs, Rob was in the room studying his Indian guidebook and I was on the rooftop with our safari driver, drinking rum and philosophising.

'You want to what now?'

'I want to read your palm, your life is written in your hand,' Dev told me seriously.

I shrugged. 'Sure, why not.' I held out my hand.

Dev took hold of it, staring intently at the lines and grooves like he was reading a book.

'You meet an Irish boy for fifteen days,' he began, pausing while he studied it some more and I reflected on how, coincidentally, I had indeed had a two-week romance just a couple months before.

'And then you come to India ...'

Well, duh! We were *in* India. But the rum had sufficiently mellowed and buffered my sarcastic retorts and they floated away, unspoken.

'What next?' I asked carelessly, rubbing my nose and gazing at the stars above.

'Well, Miss Liz, next you meet your husband!' Dev finished with a satisfied smile before dropping my hand back onto my lap and reaching over for his own drink.

'Oh, and I suppose that's you, is it?'

Dev gave me a disapproving look.

'No, no, another Indian. Really!'

'Ha! Good one, Dev, very funny.'

It made me smile, scribbling it down in my diary later on, at which point I promptly forgot all about it. But you know, perhaps it's a good thing I paid no attention to his prediction. I might just have got in the way of it …

Chapter 6

India overload

Hi Liz,

How was the safari? Guess it'll be over by the time you read this. I'm in Allepey to plan a backwater boat trip, escaped the ashram yesterday, I couldn't handle the visions of your sweet beautiful face appearing to me there anymore. Think I might have shouted your name a few times in my delirium during the afternoon meditation. The resident ashramites were not impressed but if they'd only seen the images I was seeing, they would've understood. Don't worry though, I still respect you and your purity has not been tarnished. Time to eat some chicken, drink some beer and, well, the third pleasure I'll have to wait for. Any idea how long that might be?

Yours in jest,

Jack

Oh God. I put my head in my hands. His emails were starting to infuriate me.

Hi Jack,

Funny email. If I'm honest, I'm a bit tired of all these suggestive jokes. Please be straight with me for a change

53

(if that's even possible) and just tell me what exactly is going on? On another note, the safari was fun, though one night was definitely enough. We've got today to hang around the fort and we're leaving in the evening for Agra, gonna be a long trip. Looking forward to the Taj, seeing what all the fuss is about. I'm getting used to this country, slowly slowly as they say here. Maybe another week up here till we head south, but our plans are changing all the time, you know how it is when travelling. See you!

Liz

We left Jaisalmer's slowly crumbling fort on a sleeper bus that evening, but only after twenty minutes of utter chaos as none of our tickets matched any of the seat numbers. In the mess of squabbles an Indian guy suddenly appeared and started ordering people where to go. Paul and Rob got to share an upper bunk just big enough for two toddlers. I got evicted from the single bunk I'd claimed and was told to share a double with a random Australian guy.

Just as I was about to rant and rave self-righteously, I caught sight of Noah and my outrage melted away in the calm of his blissful angelic aura. There was something almost ethereal about him, with his slender frame, long, silky ponytail, delicate features and a voice as soft and gentle as a bed of petals … I felt loud and chaotic in his presence. Noah's calmly serene nature wasn't solely an act of God, however – it turned out that a regular intake of bhang cookies had rather a lot to do with it. (A bhang cookie is much the same as a hashish biscuit and they're sold legally in certain government shops around India, particularly in the north. From the looks of it, Noah was most likely keeping several of these shops in business all by himself.) I was tempted to try one as Noah was a model example of the graceful beauty of getting high. Plus I was backpacking around India – getting stoned at least once along the way was a vital part of the whole experience for a wannabe hippie like myself. Now, before I go any further, a little disclaimer: drugs are bad. And mostly illegal in India unless you've bought yourself special cookies from an official government bhang shop, like Noah did, or you're in a Hindu temple smoking with a *Sadhu* (holy man) which, in Hinduism, is considered a way to honour the god Shiva. Just so you know.

Back to our travels and, as the bus rolled along the highway for the following twelve hours, I proceeded to get high in the presence of an angel while the boys remained curled up in foetal positions, and got drunk on yet more Indian whiskey. It was a little odd lying horizontal on a vehicle hurtling through Indian traffic to the most bizarre soundtrack of both bus and truck horns that could pass for an inter-galactic battle from *Star Wars*. Allow me to elaborate: Indian buses and trucks have unique horns that make sounds like those from a 1980s computer game with the volume on cinematic surround-sound level. The cookies turned out to be a nifty way to sleep through it all.

We pulled into the pink city of Jaipur in the early hours of the morning. No time to stop and visit the capital of Rajasthan; it was straight on to Agra for us and our celestial friend Noah to visit the Taj Mahal. We had been put off exploring Jaipur's hectic streets on the advice of a couple of tourists. It's ironic, but the one big city we skipped on our tour of Rajasthan was the one I'd later come to know better than all the others.

The road from Jaipur to Agra in October 2007 was chronically bad (that, and our bus had steel rods for suspension). My bones were rattled and jolted and battered for nearly seven hours in stifling heat. The pit stop midway provided toilets that seemed more like cattle stalls, with no doors to any of the four-foot-high cubicles. Without anywhere to properly hide, I squatted and peed as quickly as possible before anyone passed by.

Another few hours of teeth-rattling travel ensued. While Rob and I held on for dear life, Paul and Noah across the aisle from us slumbered peacefully, even as wicked craters in the road shot us all inches off our seats and smacked our tender behinds back down again. By the time we reached Agra, twenty-four hours after leaving Jaisalmer, my nerves were fried and I felt as though my body might suddenly explode into tiny pieces. The touts descended on us like a swarm of wasps but we found a cab that could squeeze in the three of us plus our bags. The last glimpse I caught of our stoned angel Noah was his crimson cotton shirt and silky ponytail billowing in the breeze as his own tuk-tuk sped off into the dusky evening.

Despite it not being the hotel we'd told our driver to take us to, Shanti Guesthouse turned out to be a gem. Stepping up onto its rooftop restaurant, we were greeted with a clear view of perhaps the most romantically famous building in the world. Standing tall and solid in the fading light of dusk and the haze of Agra's intense pollution was the awesome Taj Mahal; a testament to the consuming passion and extravagance of love; an inspiring, majestic, phenomenal work of art – that was closed to the public every Friday. Tomorrow was Friday.

Having to hang around wouldn't have been so bad in pretty much any other city in India. But Agra sucked. It sucked worse than a lemon and we had to spend an extra day there.

We decided to spend the day doing a tour of the numerous other mausoleums and less famous (and less impressive) mini Tajs. These buildings were elegant and beautiful, but the rest of the city was a joke gone wrong. It was utter pandemonium raised to a whole new level. We were taxied around for the day by a friendly local tuk-tuk driver and to this day I haven't found a city I liked less. Mumbai, Jodhpur and Jaisalmer had their own unique charms and characters. I considered Agra their aggressive, ugly cousin; if people in the West have an impression of India as a dirty, backward country, Agra could well be the reason why. As the morning wore on, we fell into a wordless stupor, careering past tattered kids pooping on the side of the main road, pigs rolling around massive mounds of stinking rubbish and hordes of men with banners chanting and protesting (hopefully against the state of their city). The sheer number of vehicles and people on the roads made it impossible to drive in a straight line or go any faster than our plodding camels back in the Thar Desert. But rather than ambling along calmly as on our safari, we lurched and swerved and endured a deafening caterwauling of fifty million beeping vehicles crammed around us, like we were stuck in a group of caged wild animals, wailing and screeching, desperate to escape the hellhole of Agra's roads.

I was impressed with our driver. The only sign of the intense effort required to negotiate such conditions was a light sheen of sweat that formed across his forehead as he dodged another manic road-user and slammed on the brakes to avoid mowing down a random cow. (The ardent fervour of religious Indians is a force to be reckoned with, so never mind if a suicidal animal flings itself in front of your car – harming India's blessed holy cow can have dire consequences.)

Along the way, we picked up random guest passengers, including a cop who perched next to the driver for a brief spell, his authoritative presence reassuring against the mental outer world that was frying my senses, and later on, an older couple who, upon seeing us in the back, giggled and bounced like young girls who'd hopped in a cab and discovered Justin Bieber was sitting inside.

Towards late afternoon, we agreed to help out our sweet driver by visiting a couple of expensive shops, a common practice in India; just by the act of us going in for a browse, he would receive a commission from each place. But after visiting maybe four different shops, we were starting to go cross-eyed with tiredness. Our sightseeing was done. We were done. Time to go back to the hotel and chill.

Out came the cheap Indian whiskey once again. We hung around our hotel rooftop restaurant for a few hours with other tourists and guzzled the burning liquor. It eased our wired minds and bodies and we gradually started to relax. It was in a very intoxicated state that I went to check my emails downstairs and saw there was a new one from Jack.

Hi Liz,

have you seen the Taj Mahal yet? Is it everything you hoped for and more? I was on a train to Cochin yesterday and got talking to these friendly locals. Forgot my "Lonely Planet" bible. Lucky I got their numbers as I already called them and hopefully I can get it back off them when I get to Goa. I know I joke a lot about us, that's just me. But you want to be straight up, fine. I like the way you talk, the way you laugh, the way you walk ... OK, I worship the ground you walk on. I like you. A lot. I hope that's clear enough. I'm enjoying Cochin. It's an interesting little town, and there's a crazy artist living here with wild hair who smokes all day. It looks like his studio's on fire when you walk past. Hotel's great, food's great. All that's missing is my bible. And you.

Jack

I sat back in my chair, a little woozily. Oh crap. I'd been pretty sure it was coming, I'd asked him to spell it out for me after all, but now I realised I didn't know what the hell to do with his heartfelt declaration. Jack was a funny, entertaining and intelligent man. We had a lot in common. But while he was sure and clear about his attraction to me, I was utterly confused about my feelings towards him; my plan of surviving India without addressing these complicated feelings was most definitely backfiring. In the last still-sober corner of my brain, a little voice told me to leave the computer and write back to him tomorrow. Of course, I completely ignored it.

Dear Jack,

Wow! That's incredible. I'm a bit drunk so this may not be the best time to write this. We're in Agra and it's completely mental. Going to see the Taj tomorrow, you can actually see it from our hotel. Agra sucks. Don't bother coming here.

Indian whiskey is surprisingly OK. I mean like it's alright. I think I'm quite drunk. Will write back again soon. Should be heading down to Goa, maybe in a few days. Enjoy the beach.
Liz

* * *

'Jeeesus, this is spicy!' I complained. It felt as though there were flames coming out of my ears as I reached for my bottle of water.

We were in a pokey little Indian café and being drunk had eased my paranoia about potentially dying of dysentery, so I was mindlessly shovelling down curry much the way you would back home after leaving the pub. Unfortunately, the food here was apparently laced with chillies hot enough to thaw Frosty the Snowman. Paul looked at my puce face – he was the only one of us not completely wasted.

'It's not that hot, Liz,' he said dismissively.

'It fucking is. I don't live on spicy food back home like you,' I retorted, swaying a little in my chair.

'It really isn't that hot, Liz,' Rob said with a little snigger. His eyes were slightly glazed and he didn't seem to realise that there was curry sauce on his chin. I giggled. Then imagined licking it off.

'I want dessert!' Rob announced moments later and burped loudly. I couldn't contain my laughter and doubled up, my head lying on the table.

'Me too. Dessert!' I sat myself back up with difficulty.

Paul rolled his eyes at the pair of us. 'Well, I'm heading back to the hotel. See you two later.'

Rob and I staggered off to locate a sweet shop still open at 9 pm. My bubble of whiskey shielded me for a small while but eventually I started feeling uncomfortably self-conscious. Everywhere I looked, all eyes seemed fixed completely and totally on me and it soon became clear why: the streets of Agra that night held a sea of men and there I was, one lone female, in a flimsy cotton dress. It felt like I was a lamb walking through a pride of lions. I wished I could swathe myself in some kind of trench coat, or better yet a burqa, anything to hide myself from the millions of male eyes that all appeared to be pinned on me. I've never been a fan of the spotlight and, if I'm being totally honest here, Indian men often stare at women in a way that could be described as 'undressing you with their eyes'. I hate to tar all of India's lovely men with the same brush, for they are not all like this, not by a long shot, but it's definitely been a general theme of my travels. It's a little intimidating to say the least, but on that first trip, having never before experienced this kind of attention, it was completely unnerving. Face flushed, I scurried after Rob and stayed close till we were back at the hotel. Once there, I changed into a T-shirt and cotton trousers and stuffed the dress in the bottom of the backpack, where it would stay till we reached the beaches of Goa. While it was quite a respectable dress, it was perhaps a little unsuitable for the more conservative northern states and I certainly felt a whole lot more comfortable having my legs fully covered from that night on.

* * *

'This is kind of boring,' I commented, holding my hand up to block the sun's glare, my head pounding from the previous night. We were in the pretty Taj Mahal grounds, having spent a couple of hours there already, admiring the iconic building. Pristine and polished, the whole place gleamed with the shine of money and careful maintenance and, although we had come early, the place was mobbed with tourists, all snapping selfies with the famous cream-coloured building behind them. A normal person would have delighted in the beautiful structure, with its insanely elegant architecture and the romantic love story at the heart of it all but, to be honest, the Taj wasn't doing it for me. It didn't have the rugged character of the forts of Jodhpur or Jaisalmer, there were absolutely no cute furry animals to be seen and I was, quite simply, dying of a hangover. I'm afraid nowhere but my bed was going to make a good impression on me that morning.

To my relief, the lads seemed as ready as I was to leave both the Taj and the throngs of Indian families thrusting babies at us and then snapping photos like crazy (don't ask, it's just one of those quirky Indian things).

Leaving via a side exit, different to where we'd entered, we ended up walking down streets that had definitely seen better days. The path was filthy with stretches of stinking open sewage and numerous tattered makeshift homes. I found myself sidestepping several mounds of unthinkable dirtiness, trying not to dwell on my exposed flip-flopped feet. It was a wretched area to walk through and to think that people were actually living here seemed unbearably wrong, all the more so given the immense wealth generated in this part of India from the Taj just around the corner. How could these two opposing realities coexist so close to each other?

At that moment, however, I was in no state to consider such a profound societal injustice. The heat wasn't helping my hangover and my tongue was rough and parched like a piece of sandpaper. I held up my scrappy shawl, attempting to shield myself against the brutal midday sun, while the stench of the street pervaded my entire being to the point of dizziness.

It was a while before the ever-observant boys noticed I was lagging weakly behind.

'Guys, do you want to have chai? Liz, are you feeling OK?' Rob asked, looking around at me at last. I could feel a sort of madness coming on.

'It's too hot. I need to get out of the sun.'

I wasn't sure how long I had left before I'd start rolling around on the filthy ground, wailing like a woman possessed.

'Could we go somewhere, anywhere, just far away from here and this heat?' I was very nearly begging now.

'Sure,' Paul said, looking around. 'There's a tuk-tuk up there, let's leave this dump.'

I can't remember quite where we asked our driver to take us but I'm pretty sure nobody mentioned Costa Coffee. Nonetheless, that's where we ended up and I could have hugged the man. Air-conditioned, spotless, my saviour, Costa Coffee hauled me back from hungover India overload to being able to cope once again.

I'm slow to promote a multinational corporation, yet it was our first taste of anything really Western since arriving in India and, I must say, a welcome reprieve that saved my sorry ass even if it was exorbitantly expensive. An hour in the cool café lounging on comfy armchairs and sipping a simple hot chocolate soothed my alcohol-battered brain and I was once more ready for India in all her glory.

That night, sitting on the sleeper bus as it drove us out of Agra, I felt nothing but relief. I was glad we'd seen the Taj but, much like the camel safari, it was something I would enjoy talking about far more than I'd enjoyed actually doing. The whole experience of Agra had been so intense, from the drive around the city on our first day to walking through it at night with Rob, to my awful hangover next morning. I have to wonder, all these years later, if I returned again and gave her another chance, would the beautiful building win me over the way she does just about every other person that's ever visited? Perhaps the poisonously cheap whiskey had blinded me to her magic. Or perhaps I'm just weird.

Chapter 7

Food and drugs, baby

The skin on my face stretched wide with the force of my yawn. It was 7 am and we were now on a cheap local bus to get from Ajmer to the nearby popular town of Pushkar. The wheezing contraption was like something out of the Flintstones – I was surprised we didn't have to actually pedal our legs – while the driver, with his fabulous turban and long, wizardy beard, seemed to belong to some equally bygone era.

Pushkar, hippie heaven, heralded a change in my eating habits since arriving in India. Initially the heat and intense spices of India had called a halt to my appetite. It wasn't that I didn't get hungry, I could be ravenous when I started eating, but after only a couple of mouthfuls my stomach sent messages to my brain saying it had shut up shop for the day. It amused the boys greatly, as they happily polished off my meals (free food for them equalled massive brownie points) but touristic Pushkar had a wide range of Western-style cafés and restaurants with deliciously bland, non-spicy food on offer. I gorged, making up for all my involuntary fasting in an all-you-can-eat buffet. At a speed that felt more like vacuuming than eating, I stuffed my face with pasta, okras in cauliflower cheese sauce, salted fries, falafels, salad, a little more pasta for good measure and finally, for dessert, deep-fried doughnuts (the heart-attack-inducing kind). When I eventually heaved myself out of the chair and waddled out of the restaurant, my stomach had tripled in size.

After a large meal, a lot of energy goes into digesting the food, which causes mental faculties to slow down and results in lethargy and drowsiness. I found a lot of my energy went into shopping. Strolling my portly belly down the one main street of the town was like indulging in another feast, this time for the eyes. Beautiful, brightly coloured clothes spilled out of shop doorways, an endless supply of hippie-style T-shirts, dresses, Ali Baba pants, bags and shawls fluttering on display, enough to entice even the most frugal backpacker. It was India's hipster paradise. Delighted, I walked the length and breadth of the main street several times, bags accumulating in my hands like gifts at Christmas. At these prices, I was going to need a bigger backpack.

* * *

'Are you getting anything yet?' Rob looked over at Paul, supping on his bhang lassi, his eyebrows raised questioningly. I do believe it was the last coherent sentence he spoke that night.

'Not much, man, these are weak as piss,' Paul said dismissively. 'You should have tried one, Liz, you're such a girl.'

'I'm grand for a yoghurt drink laced with weed, thanks very much,' I replied, sipping my innocent pineapple shake. 'There are warnings in the guidebooks about them, they're stronger than you think.'

Rob smiled nervously, looking down at his nearly empty glass.

'This is cool, it's like going to a coffee house in Amsterdam,' Paul commented a while later, looking around the slightly dingy café. 'Maybe not quite as clean and the drugs there are definitely stronger. But these aren't so bad.' He swished his drink around and swallowed the last of it. 'What do you reckon, man?'

Rob grinned guiltily at him.

'Yeah, ish-alrish-yeah …'

I looked at Paul and burst out laughing.

'Rob! Are you getting stoned?' I teased.

He looked my way and then, inexplicably, his shoulders began shaking as he started laughing uncontrollably.

'I think we've lost him,' I told Paul. We grinned at our Austrian hulk who had leaned back in his chair in a puddle of limp muscles and rubber bones, practically convulsing.

A while later we headed elsewhere for a change of scene. In another pokey little café, sitting at a small wooden table, I took a proper look at Rob across from me and realised that, much like me during my near-meltdown in Agra, he possibly wasn't doing too well.

'Are you OK, Rob?' I asked. He swung his head loosely in my direction, moving his mouth wordlessly and frowning in concentration.

'Paul, I don't think he's doing too good, maybe we should get him back.'

Paul glanced at him in surprise.

'Rob, man, how's it going?'

Rob turned his head slowly towards Paul. The lights were on but the occupant had left the building.

'Yeah, he's off his face. Let's get him back while he can still walk.'

I linked arms with the Austrian giant and literally steered him down the street to our nearby hotel, guiding his ninety-kilo frame back on track each time he veered off course like a doddery old man. We got him back to our room where he lay down on the bed, fully clothed, shut his eyes and didn't budge for the rest of the night.

He shared some of his post-weed paranoia with us the following afternoon as we hung around our hotel courtyard drinking chai.

'Once I lay down I couldn't move, *ja, meine* arms felt like they weighed twenty kilos each. I was so sure that the ceiling fan was sinking lower and lower and was going to slice me into tiny pieces. When I woke up this morning I thought to myself, well that's it, Rob, you've damaged your brain for good.' He smiled, shaking his head in disbelief. 'Thank *Gott* it's over now, what a horrible experience!'

'I warned you they were strong,' I told him smugly.

'No, they're not, he's just not used to it,' Paul countered. 'On another note though, have they no Western-style toilets anywhere here? I'm sick of squatting every time I've to do my number twos.'

'I think the Indian toilets are really good for you,' I answered. 'It's scientifically proven that the angle of squatting makes it easier for your body to relieve itself with your knees pressing against your bowels.'

Paul shuddered. 'Disgusting, Liz!'

'She's right,' Rob spoke up. 'Squat toilets are much better – I actually prefer them, even though they're not exactly easy for me to use.' He slapped his enormous, muscular legs.

Paul was adamant.

'No, man, no way. I need to sit on my throne with a good book for at least twenty minutes.'

Rob coughed on his chai as he and I burst out laughing.

'*Ja*, I'm changing your name to the Dark Lord from now on!' he spluttered. 'The Dark Lord and his Throne of Evil!'

By the time we'd finally calmed down Paul was already sick of the joke but Rob and I kept it going for pretty much the rest of the trip. That's what friends are for, you know?

Pushkar was a little cosy nook in the hectic chaos of northern India so we stayed a few days, enjoying the food, the shopping and, with a fair amount of caution, the bhang lassis. To clarify, a lassi is a delicious yoghurt drink, usually mixed with fruit such as banana, mango or coconut. In Pushkar, one of the novelties for us hippie wannabes was the preponderance of little cafés that served lassis mixed with weed, which were completely legal. It really was like the coffee shops in Amsterdam and, despite our caution, there was more than one occasion when we found ourselves sat at the back of one of these cafés with tears rolling down our faces in utter hysterics. Even the bored waiters couldn't help smiling at us.

On our final evening in Pushkar we came up with a bright idea to help us sleep on the overnight bus journey: a bhang lassi, of course. It might have been a good plan except that we hadn't factored in that the café closed at nine, three hours before we had to go catch our midnight bus and, well, we probably had a bit (a lot) more than was necessary.

As we passed the time afterwards back in our hotel courtyard, I was so high I would have sworn on my life that the earth most definitely does spin around the sun because I could see it moving.

'Oh my God, I'm so stoned!' I half-moaned, half-giggled to the others. Rob had passed out on a chair with his head leaning on his hand while Paul was chatting to a few other tourists, once again the only one of us someway sober. Everything I did felt warped and oddly removed from reality. I *really* wanted the world to stop moving, and I would have liked to stop laughing but there didn't seem to be an off-switch for that anymore.

When it was finally time to head to the bus stop, a friendly worker in the hotel led us three stoned Westerners through the now deathly quiet town and we'd never have made it otherwise. The normally buzzing streets were eerily still and dimly lit, and the spooky walk was doing nothing to ease the beginnings of my weed-fuelled anxiety.

Once we finally made it to the bus stop, Rob, who'd barely opened his eyes during the entire walk, sat down on his backpack and went straight back to sleep. I sat down too, wishing the world would stop its dizzying dance.

While we waited for our bus (naturally running late) massive painted monsters roared around the bend past us, blasting their Star Wars battle horns as they charged. A part of my brain was aware that these were Indian heavy-goods vehicles. Another (possibly drug-altered) part was convinced that these bellowing demons – with their windscreens framed and decorated to resemble eyes and their bizarre, blaring horns sounding distinctly like battle cries – wanted to eat me.

When the bus at last arrived, Rob roused himself enough to squish his bulky frame onto a tiny seat before passing out again, while I collapsed beside him with relief. Note to self: in future, stick to whiskey.

* * *

Udaipur (the site for a portion of the James Bond movie *Octopussy*) was a huge, sprawling city, done up like a tacky Christmas tree with strange tinsel and fairy lights strung across the tops of buildings, an overhead curtain of twinkly decoration. We didn't spend long there, we'd had our fill of Rajasthan and city-hopping by that stage, but we hung around just long enough to discover that it served some of the best chai of the entire trip in a run-down, dank little café, offered scenic views up high from Monsoon Palace, and sported unusually aggressive beggars. It was an interesting, rugged city and one that probably deserved more time and exploration, but we were all ready to start heading south and so, once more, a sleeper bus was booked; just two days after arriving, we left for Mumbai.

With its familiar streets and landmarks, rolling into Mumbai gave us a vague sense of coming home. This time the streets were full of women, most of them squatting among carpets of brightly coloured flowers and patiently threading the flower heads into mounds and mounds of extravagant garlands for an upcoming festival. It's hard not to love the kaleidoscopic colours of India.

Getting off the dirty, grimy bus we went straight to the train station to book our onward journey to Goa, hoping to get tickets for that very night. Given our last-minute booking we were lucky to get any tickets at all, even if they were for the posh and fancy 'second-class AC' costing 800 rupees each (over sixteen euros back then). That may not sound like a lot in the West (heck, that would barely get you a ticket for the bus from Cork to Dublin in Ireland) but when your daily budget is around twenty euros and you've got to make it last for months, spending sixteen euros on one journey is a real splurge. Tickets bought, we stowed our luggage in the station's locker room and headed back into the metropolis where, to use up some of the time, we stopped at an internet café. I saw there was an email from Jack and suddenly realised I hadn't heard from him for a good few days.

Hi Liz

I've made it up to Goa, drinking coconut water in the mornings, tequila cocktails in the evenings and getting nearly as drunk as you seemed in your last email. Found an interesting yoga centre here that specialises in Tantra, that's the one where spiritual bliss lies on the other side of a quick romp. I figured I'd look into it since I know how much you're interested in it... I mean the spiritual bliss, of course. I think I'll stay for a while and make the most of beach life. Let me know when you think you'll get here.

Jack

No mention of his heartfelt confession from the previous email and, once again, the jokes about sex. I found myself a little perplexed. Did he mean what he'd said in the last email? Was that a joke too? I couldn't tell anymore and quickly jotted down a reply.

Hi Jack,

we're in Mumbai for the day, catching a train to Goa tonight, can't remember which part, but hey, we'll be in the same state at least, surely it won't be that hard to find each other?! I didn't realise we'd spend so much time in Rajasthan but I'm really glad we did, it's so beautiful and vibrant. Still, I can't wait for a bit of beach life myself. Will call you once I get to Goa – looking forward to finally seeing you!

Liz

I hit send, wondering should I have mentioned something about his other email. I didn't think I'd said much in the last one I sent, given my befuddled state at the time, but then again he didn't mention anything either. Maybe better to leave it off, we could discuss it properly in person once we met. I swallowed and quickly pushed the uncomfortable thought to the back of my mind. It was something I really didn't want to deal with.

Chapter 8

City slicker to beach babe

The need to answer nature's call roused me bright and early next morning. I stretched my legs languorously, snuggling my head onto the soft pillow and feeling deeply rested. After the sticky overnight bus ride, followed by an entire day wandering around Mumbai, we'd been exhausted getting on the train the night before and pretty much any horizontal surface would've been a delight. But this time we had *pillows* to lay our heads on, real soft pillows, instead of our lumpy rucksacks. We had crisp, starched, white sheets and it was blissfully cool, thanks to the air con. I revelled in the luxury of it all. The *pièce de résistance* was when I climbed down from my bunk and cast an eye out of the window. There was so much green! Sprawling fields, bushy trees, colourful flowers, palm trees and, wait a second, was that a cow? In a *field*?? Holy smokes! After three weeks of northern India's concrete jungles, my starved eyes soaked up the landscape of lush vegetation and wildlife. It was a wonderful sight.

A couple hours later we disembarked at Calangute train station and it was as though we'd stepped into a baking oven whose humid heat wrapped itself around you like a heavy winter coat in summer. We were dripping sweat in about two minutes. Nonetheless, after the rigours of travelling up north, Goa was heavenly. That afternoon, the sky clouded over and a tropical storm blasted away the dust and the heat. The pungent wet-earth odour that saturated the air around us was an intoxicating perfume, the loud barrage of rain-drops a sweet symphony. What a contrast from the arid landscape and the general commotion of the cities we'd just left.

One brief blemish for me was the trio of blonde, tanned, German babes staying in the room next to ours. I despised their friendly, happy smiles and cheerful chatter and it had nothing whatsoever to do with the drool pooling at the corners of the boys' mouths or my sudden disappearance from their sphere of consciousness. Absolutely nothing. Luckily for me, the gorgeous girls didn't hang around long and, once the rain had stopped and I had the boys' full attention once more, we all headed to the beach. It was still overcast and humid and a dip in the rolling waves would have been refreshing. Unfortunately, a crowd of Indian men were the only other people on the beach and their eyes were instantly fixed on me. Uncomfortable with all the attention, there was no way I was going to strip down to a bikini. It's funny, in India I felt exposed just wearing shorts and tank tops, yet when I lived in Spain nobody would blink an eye when I sunbathed topless. The disparity between the two cultures was off the scale.

Paul was content to just roll a joint and lie on the sand near me. Rob, however, stripped off to his shorts and ran into the sea at full speed. His enthusiasm was no match for the turbulent waves and minutes later he came and sat next to us, cupping a dripping, bleeding nose in his hands. I looked at him curiously.

'What happened to you?'

'I hit my nose on the sea floor. *Ja*, the current here is strong.'

We remained a while, watching the Indian men across the way. With their bulging guts, double chins and balding heads, they cartwheeled and somersaulted across the sand, frolicking like I've never before seen grown men frolic. They flung themselves into the shallow, turbulent water, giggling and shouting in delight, burying each other in the sand and attempting unruly handstands. They reminded me of my cousin's four-year-old twins after drinking Coca-Cola.

That evening, I went to phone Jack from a public booth, excited and nervous that we would finally get to speak after all these confusing, ambiguous emails. My anticipation fell flat on its face. The number I was dialling wouldn't connect.

'You are missing a digit,' the shopkeeper informed me, with a sage head wobble. 'Here in India, we are having ten digits. You are having only nine.'

Bugger. I would have to check my emails again later and see where I had gone wrong.

* * *

Our second day in Calangute brought an excellent change of events with the arrival of sweet, self-assured Renee. We first met the friendly Dutch girl in our hotel in Agra and then after that in nearly every other city we visited. When we yet again crossed paths in the Salvation Army (where the boys and I had passed some of the day in Mumbai), we swapped emails, promising to hang out once we all got to Calangute.

'No way!' I stopped short, having stepped out of the hotel room only to see Renee's familiar face as she walked up with her backpack.

'How do you do it?' I exclaimed, giving her a hug.

'You guys must be magnets,' she laughed, equally surprised that she'd randomly found the same hotel as us.

'It's good to see you, how was your trip?'

'Not so great, actually,' she answered as our hotel-owner's son Hilary (at least that's what his name sounded like to me) opened the door to the room. 'I got the date mixed up on my ticket, as I discovered when I saw an Indian sleeping on what was meant to be my bed.'

'What happened?'

'Well, once we'd figured out why it was actually his bed, and I realised that I'd been an idiot, he kindly offered me the end of the bunk to curl up on. Yes, this is fine, thank you,' she said to Hilary, dumping her backpack on the ground and surveying the bright, clean room. 'But it's kind of hard to get a good night's sleep when someone's feet are poking into you and you're squashed into a tiny corner.'

I clucked sympathetically, advising her to take a nap and come to the beach with me afterwards. This time, with the moral support of another female and fewer men in the vicinity, I braved stripping down to my swimsuit and entered the unruly waves. After nearly losing my bikini top twice to the wild Arabian Sea, I decided not to risk it a third time. A couple of men had converged to leer at us and there was no way I was giving them any special viewings.

* * *

'You must try our local liquor,' Hilary told us as he served us our dinner on the hotel's terrace. While Paul had already started on the beer an hour earlier, Rob and I were waiting to try something different.

'It's made from the cashew nuts and it is very delicious. A strong drink, all of us locals are loving it.'

'I'll definitely give it a go,' Paul said with a sloppy grin, looking from me to Rob before he drained his beer. 'What about you guys, you interested?'

'If it's a break from Indian whiskey, I'm happy,' I said.

Hilary took that as his signal and went scarpering back into the hotel kitchen, shouting out behind him: 'Wonderful, I go get some fanny for you!'

To which Paul and I stared at each other.

'Did he just say what I think he said?' Paul asked incredulously, while I giggled.

'I swear he did, he said he was going to get us some fanny!'

We burst out laughing.

Rob stared at us, perplexed.

'What's so funny?' he asked, pouting at being left out of our joke.

Between us Paul and I explained how, in Ireland, fanny is a name for a woman's lady parts. As soon as he understood, he was giggling alongside us, all the more once Hilary arrived back with the bottle of clear, alcoholic liquid, announcing with a flourish: 'Here, you can see what the fanny is tasting like.'

He stared in puzzlement at the three Westerners in fits of giggles on the chairs in front of him.

'You would like to have some fanny?' he asked, opening the bottle but hesitating at our reactions. Paul was all but pounding the table and I had tears streaming down my face. He looked from one face to the other.

'Maybe I can just leave the fanny here for you to enjoy …' he said, and with one last uncertain glance at the three hysterical tourists clutching their stomachs, he left us to it.

Correctly spelled Feni, it has an unfortunate pronunciation, but we found it tasted a little like sweet vodka and enjoyed several rounds. Of course, the more we drank, the funnier the jokes became.

'Who would have thought fanny would go down so easy?' I spluttered at one point, holding my aching cheeks.

'*Ja*, imagine ringing home and telling your friends you got wasted on fanny last night!' This one was Rob.

'Ha! Drink up your fanny, guys. Liz, have you got any?' Paul exploded laughing at his one. For once, he was the most bamboozled of the three of us and his reaction was funnier than his joke.

Renee joined us just as the Feni (and the jokes) were nearly used up. More than ready for a night on the town, we caught a cab to nearby Baga and its hugely popular club, Mambo's.

The place was rocking when we showed up, with soft lighting, hip-thrusting beats and buzzing crowds of both Westerners and Indians. There were two main areas: the bar/dance floor (which resembled any club back home, except for an excess of dreadlocked hippies) and the lounge area, where people could relax, puff on shishas and sip their cocktails while surveying the many beautiful bodies on show.

The boys were interested in just one thing – girls – and sat down for the night in the lounge to puff on hookahs and try to look suave and cool. Irritated with the Austrian buffoon's inability to try it on with me, I headed to the dance floor with Renee to boogie it out of my system, and boogie we did. We danced like clowns, we danced like sexy girls from an MTV pop video, we danced like we were the only two girls in the whole room and nobody could actually see us, as we spent the night making total asses of ourselves and wiping away tears of laughter.

'I have a crush on Rob!' I yelled over the music, during a brief lull in our antics.

'So tell him!' Renee yelled back, getting caught up by a random Indian bloke who whirled her off before she could break free and dance her way back.

'I don't want to spoil the friendship.'

'Then get over it.'

'But he's so cute.'

'What?'

'He's so CUTE!'

'So TELL him!'

I shook my head resolutely. Giddy as I was, I knew I couldn't risk ruining the dynamics of our little trio; it could spoil the whole trip. Better to stick to my fantasies.

Getting home late that night, I learned a new lesson about toilet humour, namely that Paul and his farts were a lot funnier when he hadn't consumed large quantities of alcohol. I turned the fan on full and opened all the windows wide, but you could nearly see them, they were so foul. Oblivious, Paul lay on the bed, fully clothed and snoring loudly until Rob threw his *Lonely Planet* guide at him.

* * *

Anjuna flea market takes place every Wednesday, a forty-minute bus ride from Calangute and a must-see, according to the guide books.

Spread out close to the restaurants and beach of Anjuna, the market is overpriced (unless you're as ruthless at bargaining as the stall-owners are at hassling) and the aggression in the people selling borders on mild violence. On one occasion I was all but dragged into a shop and pinned to the wall till I'd agreed to give them a 'good price' for the cotton top I'd stopped to admire (alright, that may be a *slight* exaggeration but you get the idea). I found myself trying to keep my gaze straight ahead and make no eye contact. If somehow eye contact did happen, I switched from a sedate stroll to a frantic run, much the same way you might flee an approaching predator. You could say the market wasn't really my cup of tea.

During the afternoon I found an internet café where I could finally look up the correct phone number for Jack; I'd been missing an extra 8 towards the end. How had that happened? Despite having his number now on me, and despite the fact that a lot of the day hanging around Anjuna was literally spent, well, hanging around Anjuna, for some reason the thought of calling Jack there and then didn't strike me as a viable activity. Being lazy and moody on the other hand did.

So another day passed without my contacting Jack. We were heading south along Goa's beach-packed coast to Agonda next morning, unfortunately leaving behind Renee who had to go back to Mumbai for her flight home. I was disappointed. She'd slotted in so well with us we hadn't even noticed our trio had become a four-o and I wished I could tuck her up in my backpack. Nonetheless, I was looking forward to exploring the south of Goa which was said to be more relaxed and chilled out than the busier northern side.

Chapter 9

Back to basics

It was late in the afternoon when we arrived into warm, cloudy Agonda. We had no real plan for accommodation and simply began walking down a quiet, rural lane surrounded by coconut trees and cute, colourful Goan cottages, with the sounds of the nearby ocean to our left. After several minutes we came upon a tiny concrete house, almost right on the beach, with a robust Jamaican woman sitting on the porch.

'Ey mon, you be lookin' for a room den?' she asked in her sing-song accent, taking in our large bags and hot faces.

'*Ja*, do you have something?' Rob asked.

'Dis house is free, if you be wontin' to teek a luk,' she told us with a lovely smile, heaving her massive behind up off the step to show us inside. A guy with grey, curly hair approached us from a nearby hammock and smiled hello.

The small house turned out to be just a room with two single beds and an attached bathroom.

'If you be wontin' it I can get a tird mattress, nooo problem.'

I glanced at the boys. We hadn't even asked the price but I could tell – we'd take it nooo problem.

Tina and her German partner Rolf had retired to the simple quiet life in Agonda where they offered rustic ac-

82

commodation to wandering souls such as us three. While Tina was open and welcoming, Rolf's smiling eyes were always distant and he wore the scent of weed like a strong aftershave. Nonetheless they were sweet and friendly and the little house seemed perfect for us, so we donned our swimsuits under our clothes and left our bags with Tina while she arranged the extra mattress. Ten seconds around the side of the building, through a sprinkling of palm trees, and we were on the beautiful golden sands of Agonda. Unlike the beaches further north, it was devoid of restaurants or beach huts or even people, besides us. There were just some local fishing boats dotting the stretch of beach, and, bizarrely, a little cluster of cows, most of them lying in the sand and chilling.

Coming in from the beach was a forest of palm trees, which disguised the long country lane we'd walked while searching for a place to stay. Along that same lane were some cottages, the odd little local café and, at the far end of the beach, a couple of commercial hotels and one restaurant. There wasn't even one internet café. I'm quite sure it's changed radically since then, but in late 2007 Agonda was relatively undeveloped and it was a welcome breath of fresh air. Delighted to enjoy an Indian beach minus the ogling eyes of leering Indians, I stripped off to my bikini and went straight for a swim. After being bowled over twice by the wild waves I admitted defeat and once again sat down on the sand, allowing the aftermath of the current to wash up around me.

I gazed out at the horizon, digging my fingers into the wet slushy silt, relishing the peace and calm and contemplating life. The sun's orb was gradually morphing from golden yellow to a peachy orange and the sky was streaked with giant brushstrokes of reds, pinks and purples. A quick movement to the right caught my attention and I turned my head just in time to see Tina's partner Rolf, stark naked, running into the sea. I got an eyeful of his white bottom disappearing beneath the waves. It gave a whole new meaning to the term beach bum ...

* * *

For the first time in my life a rooster awoke me next morning at 7 am. After so much city-hopping and non-stop travel, we took full advantage of our new-found beach life and lazed to our hearts' contents. Or at least Paul and I did. Rob put us to shame by rising early each day and going for a long jog along the beach; after several weeks of trying out Indian beedies and little exercise other than walking around India's northern cities, our Austrian health nut was itching to get moving again. I tried to exercise vicariously through his efforts, imagining the calories burning off me as he ran while I lay on the wet sand and exerted as little physical effort as possible, but I won't lie to you, there weren't any visible results.

One of the best things about Agonda (other than its sweet rustic charm and the genuinely friendly locals who waved a hello and giggled delightedly when we waved back) was the food. In fact, our days there usually revolved around mealtimes.

We found two cafés that were special local gems, one for breakfast and another for lunch. Our breakfast 'bistro' was a small, local place near our end of the lane. It was dark and shabby and fantastic. The first time we found it (on Tina and Rolf's recommendation) we couldn't contain our delight as we dunked sweet bread rolls into gently spiced potato curry and washed it all down with cups of steaming, tea-infused milky sweetness, all for less than the price of a cup of coffee back home. Our other indulgence was in a similarly small, family-run café about halfway down the lane from our house in the other direction. Bright, clean and inviting, we literally gorged on their thalis (a thali is a dish of rice, various tasty curries and raitas). We were soon recognised as regulars, developing a routine of feasting on the home-cooked food and finishing off the spectacular event with a shared packet of biscuits and, of course, chai.

Poppa, balding slightly and imbued with the solid self-assurance of a man successfully fulfilling his role of 'provider' (while his wife did most of the work), stood behind the counter surveying his small but important domain. Each day we went there, he had his T-shirt rolled up to rest above an impressively large paunch that he could have used as a table top for a cup of tea. As we munched on chocolate-chip cookies and drank our milky tea for the third consecutive day, I realised the dream of skinny Liz up in Rajasthan was long gone and the reality at this rate was probably going to be something akin to the tubby father of this café. I glanced down at my stuffed belly with a sigh as I swallowed the last of my mouthful. Then I reached for another cookie.

Strolling home by myself one day, post-gluttony, an adorable family called me over to their garden, an earthy grove of plants, shrubs and coconut trees. Full of smiles and hellos and one-word questions (name, age, country etc.), they then invited me to drink some coconut water. I was happy to oblige, wondering what it actually tasted like (these days, regular supermarkets in Ireland sell packaged coconut water, but you must remember, I'm talking about a time when kale was considered a weed and 'tik tok' was just the sound a clock made). The father deftly hacked off the top of one of the giant green nuts and worked a hole into it before handing it to me with a straw.

There's a fair amount of liquid in a coconut. A very decent amount. A real generous amount. Oh God, a sickly amount. A few sips into the naturally sweet drink, I realised drinking the coconut water was not actually a good idea and, as the contents of my stomach began to float, I discovered that it was a very bad idea indeed. Unable to disappoint the beautiful family with their happy smiles, I ploughed on, my eyes slowly watering. Cradling my swollen, bloated stomach, I practically crawled the rest of the way home to the boys and collapsed on my bed, groaning as the liquid sloshed around inside.

'I'm so disgustingly, horrifically sick!' I complained. 'If I never see a coconut again it'll be too soon.'

* * *

Dialling the last digit, I held my breath, waiting in suspense for the sound of the number connecting, the sound of Jack's phone ringing. Nothing. I waited another moment. Finally the silence was broken by a garbled foreign language in a woman's voice, followed by Hindi and at last a musical, sing-song English.

'The number you are calling is currently not reachable. Please try again later.'

After three attempts ending with the same message, I gave up. It wouldn't be happening today either, then. We'd been in Agonda a few days and this was the second time trying to call Jack. I would have to wait until we got to Palolem (and internet) tomorrow where I could email him, find out where he was and why his damn phone never seemed to work, with or without the right number.

* * *

Dear Jack,

We're in south Goa, staying in Agonda. It has zero internet facilities so I had to wait till I got to Palolem this evening to write to you. I've tried your number a few times and got nothing, it's like it doesn't work. Where are you now? Are you still in Goa?

Liz

* * *

'Let's do some shots, man!' I bounced on the spot to the trance music pumping out of the speakers.

'Alright, you're on!' Paul grinned and took a loose drag on his cigarette, swaying a little as we went to the bar.

We passed Rob on our way, stretched out on a bench having a weed-induced nap. Massive surround-sound speakers thumped out the beats and we wove our way through the dancing bodies. Paul knocked into one guy, grabbing the man's arm so he didn't fall. Perhaps shots weren't such a good idea after all.

Palolem beach, not far along from Agonda, had a real party scene, though with a decidedly chilled vibe. The aroma of various joints drifted gently on the sea breeze, alcohol flowed and the solid continuous beats of trance parties throbbed constantly like they were Palolem's muffled heartbeats.

'Yes, my friend!' one of the handsome bartenders greeted me, oozing swagger. 'What would you like?'

'Two shots of Cointreau, please.'

He poured our two drinks and we knocked them back, the fiery orange liquid flowing down my throat like honey.

'Whoo!' I shouted. I was already quite tipsy. 'Let's go again.'

Paul nodded, though he was holding his stomach and his face was the colour of the moon.

'Are you OK?' I asked, not really paying attention, as he bent forwards, our bartender already pouring the next round.

'Yeah … shure,' he slurred, clanging his shot glass roughly against mine in a 'cheers' before we knocked them back.

He dropped his glass noisily on the counter.

'I think I'm gonna puke.'

What he'd said didn't register straight away. A rush of blood had gone to my head from the shots and I had my eye on the bartender, trying to act smooth and nonchalant as I leaned against the counter, giving him a sultry smile. What I really did was knock clumsily into the bar, bruising my hip and grabbing the edge for balance, all the while grinning impishly. I reckon I came across about as sexy as Barney the dinosaur.

Suddenly I remembered Paul and looked back to where he'd been standing beside me; I turned around full circle. Where had he disappeared off to? Five minutes later I found him staggering from behind a palm tree.

'That's much better,' he announced, wiping his jaw with his sleeve. I could already see colour returning to his cheeks.

'I just puked behind the tree. Might avoid walking that way for a while if I were you, it's a bit slippery,' he told me, before stumbling off into the crowd.

In India, all outdoor music has to be turned down at 10 pm and once the music faded, so too did the party mood that had just been getting into full swing. As the energy and the crowd started to disperse, I sought out the sleeping giant and the wasted Irish man, packing us all into a taxi and heading home to our little beach hut in Agonda. The spiritual journey of India seemed to have switched to party central; we'd all succumbed to the pleasures of mild drugs and alcohol and it wasn't exactly what I'd imagined before leaving Ireland (nor was it exactly the stuff I shared in my emails or phone calls back home). Not sure what to make of any of it, I brushed my teeth and went to bed. My two partners in crime were already out for the count.

* * *

For our last couple days in Agonda, Paul rented a motorbike and powered off to sightsee the surrounding villages. Later on, he gave Rob a spin to a local house to drop off both their laundry and, while coming home, the back-heavy bike reared up under the Austrian's weight, tossing the two boys to the ground. While Rob simply cut his toe, Paul tweaked something in his right arm that grew more painful as the day wore on. A massage in the evening didn't help, except for some useful advice afterwards: get an X-ray.

Paul left early next day to return the bike and to go for a check-up at the hospital. It was our last day in Agonda and we were moving on to Hampi in the early hours of the following morning. After breakfast, Rob and I went to pre-book our taxi to the train station and on our way back, we bumped into Paul getting out of a tuk-tuk, his injured arm in a sling.

'So how are you, Mr Invalid?' I asked curiously. We'd both offered to go with him to the hospital but Paul had insisted on going by himself.

'The doctor said just inflammation, no serious damage,' he told us.

'You're lucky, *ja*,' Rob commented, slapping him on the back with a grin that changed quickly to a grimace.

'*Gott*, you are soaking wet,' he said, wiping his hands off his shorts. Paul lifted off his sunhat to show dripping hair underneath.

'You would be too in this heat. I was walking for about forty minutes to get there.'

'You walked?' I was incredulous.

'Once I'd dropped the bike back to the rental shop, I figured it couldn't be that much further, so I just kept going. I walked most of the way back too.'

'Why didn't you drive to the hospital first and drop the bike off on the way here?'

'Because I ... because ... ah fuck it!' Paul pulled his hand down over his face and groaned while Rob and I started laughing.

'All that beer and weed must be killing off your brain cells, dude.'

'Ha ha, Liz, ha bloody ha!' Paul retorted, striding back to the house ahead of us as we followed, still snickering.

Curry, Chaos and Love

We celebrated our last night in Agonda by going back to the one official restaurant in the area, Dercy's, for dinner. Paul decided to order the hottest, spiciest curry possible.

'It's time,' he told us with a grin. 'Bring it on!'

Rob got an adventurous look on his face.

'Count me in too,' he said, ordering the same from our waiter.

When our food arrived, the boys excitedly tucked in. We barely noticed anything at first. A few sniffs, a slight sheen on his forehead, the odd sigh. Suddenly, Paul dropped his fork with a clatter, grabbed a serviette with his one good hand and blew his nose into it to such a degree that I began to feel slightly nauseous.

'How are you doing, Paul?' I asked, intrigued.

He took another tissue and wiped the wet sheen off his forehead, sniffing loudly. In the dark light his cheeks were glowing like embers. I glanced over at Rob, who looked a little pink and sweaty, and we shared a grin. Ignoring my question, Paul called over the waiter.

'Can I get another beer?'

The waiter nodded and took a step back as Paul wiped his forehead yet again and sprayed more sweat around him.

'Hey Paul, how's the curry?' Rob asked, laughing silently with me as we both watched. 'Here, you need a few more serviettes, *oder*?'

'That's really funny,' Paul answered dryly.

'Is the curry a bit much for you? You can tell us, we won't judge.' I giggled, watching another trickle of sweat roll down the side of his face.

'Shut up, you guys!' he said, mildly annoyed. His beer arrived and he took the bottle and drank straight from it.

'It's been a while since I had something really hot,' he said a little lamely, eyeing the mound of food still in front of him before gamely picking up his fork and digging back in.

'The Dark Lord has met his match!' Rob spoke in the deep voice of a wrestling-match commentator. 'Tomorrow he will sit on his throne as the fires of hell burn deep within!'

I erupted laughing and Paul threw one of his used serviettes at Rob before taking another swig of his beer. He was still sweating when we got home and packed up the last of our things for our early departure next morning.

* * *

Hampi, a small, quirky town inland in the state of Karnataka, is one that seems to capture travellers' hearts time and time again. Randomly strewn across its landscape are massive odd-shaped boulders, huge rocks and a plethora of Hindu temples. The air is arid and scorching, the land equally baked, and yet it's got life, with its bizarre natural scenery that looks from afar as though a giant had scattered his bag of marbles.

We were there for four days but it never quite caught me the way it does every single other person I've met who's visited it. I actually found the landscape pretty boring – as they say, a rock is a rock (is a rock) and, like museums, there are only so many temples you can visit before they start to blur into one another. As with the Taj Mahal, I feel like I must have missed out on something because people are always raving about their amazing time in Hampi and yet my memories of our time there revolve around the discovery of Nutella pancakes. I guess we all have different priorities. I received one email from Jack while in Hampi.

Hi Liz,

I'm in Gokarna now staying on Kudle beach. I often don't have signal here so that's probably why you aren't able to get hold of me. We had a bad day yesterday. A young Indian lad got into trouble while swimming, the current pulled him far out and an Australian tourist tried to help him but they both drowned. I think I'm a little in shock. The Indian boy's parents were here in the evening, distraught. It happened so suddenly but the current here is incredibly dangerous. Where are you and when am I going to see you?
Jack

I felt shocked and saddened at the news and my previous annoyance at him dissipated as I sent back a reply. It's interesting how hard it is to make words work for you when trying to convey the most important emotions, but I sent it anyway, adding that we were also leaving for Gokarna the next day and so, if he could hang on there a few more days, we would see each other soon. Four days after we'd arrived in Hampi, we were on the move again, having to take yet another uncomfortable overnight bus, much to Paul's chagrin ('This is the last time, guys, the *last* time!'). As the big old Volvo began the long drive to Gokarna, I leaned back in my seat feeling both excited and quite nervous. Finally, definitely, certainly, it was going to happen: I was going to meet up with Jack.

Chapter 10

Finding our way

'Gokarna! Gokarna!'

It was pitch black both on and off the bus and I couldn't work out what was going on. I sat up, drowsily pulling myself out of my dreams, and stared blearily out of the bus window. It looked as if we were being dumped at the side of the road. Surely this wasn't our stop?

Grumpy and groggy from lack of sleep, a handful of us stumbled off the bus where the conductor was already yanking bags out of the luggage compartment. It was just before 5 am and having left Hampi seven hours earlier, at best I'd had only snatches of sleep. The road we'd just travelled made the awful route from Jaipur to Agra seem like a sleek German autobahn. I think our bus driver had actually steered us over the giant boulders of Hampi because it had felt like trying to sleep on a giant loudspeaker that was pumping out dance tracks. There were seven of us in total heading to Gokarna and we were all a little peeved about being abandoned in the middle of nowhere and in the black of night.

All except Rob. Rob was absolutely outraged.

'We have paid to go all the way to GOKARNA!' he yelled angrily at the conductor. 'GO-FUCKING-KARNA! Why, *warum*, are you leaving us here in the middle of NO-WHERE?'

The young Indian remained expressionless and just waggled his head in the face of Rob's outburst, then thrust his backpack at him. There was a large vein throbbing on Rob's forehead now, one I hadn't seen before. His fury was further fuelled by opportunistic tuk-tuk drivers who had been waiting for our bus.

'Yes, my friend, Gokarna? Only 500 rupees, you come!'

'FIVE HUNDRED?'

I was starting to worry a little for Rob's blood pressure.

'There is minibus coming, minibus!' our conductor called. The bus's engine started revving and he hopped up on the steps, hanging out as they started pulling away. 'You wait minibus!'

The huge Volvo disappeared into the darkness. Rob stared after it, fuming, then spun around and kicked angrily at the dirt, muttering something about India. It was in German but I'm guessing it was rather rude. Meanwhile there was nothing to do but wait. While we hung around for our promised lift, one of the other tourists called out to his girlfriend to come and look at the stars. Perched on my backpack, I watched as he pulled her in close, wrapping his arms around her from behind while they both gazed at the expanse of star-speckled sky above. It looked so damn romantic my heart actually swooned and fell into my stomach. In the moment of intense yearning, I glanced over at Rob dreamily. He was scowling and picking at his fingernails. I sighed, cupped my chin in my hands and waited for my wishful heart to climb back up into my chest. To our pleasant surprise, twenty minutes after being deserted at the side of the road, a minibus actually did show up for us. India never ceases to surprise.

As we covered the last stretch of our journey, India roused her sleepy self and the sky gradually began to brighten. Climbing the hilly route, we passed waterlogged rice fields spanning out below us, soon bathed in the gentle, sun-kissed light of early morning and looking immensely beautiful.

We arrived into Gokarna, filled out numerous forms at the police station (a rule for all visitors given the dangerous currents and the propensity for idiotic tourists here to get off their faces on drugs and play in the sea) and then we grabbed a tuk-tuk, deciding to head to Om beach. In the brief spell between reading Jack's last email and arriving into Gokarna, I had already forgotten that he was staying on Kudle beach, the one closest to Gokarna town. Oh, did I already mention the bit about idiotic tourists?

The road to Om was winding and hilly, ending with a long, steep descent to the beautiful beach, which, nestled into the high hill behind it, was sheltered and cosy. As we stepped onto the white sands, we passed a rather fancy guest house and moved on past it, looking for something closer to our budget. The beach was quiet but it was still very early. As we wandered past beautiful trees that sprawled up the hill, halfway across we stumbled on a thatched café with a trail of basic beach huts behind it. Dolphin Bay Café: no electricity, no running water, but an entire hut to yourself, twenty seconds from the ocean and only fifty rupees a night (less than one euro). As if all that wasn't enough, there was a heap of small puppies asleep under one of the hammocks outside. I was sold!

The next beach south of Om was named Paradise beach, but heaven was right here as we tucked into breakfast and chai, snoozed in the hammocks and freshened up by going for a swim when the day started to really heat up. The water was pretty calm, and I realised that the warnings of dangerous currents were entirely necessary as it was too easy to dismiss the alleged perils of swimming here.

Gokarna proved to be the first place in India where we 'settled down' and joined a mini community of fellow travellers. When we arrived, there were a few people staying in Dolphin Bay Café who'd already been there several weeks. Om beach seemed to suck people in like a vortex and the hours flowed like the colourful blobs in a lava lamp, blurring and merging into each other seamlessly until suddenly night had arrived as if out of nowhere; our first two days were soft clouds of sunbathing, swimming, eating and napping. I called home a few times during our stay there and each time it felt impossible to relate to the grey, nine-to-five life back in Ireland; my life these days was lying in hammocks with sandy toes, feeling the golden heat of the sun on my skin and connecting with other like-minded (if sometimes a bit stoned) individuals.

On our third day Rob, myself and two friendly girls from Finland, Eevi and Helmi, decided to walk over to Paradise beach. There was no road back then – you got there either on foot or by boat and it was the most southerly beach in Gokarna's stretch of sandy coastline. It was separated from Om by cliffs, bays and a small, untouched gem, the crescent-shaped Half-Moon beach. We left at 11 am, hoping to get there before the intense midday heat.

Strolling along the beautiful rugged coastline, it wasn't long until we were stepping down the cliff to the sandy shore of Half-Moon beach. Rob went for a quick swim to cool off, the sun and humidity already high. I sat on a large rock at the water's edge, my feet in the sea, my floaty skirt bunched up, the two girls nearby chatting and giggling with each other in Finnish. The fresh air was sprinkled with salt, stray wisps of my hair tickled my face in the tiny breeze and when Rob emerged from the water moments later – a tanned, glistening, half-naked god – I wondered if we'd already reached Paradise without realising.

'We should get moving, *oder*?' Rob suggested, stashing his small towel into the rucksack and pulling back on his T-shirt.

'Yes, it's getting very hot,' Eevi stated, and Helmi smiled shyly, nodding.

'I'm already looking forward to a cool lemon soda,' I said, slipping into my sandy flip-flops. 'Let's go!'

I would estimate that my happy, carefree mood lasted for at least another hour of trekking through the humid jungle before it began to rapidly evaporate. For some inexplicable reason, we had veered off the cliff's coastal path, coming further inland and, would you believe it, winding up completely lost.

'Damn it!' I muttered, after stubbing my toe on the rocky, jagged path yet again. If I'd known in advance that we'd be trekking through the wilderness I might have chosen more suitable footwear (or opted out of the trip altogether).

'Are we definitely going the right way?' I asked the others for the third time, frowning and stopping to take a swig of water from my bottle. 'I'm sure it's not meant to be this far.'

'I don't really know!' Helmi replied cheerfully, seeming totally unaffected by our arduous hike in the boiling heat. 'Maybe we should go back?'

'No, we keep going and head towards the coast,' Rob said determinedly, squinting against the glare of the sun and looking as cranky as I felt.

'But there's no path to the coast,' I pointed out, unable to keep the irritation out of my voice. There was a small knot of concern growing in my stomach, fuelled by the (somewhat unlikely) idea that we might not be able to find our way out of the maze of dirt tracks and palm trees.

'*Also*, we must find a path!' Rob responded curtly. He grabbed the bottom of his T-shirt, dragging it across his sweaty forehead while I scowled at him in annoyance. Seemingly oblivious to our tension, Eevi laughed lightly.

'Maybe they have to search for us,' she joked. 'Maybe we sleep in the jungle tonight!'

Both girls laughed at the idea but the dark expression on Rob's face showed he didn't quite share their sense of humour. Hoisting up my long skirt, I sighed.

'OK, let's keep going, maybe we'll come across somebody local,' I said doubtfully. Since leaving Om beach we hadn't passed a single person. In the whole of overpopulated India, we'd managed to get lost in the one area that didn't seem to have any people at all.

On we trekked. Helmi and Eevi seemed genuinely carefree while Rob was as tense as a coiled spring. As we advanced, we found a path running downhill through dense, leafy forest. The shade from the relentless sun was a welcome break. Further on we finally spotted a little house nestled in the trees and, to my relief, two young women sitting outside it. Humans! They seemed surprised to see four sweaty tourists walking up to them, but once we mentioned Paradise beach they smiled and one of them gestured for us to follow her.

Despite our local guide helping us find our way, I don't know if any tourists have had a harder time locating that damn beach. We wandered around the snake-ridden rice paddies of Gokarna for probably another hour and indeed I did see a snake just several feet away. It gave me quite the adrenaline rush, a primal survival instinct surging through my body preparing me to flee, except, within seconds of seeing it, the creature had slunk away and completely disappeared (I figured it was probably best not to share this incident with my parents next time we spoke). We took one final wrong turn that landed us high up a cliff, staring down at the little beach from afar – where I very nearly threw myself down just to bloody get there. Eventually though, several stressful hours after starting out, we made it to Paradise beach.

If we hadn't been so delighted and relieved to no longer be lost in the jungles of southern India, the place would most likely have been a let-down, but for us weary explorers the very act of reaching it transformed it into heaven itself. It was a really tiny spot tucked into the cliff, with one small restaurant and a handful of huts and hammocks that currently hosted about ten people with room for another five. It was simple and natural and peaceful. Goodwill was restored between Rob and me. And I got my lemon soda.

Inevitably, a few hours later, we had to face the trek back to Om. While getting lost at midday hadn't been so much fun, the thought of it happening in the fading light was a different matter altogether, so it felt like Christmas and my birthday rolled into one when the restaurant owner said he'd call a boat for us. Our misadventure had lasted over three hours; the small, motorised wooden boat had us back in ten minutes and gave us epic views of the beautiful, craggy coastline. I smiled wryly as we zoomed past Half-Moon beach where it had all started to go wrong.

Getting out of the boat at Om beach, I noticed ominous dark clouds filling up the sky like smoke. The temperature had dropped and a cool wind was tugging at our hair and clothes like a gentle warning: storm approaching. I hadn't even finished my bucket shower before the rain started coming down. I scooted back to my hut and waited out the tropical storm there. It was an impressive show nature put on for us, with torrential rain accompanying lightning and rolling thunder. When it finally began to ease, I joined Rob, Paul and the other tourists who were sheltering in the café.

As the boys and I ate dinner by candlelight and we filled Paul in on our escapades, the remnants of the storm played out like an impressive encore around us. The lightning came less often, but each flash illuminated the entire beach, revealing human silhouettes scattered across the sand, some even swimming in the sea. The furious thunder receded to sullen rumbles in the distance and the rain lightened to drops tinkling off the thatch roofs and trees. Sitting back in my chair with a full tummy and my two buddies either side, I decided it was quite a good end to the day.

* * *

Om beach, though kind on our wallets, was not kind on our tummies. My second day, and several others after that, left me feeling very unwell. Each time it happened I took to a hammock or my hut, lying down with my hands on my stomach and trying to relax. It passed every time and I managed to get by unscathed but numerous other tourists complained of some problem or other.

When chilling out in the café, it was a common sight to see the staff from Dolphin Bay Café trekking across the beach with supplies of fresh water to fill up the large water tank. Radika carried her heavy container elegantly on her head, one hand raised to balance it as they navigated the uneven beach. She was followed by tall, cheeky Rahul and the shorter, steelier Sai, who supported a thick pole on their shoulders from which hung two huge full buckets.

As we watched the little procession nearing us, I pondered how they prepared the food here in the little café with that limited supply of fresh water, washing the vegetables and cooking with it … It wasn't hard to catch the possible link between that and the various stomach bugs that had people dropping like flies. It was just the tourists who suffered but I guessed the locals, who'd lived here all their lives, had formidable immune systems compared to our delicate Western ones.

On day five our own musketeer Rob became the next casualty, confined to his hut for the day, burning up with a high temperature while his body purged itself from both ends. It seemed a fairly simple case of Delhi belly, the typical traveller's bug in India and one that numerous other tourists had struggled with while here at Om beach. Paul and I left him to sleep it off and decided to trek the coastal route to Gokarna town. What we didn't realise at the time, however, was that there was no coastal route to Gokarna.

Unlike the walk to Paradise beach, the route to Gokarna had a neat footpath further in from the cliffs. But then I seemed to have a penchant for losing my way in life, both metaphorically and literally. An hour or so passed easily as we clambered over coastal rocks. We spotted a school of dolphins gliding through the sparkling ocean and ambled on, blissfully unaware that we were going the wrong way. The first inkling of our mistake was when the path started to change, climbing higher and becoming strewn with thorny, brambly bushes that were clumped together and painfully awkward to squeeze past. The next clue was coming upon what seemed to be an eagle's lair, the birds of prey circling overhead uncomfortably close, the trees laden with their nests.

I was beginning to get a sense of déjà vu.

'Paul, this can't be the right way,' I called to him, a few feet ahead of me. He ducked instinctively when an eagle swooped aggressively close to his head. There seemed to be a swarm of them. Snagging my T-shirt on yet another thorny bush, I tried again.

'There's not even a path through here, shouldn't we turn back?'

He stopped, looking up the overgrown hill that rose five metres, almost vertical, next to us. The only way up would have been to climb which, in my T-shirt, shorts and flip-flops, obviously wasn't an option. But Paul was already setting off.

'I bet we'll find a path up at the top of this,' he said confidently, grabbing at bushes and pulling himself up.

'There's no way I can get up there, Paul!'

Ignoring me, he carried on. I hesitated for a moment, daunted at the thought of climbing, yet panicked at the idea of backtracking all the way to Om alone. Noticing Paul halfway up the slope already, I quit thinking and launched myself after him. It was ridiculous. Two tourists, dressed for the beach, lost in an eagle's lair and scrambling up a steep overgrown hill like hairless monkeys. Let me reiterate the part about idiotic tourists in Gokarna one final time, because I think I had become the official mascot.

I had a light towel that I'd been using as a shield against the sun and it was the only reason I managed to reach the top after Paul. Wrapping it around my hand like a protective glove I was able to grab hold of prickly bushes to pull myself up an otherwise impossible terrain, as my feet slipped in and out of my flip-flops and my bare legs scraped off thorns. Ridiculous or not, we did finally reach the 'summit' and glimpsed the open stretch of Kudle beach, the last beach before Gokarna, just three hundred metres away from us. Leading up to Kudle was a clear inland path that stretched back in the direction of Om beach. The path we should have been on all along.

Despite inadvertently passing through the beach he was staying on, I never saw Jack when we stopped on Kudle beach. Communication between us was as infrequent as always. I had only managed to email him once in the five days we'd been in Gokarna so that he knew where I was staying. Internet facilities were at either end of Om beach and, on the occasions that I tried, the network connection seemed to have an aversion to my personal email account. The one email I wrote to him was from Rob's account so I could never find the previous message he'd sent, which said where he was staying. In hindsight, it's a little strange how it all proceeded; had I taken down his number correctly in the first place, we could easily have met while in Goa, or had my email account worked properly I could have gone to Kudle beach and looked for him. But then, the universe had its own plans ...

Having refreshed ourselves with lemon sodas and washed off our scrapes in a little café on Kudle beach, Paul and I followed the well-worn path from there to Gokarna town and made it without incident. Trips to the town were usually made purely for purchases we couldn't make on the beach, like alcohol, and this was Paul's main incentive for going there that day. After filling his rucksack with bottles of Kingfisher, we treated ourselves to a tuk-tuk to get back to Om beach, and while the sun began its evening descent and we strolled across our beloved sands, it felt like coming home after months away.

Krishna, the chilled-out owner of Dolphin Bay Café, smiled a hello at us from behind the counter as we strolled wearily over.

'Chai?' he called out cheerfully.

We grinned and nodded. In India, a simple trip to town can become a mini adventure and I felt like I'd just completed the jungle survival course, part two.

Chapter 11

Romantic notions

'I'm gonna check up on Rob,' I said to Paul as he settled down at one of the café tables. I slipped off my flip-flops and wandered across the soft sand to the huts behind.

'Rob? How are you doing, man?' I called, poking my head in his half-open door.

He lifted his head off his pillow and the gentle evening light filtered in, illuminating his pale face.

'*Ja*, not so good,' he smiled weakly, lifting himself up slowly to a sitting position. 'I've had everything today; fever, vomiting and shitting water. If I have to squat one more time tonight, I'll fall into the damn toilet,' he said wearily.

I walked over and pressed my hand against his clammy forehead. 'You don't seem to have a temperature at least. Here,' I handed him some tablets and sachets I had picked up in the pharmacy. 'Put the electrolytes into your water.'

'*Danke. Ja*, I think the worst is over, I'll come outside. I'm sick of lying on this bed.'

'Great, we can fill you in on today's unexpected adventure.'

Rob joined us all around the hammocks, looking pale and weary but gradually coming alive as Paul filled him in on our comical trek to Gokarna. 'Are you serious?' he exclaimed, laughing out loud and looking over at me.

I nodded, rolling my eyes. 'Look at my legs.' I stretched them both out to show off the numerous cuts and scratches.

'That's so funny, you two got lost in an eagle's lair in India? Now I feel better,' he said decisively, leaning back in his chair with a satisfied grin.

Paul continued the tale, but I was distracted by a guy coming over and sitting near us. I smiled a hello and introduced myself.

'How you doin', luv – I'm Mikey.' I found my hand enclosed in his strong, warm handshake. He had a musical cockney lilt to his words, dark curly hair and smiling brown eyes. Before we could say any more, Rahul walked over to greet him.

'Oh ho, Mikey, you come back!' he said with a big grin and Mikey went to hug the funny waiter. There was much back-slapping involved.

'How you doin', mate! Yeah, I'm back, migh' not leave this time.' Mikey was laughing.

'You stay, you stay, no problem. Here is a happy life for little money.'

'Too right, my friend. Too fuckin' right!'

Mikey sat back down next to me, pulling out a pouch of Golden Virginia from his shorts pocket. I eyed it longingly while he rolled himself a cigarette before guiltily asking if I could make myself a rollie. ''Elp yourself, luv,' he nodded, pushing the packet and skins towards me. 'I've about thirty more in my bag, stocked up in duty free. Much better than the stuff you get 'ere.'

'You've been here before, then?' I asked, placing a pinch of tobacco and a filter into a Rizla and starting to roll it between my fingers.

'Yeah, I was 'ere two years ago. Ended up hangin' out on Om beach the whole time, must've been about five months.'

'Five months?' I stared at him, mid-roll.

'You get sucked into this place, luv,' he warned with a grin, lighting up his rollie and inhaling deeply. 'I had a lot going on back home and I needed time out. They're good guys 'ere,' he added, indicating Krishna and the people working for him. Rahul flashed us a brilliant smile from under his bushy moustache.

'I guess,' I said, still a little incredulous. Grabbing his lighter, I looked over at the others at our table. Pat was staring out at the sea, his left foot raised on another seat.

'How's the ankle, Pat?' I asked the English lad.

He grinned lazily at me, an easy-going mellow guy who'd already been on Om for three weeks and didn't show any sign of moving on. But Pat wasn't one for rushing around, even when certain occasions called for a bit of haste, like when he gashed his ankle off a rock in the sea and allowed it four days to fester and develop into a swollen mass of infection, before finally going to see a doctor.

'Yeah, it's OK, ' he drawled and twisted his leg around to show me. My stomach did a little flip at the ugly mess.

'Yeah, that looks just fine, doesn't it,' I agreed, wincing.

'It's not that bad,' he assured me with a cheeky grin. 'It's only a flesh wound. I've 'ad worse!'

'Quoting Monty Python isn't going to make it better.'

'Don't worry, I'm taking the antibiotics. It'll be back to new before you know it.'

'You need to take something stronger than that,' an Irish girl called Jess piped up randomly from beside him. 'Like hula-hooping!'

And she stood up and grabbed her hoop from where it was resting next to the counter. Judging from her clumsy movements and slightly erratic behaviour, it was a pretty safe bet she was wasted, though on which substance, who knew. Another of Om beach's long-term residents, I had yet to see her anywhere close to sober.

'Hey, there we go!' she shouted, as she finally got some rhythm going. 'See, Pat, this is what you need, get your energy flowing. Yeah!'

She spun around in ragged circles until she quickly lost her balance and ended in a heap on the sand. Mikey jumped up to give her a hand while she giggled to herself.

'Did you see that? How good was that, hey?'

Limp like a ragdoll, her floppy body made it incredibly difficult for Mikey to pull her back up to standing.

'That was the good one, Jess!' Rahul called, laughing out loud, and his lightness broke the mild tension that had built up among us. Jess's druggy behaviour could often make for real awkwardness. It wasn't the first or the last time we'd be treated to such a spectacle. Om beach seemed to encourage an excess of intoxication and she wasn't the only one to indulge in various substances there, merely the most flamboyant.

* * *

My heart jumped. It was actually ringing! I was down at Ganesh hotel the next morning using the public phone to call Jack and, for the first time since arriving into Gokarna, the number was actually connecting. I sat there, holding my breath, waiting … until it finally rang out with no answer. Unbelievable. A couple more tries proved equally unsuccessful. I stared at the receiver in my hand, frustrated. This was getting to be a joke.

Walking back along the beach towards our huts, it dawned on me that while the phone actually ringing seemed like a sign of progress, it also could mean that Jack had left Gokarna. I still hadn't managed to open my own email account so I never knew which beach he had been staying at – he could be anywhere now. Why was it so difficult to meet up with this man?

That night, there was a big gathering of us in Dolphin Bay Café, sitting around the tables, smoking and chatting while alcohol was shared freely. The puppies were similarly shared round, like a game of pass-the-parcel, and for a while I had a small furball of cuteness asleep on my lap.

Mikey was sitting close beside me. We had spent the afternoon hanging out and a current of attraction had quickly started to flow in and around us. He spotted the puppy and smiled.

'Well, at least one of us is gettin' a cuddle tonigh'!'

I smiled back, catching his eye and his meaning. 'He might not be the only one.'

Mikey held my gaze. The palpable sexual tension between us filled every glance, every smile, every word with a jolt of electric anticipation that grew stronger as the night wore on. We both knew what was there though neither one of us was willing to say it.

My fickle heart had abandoned Rob, but then again, I had never received a single sign that Rob saw me as anything more than a good travel buddy. Mikey was a different story altogether. There was no second-guessing his feelings, no wondering and questioning whether he was interested, I could feel it like the warm air around us and the sand beneath my bare feet.

I let down my hair out of its messy bun and tossed the thick, wavy locks casually over my shoulder. He fidgeted a little, then leaned over.

'You look even better with your hair like that!'

I pretended I hadn't heard properly. He leaned in closer till I could feel his breath caressing my cheek as he repeated the words. I was beginning to feel a bit giddy. To diffuse the heady moment, I grabbed my glass of beer and drank deeply.

'Can I borrow your torch? I need to make a pit stop.'

'Course you can, darlin'!' he said, picking it up off the table to give to me.

'I'll swap you a puppy for it,' I teased, placing the still sleeping creature gently onto his lap and taking the light.

Returning the flashlight to him when I came back, I blatantly left my hand lingering in his before reaching over to pick up my drink. It was Mikey that finally took control of the situation, clasping my hand decisively in his, our fingers and eyes interlocked and two knowing smiles of what was sure to come. He gave a little nod of his head indicating we leave the group, to which I grinned, picking up my bag and making a discreet exit.

Mikey followed a moment later, catching up to me and taking hold of my hand again.

'Yours or mine, luv?' he asked.

Even in the dim light, I could see his eyes shining.

'Yours, it's closer!'

We didn't speak much, strolling back to his hut. His hand felt warm and solid in mine and the night felt full of delicious promise.

We entered his dark bamboo hut and I slid the flimsy door shut. Taking a lighter out of his pocket, he bent down to light a few candles planted into the sandy floor and then turned back to me and wrapped his arms around my body. I soaked up the solid strength of his builder's muscles. Slowly opening my eyes, I spotted his open backpack on the floor.

'Shit! That's a fuck-load of condoms!' I exclaimed, pulling back from him and staring at the endless packets of contraceptives spilling out of the top. 'Are you planning on having sex for breakfast, lunch and dinner?'

'Shhh! Keep your voice down! They were on offer at the airport, that's all,' Mikey admonished me, partly out of embarrassment and partly because I was practically yelling. 'Look, luv, you can't always get hold of these things out 'ere and I won't have sex unprotected. Mind you, condoms won't stop you gettin' things like warts.'

'Oh right. Lovely. Well, last time I checked I was all clear on that score,' I responded drily, feeling a distinct change in the evening's mood.

'Look, luv, isn't it better I care about it? Most guys wouldn't. We don't even 'ave to do anything now, just spoonin'.'

This should have reassured me and softened things. But instead, disappointment raised its defensive shields.

'Spooning. Great,' I answered flatly.

Mikey groaned, running a hand through his hair.

'It's not like I wouldn't like to do more stuff, if, you know, you were up for it,' he suggested, putting his hands on my waist and pulling me in close in an effort to retrieve our flirtatious, tingly mood from earlier. We hugged again but the fire of our earlier passions had fizzled out and I realised I was starting to feel tired.

'Let's just go to sleep,' I said, and he laid his forehead against mine for a moment.

'Sure, darlin', no problem.'

We climbed onto the bed and snuggled and it was good, actually really good. But when Mikey came to talk to me next day, he suggested we leave off the beginnings of our little romance.

'Luv, I only just got to India, I'm not lookin' for a relationship and I don't think you're the type for a casual fling. I mean that in a good way,' he added pointedly. 'I'm always 'ere if you want a cuddle, luv, OK?' He pulled me in for a hug.

'No problem,' I mumbled into his big, hairy chest, giving a small sigh of disappointment. He was probably right, but still, we could have had some fun.

Deflated, I wandered over to where Rob was sitting by the café, reading his book.

'Hey, man, how's it going?' I asked flatly, plonking myself down next to him.

'Absolutely fantastic,' he replied moodily, tossing his book aside and bending over to inspect his foot.

'What's up?'

He was wiping sand away from the cut he'd got in Agonda in the bike accident. Though small, it was quite deep.

'This place is infested with bacteria,' he said irritably. 'The wound on my foot has gotten worse instead of better. First I rubbed off the, how do you say, the scab thing, by wearing my boots in Hampi and then again walking to Paradise beach. I think it's infected now. Fucking dirty sand.'

I stared at him in surprise. It was unusual to find him in such bad form.

'Sorry, Liz,' he said on seeing my expression. Sitting up straight, he took a tube of antiseptic cream from his pocket, squeezed out a small amount and applied it carefully to his toe. 'I'm not in a good mood. I don't like sitting around all day but it seems like every time I do anything I make it worse. It's really frustrating.'

'I can understand that. Maybe it's time we booked tickets to our next destination.'

We sat in silence for a while and watched the crew with the day's buckets of fresh water approaching the café. Mikey appeared, going over to give Radika a hand with her heavy load and I admired his strong body from afar. It reminded me of builders back home who slogged all week and then indulged at weekends: buff but cushioned. Who wouldn't be attracted to a handsome gentleman like Mikey who would run to break up dog fights, or stop drunk Indian men from hassling bikini-clad girls, or lovingly scoop up puppies that had strayed too far? He was a gem but not for me, it seemed. I sighed a little louder than I meant to and Rob looked at me questioningly.

'We should go to Gokarna town and book our next journey,' I said decisively.

Chapter 12

Moving on

'Ma'am, the next available train to Cochin is in four days.'

I left the counter to relay the news to the boys. We were in Gokarna town trying to organise our onward trip. Rob wasn't happy.

'I am not staying another four days at that beach, guys. Isn't there something before then?'

'No other train, you want to take a bus?'

'Aw, no way, man,' Paul cut in. 'No more overnight buses. I'm serious!'

'Well then, there's only the train. You'll just have to wait,' I told Rob.

'Maybe we can go somewhere else?' Rob suggested.

'We decided on Cochin for the end of your trip and now you want to change the whole plan?'

'I'm SICK of this place and that damn beach, I don't want to hang around for four more days!'

'Well then, why don't you just take a bus by yourself?' I retorted.

It was rude and mean. Rob stared at me, an inscrutable frown on his face.

'We always stick together, Liz. If you guys are taking the train, then I guess I'll go with you.'

I was instantly full of remorse. I shouldn't have snapped at him, but my short fuse that day was covering up an underlying worry that had recently returned. It was only another two weeks until Rob and Paul were scheduled to fly from Mumbai to Thailand and my pre-India anxiety, so protectively taken care of by the boys, was returning full force as I contemplated continuing my travels without them.

'Sorry,' I apologised. 'I know you're totally fed up.'

He shrugged and his face softened.

'It's OK,' he said in a kind voice. 'Buy those tickets, though, four days is my limit. After that I go, with or without you two.'

In two months of living practically in each other's pockets, all while managing the chaos and challenges of travel in India, this was our first ever real disagreement. It showed just how easy and comfortable our friendship was. It also showed just how frustrated Rob must have been.

We left the train station with our precious tickets and pottered around the little town. With our onward journey now confirmed, it suddenly dawned on me that I would be heading in the opposite direction to Jack, since he'd already been down to Kerala. But on the few occasions I managed to log into my email account, there had been no updates from him and this was my last week or so with the boys, I felt I had to stick with them. In an internet café in Gokarna I sent him an email before we returned to the temperamental network of Om beach again.

Hi Jack,

I haven't heard anything from you for a while, not sure where you're at these days. I know I haven't been great about getting to the internet cafés to email but I tried ringing you recently and for the first time it seemed to connect. Does that mean you've left Gokarna if you finally have signal? The boys have only a week left before they leave and they wanted to see some of Kerala so we've booked tickets to go down to Cochin. I'm dreading the thoughts of being left on my own but it does mean I'll be completely free and I can come to wherever you are, and we can finally, finally hang out. So, let me know, I'll stay in Cochin with Rob and Paul for their last week in India and then I'll come see you! It's a promise.

Liz

I sent the email. It was rather callous, not that I realised that at the time. Now that I was going to be on my own, I wanted to meet up with Jack far more than before. I was missing the fact that I hadn't worried too much about it, as long as I had the security blanket of Paul and Rob at my side. I had, in fact, royally fucked up. I just didn't know it yet.

* * *

That evening, a group of us gathered down on the beach, where a few local Indians were trying to get a fire going. Even Rob was out and about socialising (his infected toe wrapped up in a thick wad of bandages). Not only was this somewhat unusual behaviour, but at 11 pm, it was also way past his normal bedtime. There was a reason, however; a few pretty, Austrian reasons. I had officially lost my hunk to ladies of his own land although for the moment, at least, I had his full attention.

'There is scientific proof to back me up,' I told him.

Rob snorted dismissively.

'How is it possible that a bit of paper stuck to a bottle of water can change the basic properties of the liquid inside, hmmm?' He stretched his endless body along the sand, laughing as if in the presence of total idiots. 'No way is it possible.'

I gritted my teeth but Rachel, who was sitting beside me, spoke up.

'It's weird but true,' she asserted in her soft Welsh accent. She took her water bottle and tore off the plastic wrapper around it, shaking the bottle to emphasise her words.

'They've tested it and the same water inside has proven cleaner and purer, just from removing the company label. So, imagine the effect of writing a positive message – peace for example – and sticking it to the bottle. The molecules in the water will attune to that vibration and that's really what you're drinking. Peace!' she finished with a smile.

Rob stared at us like we had trees growing out of our ears.

'That is such a load of hippie crap! If I write "sexiest man in the world" and stick it on my forehead, do you think it'll come true?' he asked, laughing at his own joke.

'There are some things even God can't change,' I snapped in annoyance.

But Rob had already turned back to his fancy Austrian babes and missed my retort. I fidgeted in irritation. I had already acknowledged that nothing was ever going to come of my little crush on the handsome Austrian, but that didn't mean I was happy about him ignoring me for his new female fan club. Not realising Rachel had moved away, or that there was someone else now next to me, I began to vent my frustration with the male of the species.

'Maybe men should try writing "I am not a total twat" and glue it to their foreheads. Could make the world a better place for us all.'

'What's that, luv?'

I whirled around at the sound of Mikey's velvety voice and coloured with surprise.

'Um, nothing, thought you were Rachel.'

'Firs' time I've been mistaken for a woman! Is it my man boobs?' he joked, leaning back casually on his elbows.

'Sure, that and the facial-stubble. Oh, and a certain extra package. All indicators of your delicate, effeminate sexuality.'

'Extra package? You're not referrin' to my love 'andles I 'ope, darlin'. A guy can get offended, you know.'

I could hear the smile in his voice.

'Handles? I was thinking more floppy wings.'

Mikey coughed on his beer.

'Sorry, bit too far?'

'Just a little, darlin'!'

And there it was again, that chemistry, like a powerful jolt of electricity all but crackling in the air between us. We didn't joke around anymore after that, in fact we said very little to each other, pretending to be interested in the others in the group, but the tension couldn't be ignored for long. Once again the gallant gentleman took charge, throwing his arm around me like a man finally claiming what was his all along. My feminist alter ego, meek and mild-mannered at the best of times, rolled her eyes, saying nothing. Mikey could have his wicked way with me if he wished.

Unfortunately, our little saga was doomed from the beginning. I was a high-maintenance girl who required a very patient, very tolerant partner, a big ask of anyone but especially a guy who'd just come to India to chill out. A few tantrums (fuelled mostly by Super Jack whiskey) were the nails in the coffin of our little fling. We still managed to end on good terms but the credit for that belongs solely to Mikey and his saintly patience.

On our second-last night at Om beach, my hut became inexplicably but undeniably haunted. At some point in the black of night, I found myself tugged out of slumber to that very surreal place – the in-between world of sleep and waking consciousness – by the uncomfortable sensation of heavy, immovable weights on both my hands. They wouldn't move. I couldn't move. Shit was getting very weird.

A very real rustling right outside had me abruptly wide awake and convinced there was someone else actually inside my hut. The energy of another person's presence felt as real as the beads of sweat about to trickle down the side of my forehead. In the primitive fear it engendered, I was frozen, lying there completely still except for the rapid rise and fall of my chest, too petrified to even consider leaving my hut and calling on Paul or Rob for reassurance. Eventually, lying so still, the weight of tiredness pulled me back under and when I opened my eyes next, the sun was chasing away the ghosts of the night. I got up and padded down to the toilets, then went to the café for chai and human company, still reeling from my bizarre experience.

Sitting down next to a few of the others already up, I shared the unnerving experience.

'Luv, you should 'ave called into me!' Mikey told me, sounding surprised that I hadn't. 'If it 'appens again to-night, you make sure you come to my hut. No point 'angin' around on your own, scared.'

'He's right,' Rob said, while Paul stared at me in fascination.

'Man, that's so freaky,' he said bluntly. 'I've heard of it be-fore how some spirits will latch onto a person but they can only do it while we're asleep because you're more connected to the other realms. They call it psychic rape and stuff.'

'Jesus, Paul!' I stared at my lovable but incredibly tactless friend. 'Don't be saying shit like that!'

'Ignore him,' Rob told me firmly. 'It's not like any of that stuff is even real, *ja*, last night was just your mind playing tricks in the dark.'

'The noises you 'eard could 'ave been rats, I know there's a few of 'em about,' Mikey added.

Paul didn't look convinced. 'I don't know,' he started. 'This psychic stuff is real–'

'SHUT UP, Paul!'

He finally let it go, shrugging at our fierce expressions.

That night, we went for drinks at another hotel on the beach, but after a while I started to get tired and my stom-ach didn't seem entirely well, so when Rob and a few others left early, I went with them. The moment I sat on my bed in the dark quiet hut, the disturbed feelings of the night before returned full-force, surrounding me like invisible, taunting bodies. I realised I had two options: stay in my hut, scared witless or …

'I know this might sound really stupid but I'm kinda freaked out again, can I sleep next to you tonight?'

A torch blinded me, shining straight at my face.

'Of course you can.' Rob began to move his things and make space next to him on the bed.

I scooted over with my sleeping bag and pillow and curled up beside him.

'Wake me up if you get scared in the night,' he mumbled as he drifted off to sleep.

'OK.' But I couldn't imagine feeling anything but snug and secure as I lay beside my dear Austrian hulk.

* * *

'FUCK OFF!! Stupid crows!' Rob yelled into his pillow, not even bothering to lift his head.

There was a moment's pause.

'Did you sleep OK?' he asked.

I giggled.

'Really good! Right until those birds started screaming outside the hut.'

It was true. For the first time in many days, I had slept the whole night like a baby and, given we were leaving that evening, I didn't have to worry about the demons lurking around my hut anymore (whatever lucky traveller moved into it next could deal with them). I stretched contentedly and lay still for a few minutes, finally creeping out of the hut for my morning chai while Rob snoozed on. To my surprise, Pat was sitting up outside with a joint and a coffee. I glanced at the café clock. It was just gone 8 am. The last I'd seen of Pat the night before, he was floating away in a drugged bubble of ketamine along with several others.

'Good morning, sir!' I joked. 'How are we doing today?'

Pat turned two bloodshot, fuzzy eyes towards me with a big goofy smile.

'Aw yeah, Liz, g'mornin' doll face, how ya doin'?'

'I'm good,' I paused, looking at him carefully. 'What the hell are you doing up so early?'

'Slept in the hammock.' Pat pointed vaguely at the several set up around the café. A tanned Hungarian lad was still fast asleep in one, an arm hanging loosely over the side.

'Yeah, it wasn't really too comfy. Got up to have some chai.'

'You're mad.' I laughed, slapping him affectionately on the shoulder.

'I don't want you guys to leave,' he said suddenly, switching from druggy bliss to sorrow and staring at me mournfully. 'I don't want to be around when you're going, I hate goodbyes.'

I was silent a moment, feeling a heavy pang of my own. In the background Groove Armada played on the café's little speaker, accompanied by a rumble of snores from the hammock and the gentle ocean waves nearby. I felt a deep melancholy at the thought of leaving behind my new friends and the comfortable familiarity of Om but a part of me also knew it was time to move on. I sighed, feeling a bit depressed. Not, however, quite as much as Pat.

'Krishna! One beer, mate.'

Krishna looked over at us from the counter. 'Beer, Pat? Now?'

'Pat, it's eight in the morning!' I told him.

He looked at me with that doleful smile again, though his eyes were glazing over.

'I hate goodbyes,' he repeated before standing up and walking unsteadily towards the toilets. A few hours later, he was in a foggy sleep of beer and drugs for the day, just as he'd intended.

Far too quickly for my liking, day drifted into night and our taxi to the train station arrived. People gathered around like a mini family to see us off and, just as we were putting on our backpacks, we heard Mohan shout out a cheery greeting.

'Good morning, Pat!'

Ironically, he'd gotten up right at the moment he'd wanted to avoid. Looking dishevelled and sleepy, he threw his arms around me in a quick, gruff hug, at the same that time Jess arranged a string of jasmine flowers in my hair. Rachel gave each of us a big squeeze and the last person I approached was Mikey who, despite my huge backpack, managed to wrap his arms around me in the warmest, most comforting bear hug imaginable.

And then we were gone, bumping and jolting through the darkness. We had somehow succeeded in dislodging ourselves from the quicksand of Om for our last journey together as a trio. It was time to visit beautiful Kerala.

Chapter 13

Time to say goodbye

An uncomfortable sticky heat woke me next morning as the train rolled us steadily towards the small coastal town of Fort Cochin. Located in the beautiful lush state of Kerala – aptly known by the locals as God's Own Country – Fort Cochin was a touristic little town on the peninsula, full of British architecture, colonial walls, cobbled streets, Christian churches and more tourists than you could shake a stick at.

It seemed that our need to run around and visit sights and scenes had dried up. The boys and I spent our last week together relaxing in the small town where the biggest decisions we had to make each day were usually in which cafés we should eat or read our books.

We dabbled in just a few of the requisite touristic attractions, mainly the backwaters and Kathakali dancing. The backwaters involved a day's excursion on a big, flat wooden boat propelled by a lean old man with a long bamboo stick. He sailed us quietly along the meandering, natural canals of fresh water that wound through infinite coconut forests and spice plantations. It was beautiful and tranquil and very un-Indian.

Kathakali, on the other hand, couldn't have been more Indian if it tried: noisy, colourful and completely incoherent to us Westerners. The ancient theatrical dance involved weird warbled singing, clanging drums and bizarrely costumed characters that told an indecipherable story through subtle dance. Our touristic, diluted version lasted a single hour as opposed to the *six* it would traditionally have been and thank God for that, as five minutes in, the story was already lost on me and the drumming was giving me a headache.

The only thing to tarnish those peace-filled days was the email I finally received from Jack. I had tried to call him again on the second day in Cochin and, to my shock, it had actually answered. Only, it wasn't Jack's voice at the end of the line, but Cathy, a bubbly Australian girl. Apparently, Jack was away for two days on some excursion, but she'd let him know I'd called. I hadn't heard anything from him in over a week at that stage. But I did hear from him at last and it wasn't pretty.

Hi Liz,

I'm inland for a few days, not far from Hampi, and having a damn good time. So now that your precious boyfriends are leaving you're getting lonely. Well, to be perfectly honest, I don't care. You're not who I thought you were. Admittedly it's my own fault for creating a totally imagined person. You berate me for joking around about my feelings but when I offered my heart to you, you pissed all over it. I have a solid group of friends around me here so you can stop emailing or trying to call me. It's tiresome. Enjoy the rest of your travels all on your own. You deserve it.

Jack

Ouch. He did have a point, or several points to be honest. Nonetheless, my wobbly self-esteem took a blow and I had to explain myself to the boys later that evening, given the sudden plummet my mood had taken.

'Fuck him! He's an ass if he said all that. You're better off without him,' Paul told me with full conviction. His automatic rise to my defence was typical and sweet, even if maybe I didn't deserve it.

'You know what I think?' Rob said thoughtfully. 'I think he's probably in an old people's home out here in India …'

'Rob!' I exclaimed, giggling.

'… and he keeps saying he's in this place or that place when really he's sat in a wheelchair being fed cookies and milk by some hot Indian nurse.'

'Rob, stop!' I was laughing properly now.

'That's what old people do, Liz,' Rob told me with a sly grin.

'He's only in his forties, give the man a break.'

'I was trying to give you a break, Lizzy,' Rob answered back. 'Don't be too upset about it. You tried to contact him a million times, it obviously wasn't meant to be, so cheer up. You will both get over it.'

I didn't really believe either of them but I felt a lot better. They were good friends.

* * *

Finally, dreadfully, D-day arrived. To mark our last meal together we dined like royalty in a fabulous north-Indian restaurant. It had bare, whitewashed walls, dark wooden tables, an eccentric, white-haired owner and the most superb, soul-satisfying food.

'Let's have chai,' Rob suggested, as our empty plates were cleared away. He glanced at his watch, but their train back up north wasn't leaving until 10 pm, still two hours away.

We called the owner and ordered three *masala* chai (sweet milky tea with extra spices added).

'For our last supper together, that was pretty spectacular,' I said, patting my stuffed belly.

'So, you're going to be flying solo now, Liz,' Paul reminded me tactfully. 'Where are you gonna head next?'

I shrugged.

'Maybe Munnar and the tea plantations. It's meant to be beautiful. I'd like to go to an ashram too, maybe do some yoga. God, I haven't a fucking clue!' I blurted out, biting on my lip as I began to feel my overwhelm spreading like wildfire.

'You'll be fine, you'll figure it out,' Paul said confidently, just as our hot drinks arrived.

'A toast!' Rob declared, lifting up his little cup. 'To the three of us! And to India and some truly great memories.'

'Absolutely,' I agreed.

'Cheers!' Paul chimed in and we clinked cups.

'I'm really going to miss you guys,' I told them. 'These past two months have been amazing.'

'I'll miss you too, little Irish sister.' Rob smiled at me and I allowed myself a moment to groan inwardly at his declaration of platonic friendship, before realising how right it was. We were much better as good friends and deep down, I had always figured as much (he was far too tall for me anyway). 'I'm looking forward to the next part of the journey, I'm ready to see a new country. But I'm going to miss India and travelling with you two.'

'Yeah, me too. It'll be strange to be back up in Mumbai without you,' Paul said. 'Hey, if you get too lonely here in Cochin, you can always head back to Om beach, find a certain guy …' he added with a cheeky smile.

Rob gave me a little dig with his elbow. 'That's right, there was a little romance there, *oder*? Between you and Mikey, hmm?'

I tried to laugh it off but I could feel my cheeks going red. 'Whatever, you guys.'

'Hey, look at her going all red!' Paul laughed freely at my obvious embarrassment.

I covered my face, still giggling and blushing even more.

'We held hands and … stuff,' I mumbled.

'Stuff?' Rob asked with exaggerated curiosity. 'What kind of *stuff*?'

'Aw man, India's the land of the *Kama Sutra*,' Paul said, grinning. 'I reckon she means kinky tantric shit!'

'Alright, alright! Please, enough.' I laughed, covering my mouth as I looked from one overly innocent face to the other. 'You're such bastards!'

'Aw now, Lizzy, come on, we're just looking out for you,' Rob told me, a big grin on his face. 'You've still got two months left, *ja*? You're so lucky, I wish we had more time to explore this country. Have some great adventures but make sure you look after yourself.'

'Don't go falling for any weird Indians,' Paul snickered. Oh, the irony.

'Seriously, little Liz, travel safe. Promise me!'

'OK, OK, I promise, Rob.'

He looked at his watch. 'I guess we should head back to the hotel.'

Once there, the boys got their luggage from our room while the receptionist called a tuk-tuk to bring them to the train station. It wasn't long till we heard it pulling up outside. Emails and other contact details had already been exchanged along with heartfelt promises to always keep in touch. After two massive, love-filled hugs, I waved them goodbye as their taxi carried them off into the night and then went back up to our quiet and seemingly empty room, with just my one lonely backpack in the corner.

I felt their departure like a deep abyss inside that was rapidly filling up with loneliness. It was as if I were all alone in the big scary world and it made me curl up into a ball of tears. My Indian adventure had come full circle to the blank canvas it had been when I'd boarded the plane in Ireland; a pure white sheet of unwritten experiences and still-to-be-discovered friendships.

Chapter 14

Drifting

I spent several more days in Cochin after the boys left, trying to get used to doing things by myself, and it was a soft transition as I soon got to know a sweet Argentinian, Mateo, over breakfast in Kashi Café (my favourite place in Cochin for cakes and iced coffee).

'Liz, how are you?' he called me over one morning. 'There is a concert here tonight, my sitar teacher he's playing and it's gonna be great. You must come!'

I joined him, fanning my face to cool down. Mateo was spending four months in Cochin to study sitar with an Indian maestro and was a dedicated, disciplined, passionate student. His enthusiasm was infectious.

'OK, I'm in. When is it?' I inquired.

'8 pm. You can get a ticket at the door. So hey, you decided when you're going?' he asked, biting into his omelette.

'Yeah, I finally made up my mind. I'm taking a bus to Munnar tomorrow,' I answered, glancing at the menu, though I already knew what I'd have. The fresh fruit salad here was amazing.

'OK, so after the concert we go to Dhal Roti with Carl for a meal,' Mateo told me with a trademark wink that he did after pretty much every second sentence.

'That sounds good,' I smiled. Carl was a German tour operator working in Cochin. The three of us had hung out already a couple times and the irony wasn't lost on me that, once again, I seemed to have attracted two kind, entertaining guys for company. I wasn't complaining; their banter and boyish energy had lifted me right out of my post-Rob-and-Paul slump.

That evening I sat in the little room off Kashi Café along with nearly twenty others from different corners of the world, all of us bound together for two hours of divine communication via the sitar and tablas and their two humble artists. The eastern music was intricate and beautiful. With a presence that enthralled their small audience and transported us to a realm of magic, the two musicians channelled a force much grander and more powerful than mere humans playing musical instruments. I felt grateful to have been a part of the special concert. When the music finally drew to a close, Mateo's teacher spoke gently to us, imparting some words of wisdom in his quiet voice.

'In these days of modern technology, with our high-paced, stressful lives, it is absolutely imperative that you set aside some quiet time to yourself in each day.' He paused, taking his time to reflect before continuing. 'Sit in silence or listen to beautiful music. Take just thirty minutes out of every twenty-four hours. It will bring you great peace, I promise.

'Now,' he smiled warmly, bringing his hands into the typical Indian prayer greeting. 'Please go out and enjoy your evening. Thank you so very much for coming. *Namaste!*'

In India, even a small concert becomes a deeply spiritual event.

Curry, Chaos and Love

* * *

Munnar, a hill town full of tea plantations, was my first experience of India's picturesque landscapes – to be honest I had begun to wonder if there were any. It took me five hours to reach on a packed local bus and I was the only foreigner the whole trip. Great expanses of green valleys rolled below us as we neared the hill station, the bus filling to bursting point with locals, the sky clouding over and the temperature dropping a good fifteen degrees. I found a beautiful, bright, clean guest house and, after a luxuriously hot shower, ventured out for dinner.

The light was already fading and my guest house was more than a ten-minute walk from the centre of the town on a very quiet road, so I opted to have dinner in an unappealing hotel close by, rather than venture all the way to town by myself. The large restaurant was empty save for two Indian families also having dinner. As I sat there quietly, chewing my rice and curry and staring out of the window, I realised how easy travelling with the boys had been. I'd unwittingly taken for granted all the little things we'd done together, like exploring a new place at night, having company at meals and, of course, splitting the cost of accommodation and tuk-tuks. Most of all though, I realised how much I'd loved their friendship. India just wasn't the same without them.

I went back to my room that evening, trailing wisps of boredom and loneliness behind me. There didn't seem to be anybody hanging around the guest house for company. By 9 pm I gave up and went to bed, watching Discovery nature documentaries on the little TV and snuggling under a heavy blanket. I already missed the tropical heat of Cochin.

Most of the following day was spent seeing the touristic sights of Munnar with a tuk-tuk driver called Ravi. He was a good guide, pointing out different plants native to the area, explaining the tea plantations and how they benefitted the local economy and taking me on a tour of the whole place from top to bottom. Much like the caves back on Elephanta Island, though, the information went in one ear and out the other, while the breeze from riding in the taxi drove a chill through my bones that they hadn't felt in months. I longed to be hot and sweaty again.

By that evening, I felt like I'd done the required 'moving on'; I'd travelled alone to somewhere new, visited the sights and been a big brave girl. I was still desperately missing the boys' company (whose emails seemed to suggest they were having an absolute blast in Thailand) and so, the next afternoon found me already back in Fort Cochin. The hotel receptionist flashed a big, welcoming smile when he saw me back and the familiar streets and buildings felt like old friends; a wave of contentment settled in my tummy.

OK, so I hadn't exactly been massively adventurous, I had taken a five-hour bus ride to a nearby hill town and then scurried back to Fort Cochin after just two nights. But you must understand that venturing somewhere new and different by myself pretty much always scares me. I do it anyway, because my yearning to travel and explore is just that tiny bit stronger than my fear, but that doesn't make it any less daunting each time I set off somewhere new. The brief trip to Munnar was significant in that it proved to me that I could manage travelling in India, even without the boys, and it gave me a much-needed boost of confidence. My reward was to return to the town of Fort Cochin where

I could relax and gradually decide my next port of call.

First stop of course was lunch in Kashi Café and sitting in his usual spot was my winking Argentinian amigo.

'Liz, you're back already! When did you get here?' Mateo smiled in surprise and came over to give me a hug.

'Just now. I missed the heat too much.' I grabbed a paper serviette and wiped my sweaty face. 'So tell me, what's been going on?'

We quickly settled into conversation around food and coffee. I spent four more days in Cochin before finally moving on and it was a random role as an extra in a Bollywood movie that got me going in the end. It's a common event in the Indian film industry for movie organisers to seek out white tourists as extras, either because the movie is supposed to be set in a foreign location or just for the novelty of having foreigners in certain scenes.

At any rate, thanks to my two minutes of Bollywood fame, I got free beer, 500 rupees and made friends with a bunch of Swedish girls and a fellow Irish lad. The girls were fun, oblivious to the male attention caused by their ample cleavage and skimpy outfits, and I envied their self-assurance and strong personalities; they reminded me of warrior Vikings.

We hung out that evening after the Bollywood shoot and all next day and when they said they were going to head further south to a touristy beach town, I decided to tag along. It was time to take a deep breath and leave Cochin at last and besides, Varkala sounded like a nice spot to visit.

* * *

'What platform does our train arrive on?' I asked Selma, as we squinted at the small print. Selma was one of the Swedish girls from the Bollywood shoot and we had just bought our train tickets.

'I don't know,' she answered. 'Excuse me!'

She pushed her way back to the ticket counter, jostling the men in the queue. 'What number platform should we go to?'

With a blank expression, the man ignored her and continued dealing with the other customers. Recognising an imminent battle of wills, I left her to it.

'I'll go ask Babu, maybe he can figure it out.'

Returning to our little band of travellers, I went to our new Indian friend to see if he could enlighten us. Babu had got chatting to the others while hanging out in Cochin and, much like me, decided to tag along with them to Varkala. He was the first Indian tourist I'd met so far, originally from the northern state of Gujarat, and an extremely easy-going and open-minded individual. The only problem with Babu was that he was so stoned out of his mind all the time, he probably couldn't have told me the time of day, never mind figure out the confusion over the platform. To his credit he was pretty sober that morning as we travelled but no clearer than we were as to which platform to go to. We eventually worked it out by asking around.

This might be a good time to clarify the scope of India's diversity. The language spoken in Kerala, Malayalam, is as different in both structure and script from Gujarati (Babu's northern mother tongue) as, say, Chinese is from French. In fact, northern and southern Indians very often use English to communicate with each other, although they may sometimes speak in Hindi, which is considered the official language of the subcontinent. Hindi is the language of the central government in Delhi and the most widely spoken language in northern parts, but not all southern Indians speak it. Long story short, despite the fact that he was travelling around his own country, Babu could no more understand the Keralan locals than we could.

From Varkala train station some five hours later we took a taxi to the main attraction of the area, the nearby cliff top, and were dropped off at a cute hotel with an incredible view of the ocean and the horizon beyond. Walking up to the cliff edge, I peered over; it was a long way down. I stepped back hastily then joined the others who were already haggling over the room prices with a guy from the hotel. I couldn't wait to change into my swimsuit and head to the beach; I hadn't been in the ocean since staying at Om beach in Gokarna.

Varkala wowed with its views but aside from that it seemed to be a compacted rehash of Goa and Pushkar. Lining the length of the cliff were countless shops, hotels and restaurants, all selling exactly the same clothes/food/accommodation as all the previous touristic areas. It was disappointing not to find something a little different in a country so big and diverse but there was no denying that it was a pretty spot in which to relax with my Swedish crew. Four days passed with Babu smoking his bong for breakfast, us girls sunbathing on the beach (with me dipping my toes in a sea whose undercurrents seemed ten times stronger than anything in Goa) and everyone partying at night. Eventually, though, my new circle of friends moved on; it was early December and they were heading up to Goa for Christmas so, once again, I found myself alone.

It may be useful here to expand on my earlier point of the fear that solo travel tends to induce in me. Although I had spent a couple years travelling around Europe alone and had made the journey to India by myself, as far as travelling solo goes, to this day it still doesn't come naturally. On my arrival into Mumbai I had latched onto Paul instantly and gratefully like a lost child who's been found. Once the boys left and I was on my own, I had ventured cautiously to Munnar before running back to the familiar little town of Cochin and I had only moved on from there when I had found a new group to adopt me.

In many ways, I am as easy and content by myself as I am when hanging out with friends. But when it comes to exploring new lands I really do crave company; making that initial journey to India on my own was a mighty feat of accomplishment.

The evening that my Bollywood crew departed, I found myself in the Funky Art Café, back to dining by myself and sinking inexorably into a funk of my own. I missed the boys terribly. I had received a couple of emails from them both with news of their adventures in Thailand, including a jungle safari (Rob) and a fair few parties already (Paul) and it felt as though they had moved on to bigger and better things while I was just drifting aimlessly around India. There were two months stretching out in front of me, but I had no clear idea of what to do and trying to decide, given the vast range of options before me, felt impossible. Filled with doubt and worry, my sunny internal landscape was clouding over.

While polishing off my garlic *naan* (the most comforting of all comfort food), some French girls I'd met in Cochin and then again briefly in Munnar entered the restaurant.

We chatted together a while and it turned out they were heading south to Trivandrum, somewhere I had considered going before I buried my head back in the sand. I was already two months in India, hadn't done a single yoga class and there was a popular yoga ashram very close to the city. We agreed to leave together the next afternoon.

Chapter 15

Just one more day ...

Well, you make plans and then the universe shakes its head and tuts no, no, no, that won't do at all. The following afternoon I met one of the French girls near my hotel and discovered that instead of spending time in Trivandrum before their flight home, they were going to get a cab straight to the airport around midnight. It was only mid-afternoon now but if I was going to arrive in a strange city on my own, I didn't fancy searching for accommodation knowing that sunset and darkness were fast approaching.

I decided to stay put, just one more night. I would leave bright and early the following morning and spend the next week in the ashram: plan of action in place. But then I met Shannu, this persistent little Indian dude who seemed to be always hanging outside a small shop on the cliff just round the corner from my hotel. I passed by it several times that day and on one of those occasions Shannu stopped me, with the pretence of looking at my *Lonely Planet*. It was incredibly hot and I was convinced that he either wanted to sell me something or chat me up.

'I really want to go to the beach; can I have my book back?'

I didn't like to be rude but along the cliff every shop/ restaurant had people standing outside trying to talk to you and sell you things. It was constant and annoying and I presumed Shannu was no different, so when he tried chatting to me again that evening, I carried on walking and ignored him completely. He wasn't letting me off that easy.

'Why is it you guys never talk to us?'

Like a fish on a hook, he had me. I wheeled around to face him and give him the whole indignant white-tourist spiel of why exactly it is that we don't talk to them.

'There's over a billion of you guys and only one of me and you ALL want to talk to me. You know what, sometimes I just want to be left alone!'

He smiled patiently, tolerating my little tirade the way one would a kid throwing a small tantrum.

'If you want to be left alone, you should have stayed at home, no? You come to one of the most populated countries in the world, what do you expect? Tell me, why did you come to India?'

I hated that question. I *still* didn't exactly know why.

'To see somewhere new, experience a new culture, I guess.'

'You come to India to open your mind!' Shannu told me assertively. 'If you stay closed and alone here, then how will it be possible?'

He raised his thick black eyebrows at me questioningly but before I could get a word in he answered for himself.

'You see? To learn something new, you must be keeping an open mind. Not all fingers on the hand are the same. Come, sit with me.' He motioned for me to approach the step in front of the shop. Still not totally convinced, I walked over warily.

'I'm Shannu, what is your good name?'

'Liz.'

'So Liz, tell me, where have you been so far?'

'I flew into Mumbai, spent a few days there, then up north–'

'Did you go to Rajasthan?'

'Yeah, we did, visited most of the cities there. I loved it,' I answered.

'So, you saw Jaipur then, the 'pink city'?'

'No, we skipped that one.'

'What?' he looked at me, incredulous. 'You skipped it? It is the best city in India!'

'Well, we didn't have time to see everything.'

He shook his shoulder-length glossy hair out of his eyes, laughing.

'You skipped Jaipur, you're crazy! That's my hometown, the best city in Rajasthan. OK, so what other places did you see?'

I carried on listing out my travels, with Shannu listening attentively, often smiling and greeting people as they walked by and offering me a soft drink while we chatted.

'You must go back to Rajasthan and see Jaipur. Have you been to an Indian wedding?' he asked suddenly.

'Nope.'

'My sister is getting married soon; come with me to Jaipur for the big ceremony.'

'Oh. Really?' I was a bit stumped at the sudden invite given I'd been talking to the lad for less than ten minutes. But, as the saying goes, in India everything is possible.

'Yes really!' He smiled at my obvious confusion. 'Here in India, we are having very big weddings, big huge celebrations, you come no problem.'

'Um, OK, I'll think about it.' I was uncertain but intrigued. Rajasthan and the north of India were so chaotic and hectic and bursting with life in all its colours while Kerala, though beautiful, didn't have that same raw, rugged energy. Perhaps *that* was what I should do for the rest of my trip, head back up north?

While I was pondering all this, a tall, afro-haired Indian arrived, walking over to Shannu and speaking in Hindi with him.

'Liz, this is my brother, Ballu-*bhai*. Dinner is ready back at the house,' Shannu told me, while Ballu flashed a warm yet shy smile at me. I really wanted to grab his fabulous mop of curls. 'Come meet the others and have food with us.'

'Is it somewhere on the cliff?'

'No, it's a little farther but I can take you on the bike no problem.'

He was a complete stranger, I was alone in India and it was nearly ten at night.

'That's really kind of you to offer, but no thanks.'

'You come no problem. We do not bite,' he tried to persuade me with a grin.

'No, really, not tonight,' I told him firmly.

'OK, so you meet me tomorrow morning instead, 11 am. I can take you to see the beaches nearby on the bike.'

It seemed it was already decided for me. Until I suddenly remembered.

'I'm supposed to leave tomorrow.'

Shannu looked at me. 'You can stay one more day, no?'

He seemed harmless and one more day in Varkala couldn't hurt, could it?

'I guess I could stay *one* more day.'

Next day Shannu duly brought me on a tour of the surrounding areas on his speedy Yamaha. He was so short his feet only just reached the ground from the bike and it felt wild and crazy, as we roared down roads with no helmets on and my floaty knee-length skirt rode a lot higher than my knees (I imagined all kinds of scandalous expressions on the faces of the locals we flew past).

Shannu then brought me back to the house where he and several other Indian guys were staying. It was a very grand building, two stories tall, with cool marble floors, high ceilings and a large spacious entrance. As we entered the main living room, I spotted another tourist, about my age, lounging back against cushions on one of the three mattresses that filled the end of the room.

He smiled a shy hello as he rolled up a joint.

'Hi, I'm Liz,' I introduced myself.

'Hey Liz, Jann,' he replied, shaking my hand.

'What are you doing here?' I asked curiously.

'I'm staying with the boys.' He laughed upon seeing my face. 'Manju, one of the guys here, he met me on the cliff and invited me back to the house with him a few days ago. I haven't really left since.'

'Oh.' I pondered this news as I watched the sturdy Swiss lad light up his expertly rolled joint. Shannu strolled over to us a moment later.

'Are you hungry?' he asked me.

'Sure.'

He went back into the kitchen and a few minutes later came back with a big plate of curried rice, which we shared while sitting on the floor. A few other guys came in and out, introducing themselves although I promptly forgot all their names. (No problem, there would be plenty of time to memorise them all later.)

There was one guy, though, who I found easy to remember. As I was getting ready to leave with Shannu he came striding into the room, exuding an irrepressible energy. Thin and wiry, he had an open face, big eyes and an even bigger smile.

'Oh, hello!' he said enthusiastically when he saw me, shaking my hand and introducing himself as Alex.

'So where are you from, Liz?'

'Ireland.'

'Ah, Dublin?'

'No, Cork.'

'Where are you going now?' he asked, distracted by a message on his phone. He was still absentmindedly shaking my hand.

'I was gonna head to the beach.'

'So, Miss Irish, you do one thing, you come and join us all for dinner tonight, OK?' he asked, turning his full attention back to me.

I looked at Jann laughing with two of the guys who had joined him as he lit up the joint. The Indian boys seemed nice and Jann certainly looked at ease with them. If he thought they were OK, then maybe they were. Besides, I couldn't put my finger on it, but the house just had a really good vibe.

'OK, sure. Dinner sounds good.'

* * *

'You do it like this,' Ameer stated, a chunk of dough in his hands that he was rolling into a smooth, round ball. 'You see? Then you roll it out flat.'

Ameer was the teddy bear of the guys that lived in the house: soft-hearted, cuddly and chilled as fuck. He and Ballu, who I'd met briefly the previous night, were preparing food to feed the masses, or so it seemed. In a massive steel pot that closely resembled a witch's cauldron, a mouth-watering curry bubbled furiously which Ballu stirred while occasionally adding in some magic spices. Ameer and I were starting to fashion *chapatti* from the enormous lump of dough that Manju, the oldest member of the bunch, had just made.

When Alex bounded into the room moments later, accompanied by Shannu and two German girls, I was learning the art of rolling balls of the dough into flat circles with a rolling pin. As it turned out, I wasn't very good at it.

'Oh ho, are you making a map of Ireland?' Alex asked curiously, inspecting my handiwork.

'*Arrey* no problem, *yaar*. Watch how we cook in India,' Shannu told me smugly and, taking the rolling pin from me, he began deftly rolling out picture-perfect circles that Alex and Ameer then cooked, creating a delicious tower of stacked *chapattis*. Manju, in true Indian style, sat cross-legged up on the countertop, dousing each freshly cooked *chapatti* in rich, oily ghee. It turned out I wasn't far wrong with my notion of feeding the masses as there were at least eleven of us in the end, including the two polite German girls.

The dinner table was a plastic tablemat rolled out on the living room floor, our cutlery was our fingers and we all shared bowls two-a-piece. It was utterly delicious. The moment any of our bowls began to run low, the boys would take them and dole out more helpings from the big cauldron, followed by another heap of *chapattis*. I was almost ready to puke by the time I finally resisted any more servings, but it was totally worth it. As we digested the food, the boys sat around on the mattresses chatting, beers were offered round and a pack of cards appeared.

'Do you know, why do Egyptian kids always look confused?' Alex asked me, a cheeky grin on his face. He was sitting next to me and was full of energy, a bit like a kid who'd had too much sugar.

'I didn't realise they did.'

'*Arrey*, go to Egypt and you'll see. You want to know why?'

'OK, why?'

'When their father dies, he becomes a mummy.'

It went on like this the entire night, a whirl of card games and beer, entertained throughout by Alex who seemed to have an endless supply of jokes and wit. The other guys joined in the games as well, but never for long; they were too busy getting stoned off their faces. The couch in the corner was obscured by a perpetual cloud of thick white smoke and whoever entered it re-emerged with a decidedly distant glaze to their eyes.

Out of everyone, Alex was perhaps the only one fully sober and with enough energy to carry on for days; he was like a vamped-up Duracell bunny. Not only was he highly amusing but he properly excelled at card games and, only for the fact that he had me giggling most of the night, I might have slapped that cheeky grin right off his overly innocent face after I lost yet another game to him. The German girls, though friendly and chatty, had made their excuses and left a little after dinner. Me? I was having far too much fun to leave, I may have even peed my pants a little (that was one of Alex's jokes to do with Indian cows being traffic wardens). Finally, however, tiredness caught up with me and I checked the time.

'Shit, it's 4 am!' I exclaimed.

'We can drop you back,' Shannu told me. 'Or if you prefer, you stay no problem, you can go back to your hotel in the morning.'

I suppressed a deep yawn and looked down at the mattress I was lying on where I could literally close my eyes and drift off right now if I wanted. A thought bubble floated up in my head: Liz, you're thinking about falling asleep in a house full of strangers? In India, thousands of miles from home? Are you mad?

'I'll stay.'

It's not that I want to encourage anyone travelling solo to just randomly stay over in houses full of unknown men but it felt safe and they seemed genuine. And to be perfectly honest, while Alex still seemed wired enough to run laps for the night, the rest of the lads were too high to do much more than giggle lazily at each other like Beavis and Butthead. I figured I'd be OK.

Waking around 10 am next day, I sat up and rubbed my eyes. Ballu came out of the kitchen and on seeing me his bright-eyed face lit up.

'Chai?' he asked cheerfully.

I nodded, smiling back. It was a while before the other guys began showing their bleary faces. Alex appeared first, flopping down on the mattress next to mine and holding his throat.

'Pain,' he said, pointing to his throat. 'I stay up until sunrise with Jann on the balcony. Now I am sick.'

I rolled my eyes. When Shannu came downstairs, he and Alex chatted in Hindi for a while before he turned to me.

'You're going back to your hotel?' Shannu asked.

'Yeah, I'm going to head back soon, actually.'

'If you like, you can get your bag and come stay here. Why to pay for accommodation while you're in Varkala?' he pointed out, like it was the most natural thing in the world.

I pondered a moment. It was much the same dilemma as the previous night. Move into a house full of strange Indian men: good idea/bad idea? A few hours later, walking back towards the house with my backpack, it seemed clear what the answer was. I would stay just a few more days in Varkala with the guys and decide where to go after that. I met Jann as I was walking up the stairs to the spare bedroom and he eyed my backpack in surprise.

'You're moving in already?'

'Yeah, the guys invited me this morning,' I replied. He laughed.

'Hey, why not?'

I spent the day hanging out with Alex and Jann. Coming up to sunset, Alex drove the three of us to the nearby Kappil beach where we sat on the rocks, quiet and peaceful, frequently lapsing into companionable silence as the sky gradually changed colours.

'Can I borrow your glasses?' Alex asked me suddenly. I handed them to him and as he put them on he started messing up his hair to one side.

'What do you think? Jimi Hendrix, no?' he said, striking a bizarre pose.

'Um, yeah, sure,' I said doubtfully.

Jann was shaking his head laughing, as if to say, here we go again.

'What?!' Alex asked, feigning innocence and looking at me. 'What happened to him?'

Chapter 16

Love is in the air

It wasn't long before I felt like I'd found myself a new adoptive family (a common theme of my Indian trip, it seems). There were six guys altogether, all of them from Jaipur, the capital city of Rajasthan. They had arrived in Varkala only recently and rented the rather grand house we all stayed in from a wealthy local family. Their plan was to open up a posh jewellery boutique in the premises on the cliff that they were currently renovating (the shop where I'd first met Shannu). All of them had experience either in the field of gemstones and stone-cutting or simply in selling such luxurious goods to tourists. Kind and funny and incredibly respectful towards me, the thought of leaving them, or indeed Varkala, soon faded to the background, as did any residual lonely pangs since the departures of Paul and Rob. I was no longer overwhelmed or anxious about deciding what to do with the rest of my trip. In fact, having found myself such good friendship and company, all thoughts of further travel were temporarily put on hold.

While it was Shannu that had invited me to the house and indeed suggested I stay there, I actually ended up seeing very little of him during those initial few days. He was constantly on the cliff supervising the carpenters working in the shop (hence the reason I'd met him there in the first place). Alex, on the other hand, was always around the house, seemingly doing very little other than hanging out with me and Jann.

He was easy company, bright and intelligent and even when the jokes had eventually run out, his quick wit and snappy remarks were highly entertaining. He also had a kind heart that was truly endearing. I spent the first few days completely unaware of what was happening to me but by the fourth day, it finally hit me when Alex had to leave for Bangalore overnight on business. One of the guys, Sid, was driving him to the train station so Jann and I tagged along.

Once there, Sid got out of the car and hugged Alex, followed by Jann. Alex looked in at me.

'Yes, Miss Ireland, you can come out too!'

I got out and happily wrapped my arms around his slender frame.

'Are you gonna take that with you?' I asked curiously, stepping back and indicating my little shawl, slung around his shoulders since earlier in the day when he'd been acting the clown, as per usual. I was very much aware that he was still holding onto my other hand and had to shush the excited butterflies fluttering in my stomach.

'It's nice to have something to remind you of the people you miss,' Alex answered simply. To which several of the dancing creatures within me swooned and collapsed in delight. 'I'm coming back soon. You please don't disappear.'

Did I imagine it or was that worry in his voice? (One of the butterflies did a little fist pump for victory.) 'I'll be here,' I said firmly.

He finally let go of my hand, said goodbye and joined the crowds entering the station, my little butterflies watching him go sadly. The house that night felt quieter and emptier. The shop was finally ready and Ameer and Manju were sleeping there for security and without Alex's happy-go-lucky energy, everything felt a little dull, as if a bulb in one of the lights had gone out.

The following day I dropped off some clothes to a tailor for adjustments; I spent some time in the boys' jewellery shop cleaning silver with them; a rainstorm cleared the hot, sticky air in the afternoon and I met a sweet Australian girl to share chai and chats with. But still, it felt as though I was just biding my time, waiting. I sat across from Sid in the living room that evening while he played around with the laptop, selecting music. The first day or so, I'd barely noticed him – he often wore an obscure pink baseball cap and in the evenings his eyes usually closed to bare slits once the joints were going. But that morning he stepped out of the bedroom fresh from a shower and I did a double-take. He was, without doubt, one of the fittest, hottest guys I had seen anywhere. Ever.

His face was perfectly sculpted, a mix of delicate effeminate features with a strong masculine energy; his dark silky hair was just long enough for a small ponytail, while his tall, straight-backed stature suggested utter self-assurance. He was freaking gorgeous.

I was stumped for a moment as he ran oil through his sleek locks, muscles visibly rippling under the tight, long-sleeved T-shirt. How had I missed this Adonis first day? Easy. The charismatic, hilarious whirlwind of Alex had swept me off my feet to the oblivion of all else. That evening, as I scribbled notes in my diary and glanced across at the male model on his computer, I wondered how to broach the topic on my mind without being too obvious.

'Sid, what time is Alex coming back?' I finally ventured, trying desperately to be off-hand.

'He is coming back tomorrow,' Sid answered, still looking at his computer. 'I think it will be early morning, 8 am, something like that.'

'OK, great.' I focused all my energy on writing, trying to stop a grin from stretching across my face. Not bad, not bad, he'd be back when I woke up!

He wasn't. It wasn't until after midday when I was in the kitchen making chai with Jann that he suddenly appeared. With just a cool, confident 'hello', he dropped some things on the table and headed back to the living room, chatting all the while to Sid in Hindi. My sweet little butterflies drooped and huddled up together miserably. So much for my ridiculous ideas, I thought.

After all my imaginings of excited hugs, of the big moment of his arrival, I felt like a deflated balloon. Minutes later I joined the boys in the living room and placed the tray of cups on the wooden coffee table (like the good little Indian housewife I would never become). The guys were sitting on the few chairs available so I went over to the stairs across and sat on the second one, watching them and sipping my own sugary brew, quietly impressed with how it had turned out.

Alex sat cross-legged, drinking his chai and eating some Indian snacks. After a moment he reached down to his rucksack and pulled a thick book out of it. Opening the first page, he took a pen, scribbled something down, then closed the cover.

'*Shantaram*. I like this book,' he said to me with an approving face.

'You read it?' I asked in surprise. I'd mentioned before that it was on my booklist while in India (fully recommended by Paul, of course). He hadn't said he knew it then.

'*Arrey* no, I try to read all of this, I die!' he said resolutely, indicating the book's thousand or so pages. 'No, I read just the first page. Very true.'

He opened the book and quoted the first paragraph, the opening part where *Shantaram* philosophises on the one choice we all have that makes us human; the choice, always, to forgive.

'Is true, no?' he asked, nodding sagely, then motioning for me to catch the book as he tossed it towards me.

I caught the thick volume in my hands, wondering – was he giving it to me? Or offering it to me to look at? I opened the cover and spotted the little note he'd written a moment ago:

For the one who is kind and lovely, called Liz.

My heart melted and the butterflies started up a joyous rendition of the can-can because he'd been thinking about me while he was away. It was confirmed, totally and *utterly* confirmed: he liked me! Alex hopped off his chair and came over as I sat still gazing at the book.

'You like your gift?' he asked, clapping me loudly on the back. I winced, more from the sound than the actual impact.

'I love it, thank you.'

'*Arrey*, no "thank you"!' he admonished me. It was an Indian thing, they all believed love should be shown in your actions more than your words. Grabbing my hands, he mock-wrestled me for a moment.

'You want to come to the cliff?' he said suddenly. Our hands were still linked and he leaned playfully against me. At that moment he could have asked me to jump off the cliff with him and I'd have agreed.

As we walked, a funny awkward silence ensued. It was funny because it was the first time I'd ever seen Alex so quiet and it was awkward because I didn't know how to break it, or if I even should break it, or if I should somehow bring up the fact that my heart was fluttering in my chest like a nervous damsel fanning herself. In the end the silence became too much.

'You're very quiet,' I told him, my voice sounding unusually loud, as we turned off the main road to the narrower, rougher paths. The air felt thick and heavy in the heat.

'Sometimes it's good to be quiet, no?' he laughed, a bit nervously.

We became silent again.

'Alex, what–'

'Liz–'

We broke off, giggling.

'Very good!' Alex teased and offered his hand to shake. We shook. Then we kept shaking. And then, suddenly, we switched from shaking hands to holding hands, in one fluid, divinely orchestrated movement as we ambled along the quiet back streets.

I didn't know what to do with myself: jump for joy, hug him, kiss him or pretend nothing had happened and it was totally normal to be walking together, our fingers interlinked? My heart had officially fainted while the butterflies in my stomach were cheering and applauding and popping open champagne bottles. It was a lot to contain.

'Why did God create gaps between the fingers?' Alex grinned at me, repeating a joke he'd told several times before.

I laughed and raised our interlinked hands, losing myself in his eyes until I stumbled on the uneven path and decided to turn at least some of my attention back to walking.

As we reached the cliff, in an unspoken agreement we released each other's hands, feeling too new and shy for public scrutiny. Approaching the shop, everything about the familiar cliff top suddenly seemed fresh and beautiful: the sea was sparkling as if a million iridescent diamonds floated on the surface; the colours of the plants and flowers were bright and vivid; people's laughter and cheerful voices tinkled like wind chimes. I was all but floating with happiness.

While Alex chatted to Manju, I leaned up against a coconut tree, trying to act as if everything was normal when what I actually wanted to do was to shake each person who wandered past and shout at them: 'HE LIKES ME!'

I needed to remember to breathe.

'Liz, we go?' Alex suddenly appeared beside me. 'I need to get some things from the town, do you want to come?'

Does a girl like chocolate?

We walked back home, giggling like teenagers as we again held hands along the way. Once at the house, Alex got the keys to the car and steered the vehicle out of the small gateway, navigating the narrow path to the main road, all the while mindlessly humming. Throwing a glance at me, he flashed me a big smile and placed his free hand in mine. He seemed really distracted. The engine began whining in distress, yet he remained in second gear, seemingly oblivious.

'Um – maybe you should move up to third gear?' I suggested with a wry smile. 'Before the engine explodes?'

'What? Oh, oookaaay,' he breathed, taking back his hand to focus on driving.

'Hey, not just a pretty face, huh?' I joked to ease the nerves.

Alex frowned, looking over at me, clearly having trouble concentrating on both me and driving. 'What is this? I think you have a pretty face.'

'No, it's a kind of joke, it means like I'm not dumb just because I'm pretty, I'm smart too, you know?'

'And how do you say it? Just not a pretty face?'

'No – *not just* a pretty face,' I corrected him.

'OK. *Arrey* I don't understand, it means you are pretty?'

'Yeah but, look, it doesn't matter, forget about it!' I told him with an affectionate smile.

'No, I want to understand; explain it to me.'

So I began going through the nuances of the English language and discovered that he'd only ever learned the basics at school, leaving at sixteen to work in the tourist trade in Jaipur and, quite incredibly, learning English simply from talking to tourists over the years. It wasn't grammatically perfect and he had created a few quirky expressions of his own but damn, I'd never been able to learn a language so well without endless books and lessons. I was impressed.

'Where will we go?' Alex asked as he sat into the car a little later, the groceries stashed on the back seat.

'It would be nice to go somewhere together, just the two of us,' I answered.

'Let's go to Kappil beach,' he suggested.

By the time we arrived the sun was setting. A nervous anticipation niggled in my stomach. This was surely going to be the first-kiss moment and quite possibly the entire future of our relationship was at stake here. I felt like a teenager with my first crush. We slowed down and pulled off the road, Alex now humming quite intensely. As we came to a stop, he forgot to press the clutch and the car lurched crazily, the engine automatically cutting out. We shared a jittery giggle and stepped outside. The small, quiet beach was completely deserted save for a solitary figure further away from us, an old man.

A gentle breeze blew the soft sound of the waves our way and the evening air was light and warm. Alex came around to my side and leaned back against the car. I turned to face him and he pulled me into him, his hands grabbing my waist with a nervous smile. I smiled back, trying to seem cool and confident. Next thing, we were kissing.

I would love to say that we melted into each other, our lips softly touching, the kiss sparking a blaze of passion between us …

I would love to say that, but it wouldn't be true.

Awkward, erratic and immensely disappointing would be more accurate. After a few moments I pulled away, opting for a gentle hug instead. Alex squeezed me close as I tried to come to terms with this monumental bummer. Crap, bugger, shite.

Alex cleared his throat. 'Liz, can I tell you something?' he asked uncertainly.

'Sure.' I pulled back to look at him.

He fidgeted, looking nervous and uncomfortable. 'I have no idea what I'm doing. You're my first proper girlfriend,' he finally said.

Oh, thank holy Jesus and all the saints and angels!

'You should have told me before.'

'I was too shy.'

I laughed lightly and hugged him again before planting a tender kiss on his cheek. 'So how about we practise?' I suggested.

Alex very quickly caught on. So quickly, in fact, that my previous hopes of our first kiss sparking a blaze of passion between us soon came true. He was a fast learner! Only for the old man wandering over in pervy drunken curiosity, I could have happily stayed there all night, but we decided we should head back to the house anyway. After all, half the boys' dinner was still sitting in the car waiting to be cooked. Unsure as to how to subtly inform everyone that Liz and Alex were now a 'thing', we decided to pretend nothing had happened for the moment. Once the boys had settled down to a game of cards after dinner, Alex soon made an exaggerated excuse about showing me something upstairs and threw his arm casually across my shoulders as we headed up.

Well. It turned out *this* was how we would subtly inform everyone about us as we closed the bedroom door behind us for the night. By the time we were ready to sleep, the memory of our awkward first kiss had been almost obliterated, along with any capacity on my part for rational thinking. A new adventure was just beginning and our futures had suddenly been irrevocably transformed. I do believe mischievous little Indian cupids were high-fiving another success story because, although I was blissfully unaware of it at that moment, I had just got the answer to that pesky, perplexing, unanswerable question: 'Why *India*?'

Chapter 17

Amma

After a brief morning-after awkwardness with the rest of the boys (which amused me since it had in fact been mostly innocent kisses and cuddles), they all seemed fine with us hooking up and carried on teasing me like nothing had changed. All but one.

Shannu – who had sweetly declared he fancied me while Alex was away and who I had sweetly turned down – henceforth blatantly ignored me until he left for Jaipur a week later. I guessed the wedding invite was off but, then again, I was getting all kinds of authentic India these days.

Alex's utter devotion made me feel like a special princess, but living with the guys meant we didn't get a lot of time to ourselves. So, a week into our budding romance, Alex took me out on the bike to see some of the nearby sights. The weather was unusually grey and cool as we zoomed around the quiet roads, visiting temples and enjoying the exotic Keralan coastline. I hugged him tight around the waist, enjoying the feeling of his firm stomach under my arms and the breeze fresh against my face.

'You want chai?' he called back to me, slowing down as we neared a small, side-of-the-road tea shop.

'Chai sounds great.'

We settled ourselves into the cosy, simple interior, sitting close to each other, hips touching, feet touching, our bodies inclined towards each other. (We were in that gross, infatuated phase.)

'This is our first time doing something together, just us,' I told Alex as the shop owner prepared the tea, darting curious looks our way.

'It's good, no?' Alex smiled, resting his elbows on the worn table. 'You want some biscuits, *beta*?'

'What does '*beta*' mean?'

'It means son, but it's a pet name too, like darling.'

'You're calling me your son?'

'Yes but no! *Arrey*, darling, it's just a pet name. You want biscuits or no?'

I grinned at his reaction and nodded.

'It's funny, this is like a date isn't it?' I mused. 'I never thought I'd be in the countryside of Kerala at a tiny chai stall on a date.'

'I never thought I'd be on a date,' Alex stated innocently.

Oh my God, he was too freakin' cute.

'So how is it going then, this date?' he asked me, crinkling his eyes, a little unsure.

'It's going great,' I assured him, squeezing his hand as our drinks and snacks arrived. I dunked the Indian pastry into my chai and smiled when I saw Alex doing the same thing. As we rode home a while later, I realised I was falling hook, line and sinker for this sweet man. Any time I thought back to those first two months in India and the whole saga with Jack, I had to shake my head in wonder. How might my trip have turned out had I actually succeeded in meeting up with Jack? Would I still have found Alex? Or was that the reason I never met Jack? And what about Rob, my dear Austrian buddy? How had I moved on so quickly from him? Perhaps because, at the end of the day, part of me knew that 'buddies' was all we were ever meant to be. Plus Rob was roughly twice my height, whereas when I hugged Alex, my head slotted perfectly between his neck and his shoulder. Everything about him felt just right.

The complications of loving a person from a foreign land were completely inconsequential to my love-drugged brain in those early days: I was running on a theme of sunshine and kittens and it was just a couple weeks later we arrived at the 'I love you' stage. I blurted it out suddenly as Alex made me giggle one day and he instantly replied 'love you too, *beta*!' then sealed it with a kiss. Was it too soon and silly and impulsive? Absolutely, but our relationship's heady sprint would eventually slow to a calmer and more sustainable stroll. In the meantime, while northern India had blown open my mind in the first few weeks after arriving, both Kerala and Alex were now working on my heart. Where it would take me I had no idea yet but, as with everything in India, I was learning to let go of my plans and just flow with it. It had worked pretty well so far.

* * *

Christmas and New Year came and went in a blur of beaches, snuggles, late-night dinners, late-morning breakfasts and trips to and from the cliff. India has such a massive population with so many diverse religions and a relatively small Christian population that Christmas isn't celebrated as widely as it is back in Ireland (where it pretty much takes over the month of December). Being in such a touristy area, though, a lot of the hotels and restaurants made an effort with decorations and lights and some wacky Santa Claus pictures that looked very out of place in the sunny tropical climate. For me, 25 December always means coats and scarves, maybe some snow too if you're really lucky; Christmas 2007 found me spending the morning soaking up the sun on the soft sands and braving the wild waves of the Arabian Sea. I strolled home along the red-earth footpath past coconut trees and bamboo huts before buying a fresh pineapple juice and returning to my sweet Indian family. To celebrate the day, we all went out for dinner on the cliff top that evening. I called family and friends afterwards to wish them a merry Christmas, sharing how my day had gone and making them suitably envious. I mentioned casually to my mum and dad that I was out with new friends for dinner and left it at that. Some things require good timing; informing my parents that I had, essentially, hooked up with a random Indian dude definitely needed careful handling (never mind the fact that I was also living in a house full of several more 'random Indian dudes'). It was a conversation I was happy to postpone.

Around the end of December we got to know two girls travelling around India: Charlotte, a bubbly, outgoing Chinese-American, and Kiera, a friendly Irish lass. Snagged on the cliff by the lads (much as I had been by Shannu), they came for dinner one evening and quickly became regulars both at home and at the shop. On New Year's Day, as I was lazing around the house with Alex, a joyful Charlotte bounded through the door, closely followed by the calmer figures of Sid and Kiera.

'Liz, hey! What are you doing tomorrow?' Charlotte asked.

'Nothing much, why?'

'Come with us to Amma's ashram. It's super close by and Kiera and I are gonna check it out.'

I glanced over at Alex with eyebrows raised. He smiled at me.

'OK, I'm in!'

It's funny, I was three months in India and a typical New Age wannabe hippie (which basically meant I owned Birkenstock sandals, ate quinoa and hugged trees), yet this was my first time trying anything remotely spiritual. To be honest, I had completely succumbed to the earthly pleasures of food, sex and beach-bum life which, once again, wasn't quite the mystical Indian adventure I'd expected before leaving Ireland. But then nothing on this trip had gone as planned, neither the anticipation of finding an enlightened guru nor the fear of being airlifted to hospital with dysentery. So far, travel in India was an endless revelation, with Alex the biggest and most incredible surprise of all.

All that said, it was surely a good idea to at least try some spiritual exploration and this seemed the perfect opportunity. I didn't know very much about Amma herself, other than that she was known to sit for up to twenty hours at a go, hugging thousands of people in one day. I couldn't quite understand why she would do this, or why people would want a hug from a strange woman in the first place, but I was open to discovering more.

As it turns out, the following quote from Amma explains her hugging marathon sessions quite succinctly: 'A continuous stream of love flows from me to all of creation. This is my inborn nature. The duty of a doctor is to treat patients. In the same way, my duty is to console those who are suffering.'

Born in a remote coastal village in Kerala in 1953, she is reputed to have been drawn to meditation and devotional songs as a young girl. Over the years as she continued to pour her time and energy into comforting others, a following grew around her and she was given the name 'Amma' (a word that means 'mother' in several languages). Her journey from there to the globally recognised figure she is today is all the more interesting, given she came from a culture and society that deemed it unacceptable for a woman to come in contact with men and that women should remain quietly in the background. But Amma being Amma, she didn't give a diddlysquat about society's expectations and just carried on hugging and comforting those that came to her.

Of course, given I never research *anything* while travelling, I didn't know any of this when we took the local train south to Amritapuri, the town where her ashram is based. The word ashram comes from the ancient Sanskrit word *asrama*, which means hermitage. Generally speaking, an ashram is a place of religious retreat, somewhere to escape the busy outside world in order to pray, meditate and live a more contemplative life. The first sign that this was not your typical hermit's retreat was the huge candy-pink temple, bizarrely decorated with giant ornate lion sculptures. The second sign was the hive of activity going on around us: hordes of people of every nationality running about, busy as bees. Registration was inside the temple on the first floor and my preconceived notions of quiet serene ashram life were tossed out of the window as I took in the buzzing atmosphere around us. Charlotte spoke to a few people ahead of us in the queue waiting to register, then turned around in excitement.

'Oh, we're so lucky. She's here,' she said, her eyes shining. 'Amma's here!'

It had been such a spontaneous decision to visit the ashram that we hadn't even checked if Amma was actually there or away on one of her global tours. But her presence was the very reason the place was so hectic; crowds descended on the ashram in their thousands whenever Amma was in town. Only when its leading lady was away did the ashram quieten down somewhat, though it still retained a large number of full-time and visiting residents throughout the entire year.

'Ooh, room number 108,' Charlotte whistled a short while later as we were handed the keys for our room together. 'That's considered a really auspicious number. Oh my God, this is SO cool!'

Kiera and I followed with slightly more sedate outlooks on the whole thing and I for one was feeling dubious as my brain absorbed the surrounding chaos. Instead of tranquil monks meditating, all I'd seen so far were harried, white-robed Indians and foreigners scampering around like anxious hens.

But here's what I would gradually learn: Amma's ashram is not your reclusive retreat away from the world; it's a total immersion, a whole body-dunking in the varied sauces of life. If you want a silent, tranquil ashram perhaps it's not the place for you and for sure there is great value in seeking quietude. But if you want to really be in this world (as opposed to becoming a hermit in the mountains) then at some point you'll have to face real life and at Amma's ashram, you've every opportunity to embrace the internal journey while simultaneously participating in the daily chaos of humanity. Upon arriving I merely assumed the place was nuts, but I would learn. I would learn a lot.

When we reached our room, it turned out we were sharing with one other girl, a bright-eyed, chirpy German called Mareike. She was the sort of person you just had to like; kindness exuded from every fibre of her being and she threw herself wholeheartedly into ashram life. The thing I loved about Mareike most, however, was there was no sari uniform or plain ponytail like many of the ashram's residents. Miss Happy-Go-Lucky sported cute blonde pigtails, brightly coloured clothes and a pretty little diamond on her front tooth that sparkled every time she smiled, much like the girl herself, the sweet little buttercup.

She rose every day at 5 am for chanting, practised yoga, helped serve food in the café, scrubbed pots in the kitchen, meditated in the temple and was generally a shining example of a human being. Us three gals on the other hand mostly slept in late and sat on our asses eating cake at the Western café. Not so shining.

Amma's message is for people to help each other, that there is no greater honour than to serve. She lives by this example with her endless *darshan* sessions, her hugging marathons that can stretch anywhere from ten to twenty hours with literally no breaks in between (she barely sips on any water throughout, never mind squeezing in a meal or a nap). She is reported to sleep barely two hours a night and yet somehow, despite her exhausting timetable and frequent long-haul travel, she still oversees the running of the ashram. Her request to everyone who comes to stay at the ashram is to participate in the running of the place by signing up for *seva* duties (selfless service), which could be anything from administrative chores to sweeping up the dining hall. The ashram runs just like a well-oiled machine and yet all the work done there is voluntary which, given the sheer size of the place (there can be literally thousands staying there when Amma's around), not to mention the fact that it's all happening in India (a place not quite so renowned for its organisational skills), is phenomenal.

I think you'll agree, based on all that, she's pretty amazing. At that early stage however, I was still a little sceptical. I phoned Alex on the second day.

'Hi darling.'

'Oh, hello! How are you?'

'Good, very good. It's completely mad here, like all of India condensed into one small space. Super intense! But Amma's here and I got my hug last night.'

'How was it?'

I thought back to the event. Amma had been hugging non-stop for the better part of twelve hours that day and the girls and I had joined a queue specifically for Westerners late in the evening.

'It was cool, but bizarre too. We were sitting in line for about an hour, which actually isn't long given that the queues seemed to stretch on forever. The hall is massive but it was still nearly bursting with people, most of them Indians, and everything was revolving the whole time around this amazing little Indian lady.'

I pictured Amma on her seat up on the stage, surrounded by devotees who were organising the immense crowds of people awaiting their turn for a moment with her.

'You could hardly move it was so packed, and the atmosphere was incredible. Maybe that's where Amma gets some of her energy. Or maybe she's the one generating it, I don't know.'

'Sounds a bit crazy,' Alex commented.

'It's pretty mental alright but in a good way. No one was yelling or getting mad in spite of the chaos and the crowds. When I was right at the top of the queue, this strict Indian woman – one of the devotees – she pretty much pushed me down on my knees and grabbed hold of my shoulders from behind. Then once the guy in front of me was done she shoved me towards Amma who pulled me in close to her and whispered something in my ear.'

'What did she say?'

'I've no idea, it was in Malayalam! Kiera thought it sounded like 'nothing nothing nothing' while Charlotte thought she said 'my child my child my child'. I think it was some kind of blessing.'

'So you're enjoying it?' Alex inquired curiously.

'I guess – I mean, Amma's amazing. She runs a charity that has opened up hospitals and universities and so much more, and there are her endless hugging sessions, but …' I trailed off, fiddling with the phone cord, lost in thought, '… I don't know, there are so many people here with their heads stuck up their pure and holy arse. I get the feeling they're looking down on us because they've been following Amma for ages – like they think they're better than us.' I paused again.

'Then again, there are a few people I've spoken to who've been following Amma for years and they're fascinating and full of wisdom. I guess you find all kinds of everybody in a place like this, but there's one thing I really don't get: people keep acting like Amma's some kind of god, bowing when she's near, crying and stuff. If that happened in the West, people would think it was mental.'

'But this is India, *beta*, the spiritual land! You don't trust God, we cannot live without God. People see a guru like Amma and they see the divine in her. Do you know what I mean?'

'Hmmm … I'm not so sure.'

Alex laughed. 'You people are always doubting and suspicious. Where is the trust?'

'Alex, if I trusted every Indian I met on my trip, my bank account would be empty by now.'

'No problem, darling, you found me. Whatever you need, I pay for you.'

I rolled my eyes at his latest declaration of utter devotion, but I couldn't help a small grin. 'Love you, darling!'

There was a brief pause on the other side. 'One four three, *beta*.'

I frowned in puzzlement. 'Huh?'

'I said, one four three,' Alex repeated in a slightly joking tone, as I heard Sid and Ameer chatting in the background. Then I understood.

'Oh my God, you're embarrassed to say 'I love you' in front of the boys?'

'You don't mind?' Alex asked, laughing a little uncertainly.

'It's adorable, Alex.'

Ten minutes later, I sat back on the chair and stared at the receiver in front of me, all kinds of thoughts and ideas running through my head. Were we Westerners really too cynical and suspicious? Possibly. In my brief trip I had already encountered a level of trust and devotion in the Indian people that seemed both incredibly beautiful and strangely foreign to me. Their devotion arises out of a deep acceptance of the will of the gods, whether they believe in just one (as the Muslims and Christians do) or millions (as in Hinduism). They don't seem to see the point in arguing over the cards they've been dealt by life, things that might fill me with anger or frustration, because they believe God has willed it and God will deal with it. Our insatiable desire in the West to question everything, especially God, has led to us believing we are the ones in charge of our lives and when life typically shows us that we're not, we become enraged, like toddlers throwing a temper tantrum. The devoted Indian, on the other hand, accepts his lot and moves on. It's a lesson in humility and contentment that I, for one, could definitely do with learning.

I shook my head, coming out of my reverie and realising I should either make another call or free up the phone for someone else. Huh! It seemed that deep contemplation could occur in the midst of India's chaos almost as easily as it could during a quiet retreat back home in Ireland. Thinking of Ireland made me think about my parents. It was time for a catch up.

'Hi Mum, it's me.'

'Hello Lizzie-lou, how are you?'

I filled her in on the ashram and Amma until finally there was a natural lull in the conversation.

'So Mum, I've actually got some other news. I met a boy – an Indian boy.'

'Ooh, really?' she sounded pleasantly surprised.

I hadn't known quite what to expect from my parents upon hearing I now had an Indian boyfriend but I certainly hadn't anticipated such a lack of concern or worry. It may have helped that I omitted the part about actually living with him in a house full of Indian men ... they didn't need to know everything.

Two nights at the ashram proved to be enough for me and the girls. Amma had impressed with her endless hugging sessions and the mere existence of the ashram and all its activities, run by so many devoted volunteers, was testament to how special she was. But I still didn't really get it. The seed of Amma's powerful love had been planted and needed time to grow and develop. For now though, it was time to leave the special ashram and get back to my man.

Chapter 18

Venturing north

'Man, I wish I could stay longer in Varkala,' Charlotte sighed, staring thoughtfully out at the ocean. Back a couple days from the ashram, the three of us were sitting in the cliff-top restaurant, Trattoria, while Charlotte lamented her ill-timed travel plans.

'Why do I have to leave tonight? Why did I only get together with Sid now? Damn it!'

'I could see it coming,' Kiera said smugly, flicking through a menu. 'I knew you guys fancied each other.'

'I didn't. As usual, I was totally oblivious to anything other than Alex.' Grinning, I slipped off my sandals and tucked my feet up onto the chair seat. Kiera rolled her eyes. I think if I mentioned Alex one more time she was going to puke.

'It's such a bummer, I'd *love* to spend more time with him,' Charlotte said, running a hand through her hair.

'I don't blame you, he's a hottie,' I stated and Kiera nodded in agreement.

'He is. How many days is it until you fly home?' she asked.

'Five.'

'So who says you have to leave tonight?' Kiera raised one eyebrow suggestively.

'But I've already got my ticket to Gokarna and I never saw Hampi, which was top of my list ...' Charlotte trailed off vaguely. Kiera leaned forward in her chair, taking charge.

'Well, just imagine you're back home in the States with your big Indian adventure finished and you're looking back over all the experiences you had, would you be glad you saw Hampi? Or glad you spent your last few days with Sid?'

Charlotte scrunched her face up in uncertainty. 'Guess I'd choose Sid. But then you would have to go to Gokarna alone.'

Kiera shrugged with a smile. 'I came to India alone, I can manage.'

Charlotte stared at her, still unsure, before turning to me. 'Liz, what do you think I should I do?'

'Really?' I responded dryly. 'You're asking the girl who stopped travelling and spent the last six weeks in Varkala because of an Indian boy. Do I need to answer?'

'Ooh, I don't know, I just don't know!' Charlotte shook her head, giggling and looking from one of us to the other. 'It's so hard to choose.'

You can imagine what she decided in the end. It's hard to resist a gorgeous Indian man, trust me.

We accompanied Kiera to the train station that evening to see her off.

'Come to Mumbai with Charlotte,' she told me firmly as we shared a hug. 'Get back on the road and we can explore some of the north together. Alex will still be here when you get back,' she added with a wink before turning to the others. The idea of us exploring some of northern India together had first popped up during one of our many chats at the ashram. The more I thought about it now, the more excited

I began to feel at the idea of being back on the move again, exploring new cities, like I did with Rob and Paul back at the start.

I brought it up in conversation with Alex as we lay in bed that night. 'What do you think? Would you mind if I headed off for a little bit?'

'You want to leave me already?' he asked with a funny smile.

I lifted myself up on an elbow to look at him properly. *'Chal' pagal!'* I admonished. (It's a common Hindi expression that I liken to the Irish phrase 'ah cop on!' or, for the non-Irish people, 'get a grip!')

Alex tried to pull me in for a hug, but I resisted, sensing something was up. 'Are you upset?'

'It's fine, no?' He tried to brush it off, reaching up to kiss me on the cheek. 'Go with the girls and see some more of India, *beta*, no problem.' And just like that, he sounded more like himself again.

'It won't be for long, probably a week or two max,' I said, trying to reassure him as I realised how much I wanted to travel again and get back to the ridiculously delightful chaos of India's northern states.

'*Arrey* no problem, *beta*. I just wish you come back.'

And then I understood. He was worried that his sweet Irish lass might have too much fun and forget all about him. I leaned down to give him a kiss before grabbing his face in my hands and eyeballing him sternly.

'Alex, my dear, all the gods of India couldn't stop me from coming back to you.'

* * *

'Liz, you ready? We gonna be late.'

'OK, I'm coming!' I snapped, finally zipping up my backpack and hoisting it on. Charlotte was already in the car and Sid was pulling open the large gate as I followed Alex outside.

Our blissful honeymoon period was definitely over and we'd been having the odd mini-scrap over the past few days. A lot of it was down to our very different ideas about sleeping arrangements.

I, having grown up in a typically Western family where the child sleeps alone, practically from the moment they're born, was having trouble getting used to sharing my bed with another person. Added to that challenge was the fact that Alex had grown up in a typically Indian family where they all sleep together like a pile of puppies. This meant that while I liked to keep to my side of the bed, Alex liked to wrap himself around me like a kid hugging his favourite teddy, all available limbs tangled up and every possible part of our bodies pressed together. While it was fun at the beginning when we couldn't get enough of each other, the novelty had worn off now to the point that I sometimes woke up hanging off the edge of the bed with Alex snuggling into me and enough space behind him to fit a baby elephant. It was a minor issue in the bigger scheme of things, obviously, but my sleepless nights, combined with a spot of pre-travel nerves, made me tense and crabby.

As I dumped my bag in the boot, Ballu and Manju came to say goodbye.

'See you in a couple of weeks, my friend,' I said, shaking Ballu's hand.

'I am waiting for you!' he answered cheerfully with his big smile, grabbing hold of my hand in both of his.

'Bye, Manju,' I told the older, dark-skinned man. He flashed a toothy grin my way and shook my hand.

'OK, Liz. See you. Enjoy!' he said briskly.

Since someone had to always be at the shop, I'd already said goodbye to Ameer the night before.

As we drove to the station, I held Alex's hand tight in mine, my annoyance rapidly fading and replaced by a yearning to go back home with him and have chai together. Typical! All too soon, we were at the station making our way to the platform. Charlotte and Sid were joking and teasing each other. They seemed to have spent the majority of their time together laughing. I hugged Alex tightly as we heard the train approaching. It wouldn't stop for long, Varkala was a tiny station. The boys helped us find our seats and stow our bags, then we all got off and I wrapped my arms once more around Alex. I couldn't get over how hard it was saying goodbye to him, I was only going to be away for a few weeks at most. A little voice whispered in the background that if parting was hard now, what would it be like at the end of February when I was due to fly back to Ireland? And then another little voice suggested I didn't necessarily have to leave in February … The warning blast of the train's horn snapped me out of these musings and Charlotte and I quickly climbed back on, just as the locomotive started to move.

'See you soon, darling, real soon,' I promised as Alex walked alongside the slowly chugging train.

'Be careful, *beta*, call me from Mumbai.'

We managed one last kiss with me leaning out of the door, then suddenly Sid was there, jogging to keep up.

'Charlotte! Come say goodbye!' Charlotte held both my hand and the doorframe as she leaned right out to snatch a kiss from him, laughing all the while.

'Goodbye, Sid. Miss you already!'

And a moment later the train had overtaken him, picking up speed as it left Varkala. We went back to our seats and Charlotte sighed deeply, a lovesick smile on her face.

'Oh man, I'm gonna miss him,' she said wistfully. We were both quiet for a moment before she turned to me.

'You know, we were sitting on the roof of the shop last night, just the two of us, and I was like, is this really happening to me? Am I really here in India, by the Arabian Sea, with this amazing guy?' She sighed deeply again with a big soppy grin and put her hands on her heart. 'Oh my gosh, what an amazing trip this has been!'

I smiled at her. I was pretty sure I knew exactly how she felt.

The journey to Mumbai was long despite being in good company. By evening of the next day we were relieved to reach Lokmanyatilak station and we caught a taxi straight into the city centre, having arranged to meet Kiera, who'd already arrived in Mumbai that morning, at the Salvation Army hostel, the same place where I'd stayed with Paul back at the very start of my trip.

'Hey guys!' she called, entering the main entrance where we waited for her, an elegant shawl draped over her shoulders. We shared hugs and she brought us to another hotel nearby.

'Salvation Army was full, but this place is pretty cheap and it's clean too, which the other five I checked out this morning certainly weren't.'

We entered the small building and signed in at reception before following Kiera upstairs.

'It's great, well done you,' I said, taking in the neat, clean – and tiny – room.

'Dibs on using the shower first!' Charlotte called, already stripping off.

Glad to have a moment to lie down, I flopped onto one of the beds while Kiera flicked through her *Lonely Planet* guide.

'So, how did you like Gokarna?' I asked.

'It was OK, just more beach life. Hampi I loved, though, wish I could have stayed there longer but there just wasn't enough time on this trip.'

'You'll have to come back to India again, huh? I'm excited about going up north, being here in Mumbai feels like I'm back in 'real' India again. Varkala was getting boring,' I said, snuggling into my pillow and yawning. 'It's like a little bubble there, you nearly forget where in the world you are.'

'Until a shopkeeper tries to charge you triple. Then you remember pretty quick,' Kiera said with a wry smile.

'Ha! True.'

I was just starting to doze off when Charlotte came out of the bathroom wrapped in a towel, her black hair dripping over her bare shoulders.

'That feels *so* much better!' she exclaimed. 'It's all yours, Liz.'

A little later we wandered along the busy streets looking for a good place to have dinner and in the crowd I fell behind the others. So I was completely baffled when Charlotte suddenly whirled around, a look of utter fury on her face, yelled 'Fucking ASSHOLE!' at the top of her lungs and flung her small packet of raisins at a random man walking past me. I stared in astonishment. She caught my eye and her anger was momentarily distracted.

'Piece of SHIT!' she roared as a parting shot, before carrying on with an angry shake of her head. Astounded, I quickly caught up to the two girls.

'What the hell was *that*?'

Charlotte was radiating anger like there was an inferno inside of her. 'Sorry, Liz,' she said, still fuming. 'That dude just grabbed me right in the crotch!'

'Unbelievable!' Kiera shook her head in disgust.

'And then he just kept on going like he'd done nothing, which got me even more mad. I was gonna go after him only I saw your face, Liz, and it made me stop. Maybe 'cause you looked shocked.'

'I was wondering what was going on.'

'Damn it!' she added, with a little laugh. 'I wish I hadn't thrown my raisins at him, I'm starving.'

'Let's just eat here,' I suggested, seeing the restaurant beside us. 'I've actually been here before, it's good.'

It took Charlotte most of the meal before she'd calmed down but, as we chatted, she soon began to shrug off the incident and it's testament to just how good her trip was that she didn't consider it spoiled by the unfortunate parting shot India had thrown at her. Next evening she said goodbye to India and to us. We shared hugs and Kiera and I watched her leave, wiping her eyes as she stepped into the waiting cab, her backpack nearly as big as her.

Kiera glanced at me with a rueful smile. 'I'll miss her.'

I nodded in agreement. Charlotte had been the bounce in our trio, thoughtful and kind but also incredibly enthusiastic and full of energy. Even the incident the previous night hadn't been enough to dampen her spirits for long before she was laughing and deciding it would simply be an addition to her adventurous tales once home. I would definitely miss her resilient, upbeat attitude, not to mention how darn cute she was; my Irish genes were no match for her exquisite Chinese features.

'I guess it's just us two now. I'm ready to leave here and see Varanasi,' I replied.

We had spent the day wandering around Mumbai and I was beginning to realise that the big Indian city had been more charming back when I'd been flanked either side by two tall Western lads. Being with the girls this time had provided me with a very different perspective on the place and I felt noticeably more exposed and vulnerable than I had with Rob and Paul. It's not to say I didn't feel safe while out and about with the girls, but there were many minor incidents (being leered at or, ironically, being totally dismissed) that had definitely not happened while cocooned in the company of my two male 'bodyguards'.

For the most part, India's men had been good and kind to me so far, Alex and the Jaipur lads being the perfect example of this, but reliving Mumbai's intense energy with the girls reminded me that the subcontinent was still very much a man's world. Coming back up north with the girls had been eye-opening. I was intrigued to see what the next few days would bring.

Chapter 19

Mystical Varanasi

The train ride to Varanasi was even longer than the one to Mumbai had been and it was cold, very, very cold. I hid myself completely inside my light sleeping bag trying to stay warm and it just about worked (though it made for a rank sleep).

Supposed to arrive at 9 pm, the train was delayed and ended up stopped on the tracks for nearly two hours. Delays like this on a thirty-hour journey, especially so close to the end, are nearly as frustrating as a mirage on the desert. Concerned about finding our way late at night in this city, Kiera phoned ahead on her mobile and managed to book us into a hotel Charlotte had stayed in when she'd been here. Varanasi had a reputation for sneaky tuk-tuk drivers persuading travellers that the hotel they wanted to stay in had gone out of business, or had burned down, and then bringing them to a more expensive hotel of their choosing in order to get a commission. (This was of course before the days of instant internet access on your phone and being able to google such details at the drop of a hat.)

It was a relief to step off the train into the cool night air at last. We headed towards the exit, using the flyover to cross the many tracks. As we did so, a group of three or four men followed us, offering lifts and accommodation, both of which we politely declined. As we came down the steps by platform one, Kiera, overloaded with her two heavy bags, suddenly stumbled and fell awkwardly. The men instantly went to help her.

'Are you OK?' I asked, concerned.

'Um, I think so – thanks,' she said, as the guys assisted her in getting up. She made her way gingerly down the last few steps, limping a little.

'I think I've twisted my ankle.' She winced, looking a little pale.

'OK, madam?' one of the men inquired as they headed off.

'Yes, thank you,' Kiera reassured him.

'Let's head straight to the hotel, we'll check your ankle out once there,' I suggested.

Fifteen minutes later, we pulled up outside Hotel Divya. I took some rupees out for the fare, but Kiera seemed to be searching around for her purse.

'I had it right here,' she muttered, stopping for a moment and frowning. 'It was right here in my pocket.'

'It'll probably turn up in your bag; I'll pay for now,' I told her.

'OK,' she replied looking doubtful, and grimaced slightly as she stepped on her injured foot. She was still trying to work out what she'd done with her purse as we walked up to the hotel entrance. 'I definitely didn't leave it on the train because I remember checking that we had everything before getting off. I'm sure I just stuffed it in my jeans pocket before I fell– oh!' she stopped in her tracks.

'What?' I turned around to look at her and saw her expression before finally catching on. 'Those men?'

She nodded with a grim smile. 'And I was so nice to them, thanking them,' she berated herself with a sigh. 'I bet they even tripped me too, set the whole thing up.'

'What a dirty rotten thing to do!' The fact that they'd pretended to be so kind and helpful bothered me as much as the fact that they'd stolen her wallet.

'At least they didn't get all my bank cards – there was only one in the purse.'

We entered the hotel feeling out of sorts but things started looking up a little as the kind receptionist showed us to a clean, cosy room, we were able to have instant hot showers and Kiera discovered her ankle wasn't as bad as she'd first thought. I gave Alex a quick call before going to sleep to let him know we'd arrived safe and (more or less) sound. Hearing his sweet voice filled me with happiness. Damn, I missed him a little already. Kiera rolled her eyes and groaned when I told her.

'Jeez, girl, you've only been gone a couple days. What are you like?'

'Aw, what's wrong with being in luuurve?'

'Good *night*, Liz!'

We spent just three full days in Varanasi but the city had a special energy and charmed us like a wise and slightly weather-beaten old dame. Varanasi lies right alongside India's most sacred river, the Ganges, and is one of the holiest pilgrimage sites for Hindus who consider it the most auspicious place in which to be cremated after death. I could imagine this packed and rather polluted city being less fun in the thick heat of summer, but in January it had gentle sunlit days and cool nights that required thick shawls and numerous cups of hot sweet chai. For the first time since leaving Ireland I revelled in the cold weather, enjoying the need to snuggle up in scarves and socks and long sleeves.

Despite only staying there a short time, Varanasi managed to wrap us silkily around her gnarled fingers, crooning to us until we were blind to anything but her mysterious charm. There was such a sense of energy and movement all around us: the city felt like a breathing, living organism. Every facet of life was present, the good, the bad and everything in between, all imbued with a vitality that had us entranced. Women passed us garbed in a magnificent array of colours, car horns sounded like trumpets, cows bellowed, people shouted, roaring diesel engines often drowned everything out and their fumes battled with the heady scents of spices and incense. Throughout it all, the city swayed and swirled and heaved and sighed like a dancing body. It was magical.

Our hotel was located alongside the *ghats* but towards the calmer, quieter end of the town, a good thirty-minute walk from the areas where the cremations took place. A *ghat* is the term for a quay that has steps leading down to the river and the burning *ghat*s are the ones with the pyres where the cremations take place. On our first day, with Kiera's ankle already on the mend, we went for a wander through this strange, alluring city. Along the way, a young Nepali guy called Laki latched onto us with persistent conversation until we finally gave in and chatted back.

'So, you are into astrology?' he asked us as we meandered through the busy streets.

'I am, definitely,' I said brightly. Friends had gotten me into it several years back and on discovering all the information mapped out by my birth chart I had felt quite reassured (so that's why I'm so weird) by the astoundingly accurate descriptions of me – little old Liz – in books written decades before by utter strangers.

'Yeah, I've heard a little about it too,' Kiera said.

'Oh, that is very good, because I am knowing a really great astrologer here in Varanasi. I can take you to see him if you're interested?'

Despite being three months in India, I was still as gullible as ever and both Kiera and I were fully sold. As I look back, I can't understand why I wasn't at least a tiny bit sceptical of his friendliness. God knows I had been taken for quite the ride in Jodhpur with Sharma. I guess sometimes it takes a while for me to catch on and I willingly followed Laki as he led us through some narrow streets where the buildings blocked the sunlight and the shadow left a noticeable chill. We entered a building and found ourselves in a sparsely furnished room. Sitting cross-legged on a cushion in front of a low table was a portly, middle-aged Indian man with white robes, a grey bushy moustache and a red *bindu* (Hinduism's signature inky red dot) in the middle of his forehead.

'Welcome, welcome!' he told us with a grand gesture, and we knelt down on cushions near the small table while Laki talked to him in Hindi. Sai nodded sagely and turned to look at us with a smile.

'So! You have come for the astrology readings. That is very good, you are most welcome. It is just 1,100 rupees and I will be going through many things, your past lives and your current life and what is to come.'

We both paid up front (around twenty euros each then) and Kiera was eager to get going so I waited to the side while Sai took her date of birth and did a few calculations. He finally started talking and to everything he said, Kiera nodded affirmatively, or smiled and rolled her eyes as if to say 'don't I know it!' She was definitely getting her money's worth.

Despite my initial enthusiasm, I was starting to feel rather dubious. This was India and Laki must have been making a few bucks' commission out of us. Plus there was something about dear old Sai that I didn't fully buy into. Tuning back into what was going on, I heard him mentioning the snake energy in Kiera's lineage and she turned around to me, her eyes shining.

'Oh my gosh, this is so spot on, we've always had a thing about snakes, me and my Mum.'

I couldn't help notice Sai's expression: it seemed pretty smug. Well duh, I mean, besides the legendary wildlife expert, Steve Irwin, I've never heard of anyone who actually likes snakes, they're not exactly friendly creatures. I was regretting having paid up front now because, although I had decided that Sai was full of shite, I didn't have the guts to ask for my money back. He carried on going through Kiera's chart and eventually reached the crux of the reading.

'Now, in order to get rid of these seven generations of sin that are coming in your family history, there is one thing you must get and that is a special gold talisman,' he told her with a grave expression.

'Oh, gold, that's going to be expensive,' she hesitated, disappointed. 'I don't think I'll be able to do that.'

Sai rapidly went through some calculations before jabbing the air with his finger and nodding in confirmation.

'Yes, yes, there is another way. This problem can also be fixed by means of a very special holy plate – you must drink milk from it every morning and evening for twenty-one days. Only then, these seven generations of sin can be cured.'

'Oh!' Kiera looked surprised. 'How much does the plate cost?'

'Very reasonable,' Sai spoke dismissively. 'For you it is only 2,000 rupees.'

Kiera considered it for a moment.

'That's around thirty-five euros. I guess I could manage that,' she decided out loud.

'No problem. You must come back to me in two days. Meantime I will be performing the necessary *pujas* and blessings, by way of purification.'

'Cool.' Kiera seemed satisfied with that. I on the other hand was not impressed but as it was my turn I reluctantly switched places with her. Our astrologer shuffled papers and began to do calculations based on my own details. He soon started chuckling and shaking his head.

'Oh dear, oh dear! Just the very thing I was saying earlier, that example of difficult planetary energies and you are having exactly all of them in your chart. Jupiter and Saturn both retrograde. You must be having a hard time of it, no?'

'Sometimes, I guess. So what, am I totally screwed?' I joked, but he didn't seem to notice, frowning instead as he looked at the numbers in front of him.

'Let me see, you are not finding it easy to trust people, you are very suspicious at the beginning.'

This little insight was probably written all over my face in the moment but if you think about it, it was actually quite inaccurate; I had spent a lot of my time in India so far trusting people the second I met them. He was going to have to do better than that. Instead he spent about twenty minutes rattling off vague generic information that could have applied to anyone and in the end it seemed I too had malefic energies that needed fixing with a gold talisman – something conveniently expensive to balance all those pesky retrograde planets. I wasn't buying it, literally or figuratively, and I politely declined the pricey 'lucky charm' idea, as well as his cheaper alternatives, preferring to take my chances. I figured I'd managed pretty well so far with things just as they were.

* * *

'Did you really believe all that stuff he said, like needing to drink milk off a holy plate to cure your seven generations of sin?' I asked Kiera later over dinner.

'OK, I'm definitely not taking it all as fact,' she replied, putting down her fork to take a sip of water. 'But I'm keeping an open mind because who knows, right? And it doesn't hurt to give it a go.'

'I guess,' I conceded, poking around at my food.

'Besides,' she added. 'It's such an interesting thing to show everyone back home, it almost doesn't matter if it's real or not.'

'And the thing he said about free will?' I asked, seeking her opinion. 'I can't get my head around that.'

Sai, despite being a total money-making spoofer, had somehow managed to rattle my belief system, stating emphatically that according to the laws of the universe, we have no say or control whatsoever over our lives. Despite the fact that he hadn't convinced me about anything else in the entire time we'd been there, his conviction in an outside power running the show had in fact struck a chord in me, a rather uncomfortable one that left me feeling small and defeated. Interesting, given the deep devotion and acceptance it seems to generate in the general Indian population.

'We have such a different way of looking at life in the West,' Kiera responded. 'We want everything to happen our way and we fight and resist when it doesn't. The culture of India seems to be very different. Their spiritual practices are completely devoted to God; they accept the life they're handed. A lot of us in the West don't have that deep faith so when life decides to play around with our plans and ideas we freak out. But at the end of the day, how much control do we really have over anything?'

'Well, don't we have like – I don't know – this power inside of us, this ability to do anything, to be anything, to heal from anything ...' I trailed off, not really knowing where I was going with that one, but pretty sure I'd read it in a book somewhere.

'Maybe if you're an enlightened yogi up in the Himalayas,' Kiera said kindly. 'But for us mere mortals I don't think it works quite like that. You can only do so much with anything and at a certain point, it's in God's hands, or at the will of the universe, or whatever you want to call it.'

'So what, if we've no free will, if it's all actually up to God or whatever then why bother even trying? I mean, why not, I don't know, just give up and go lie on the street. Either I'll stay there or I won't but hey, it's out of my hands.'

'But would you actually quit and give up like that? Really? Even if we don't have free will exactly, I think we do simply because we *think* we do. I mean, when things don't go our way, but we end up with something even better than what we'd hoped for … there has to be a force of some kind, *something* else that's working there. Instead of thinking we've no power or say in anything, maybe we just need to actively work with what life is offering us, not fight it. You get me?'

I stared at her, my brain in turmoil but sensing some truth in what she was saying. 'All this deep philosophical talk is making my head hurt.'

Kiera smiled.

'On a slightly different note, are you still on for walking along the *ghats* at dawn tomorrow?' I asked, using a chunk of flatbread to scoop up my dhal.

'Definitely. I love this city, I wish we could spend more time here. But just a week or so to go and I'll be on a gorgeous beach in the Philippines, reunited with my sweetheart. I can't wait!'

Our conversation strayed to slightly less soul-searching topics as we finished our meal but it seemed that my time in India was finally taking a turn towards the more spiritual.

* * *

At 6 am next day we dressed quietly and headed out, strolling along the near-empty *ghat*s in the haze of dawn. There was a softness to everything at this early hour, as though the world was cloaked in velvet. The water of the Ganges lapped gently beside us, people's voices spoke in measured tones and a few of India's most iconic spiritual seekers, holy *saadhus*, sat peacefully by the river, deep in meditation. The atmosphere affected me profoundly and at that moment, I couldn't have felt further away from the West. India's magic is special, the land holds a unique and deeply spiritual energy and I truly hope no amount of modernisation or technological advancement ever changes that.

Later in the day we sorted out our onward journey to Delhi, buying the slightly more expensive train tickets for 'third-class AC' as it was the only option left at such short notice. Despite having several full days in Varanasi in which to see the burning *ghats* where the cremations took place, we left it till the very last evening to go there.

The cremations take place alongside the river bank, where special fires are kept burning continuously as body after body is placed on its designated pyre; funeral after funeral, one long procession of bodies discarded by spirit to be returned to the ashes of the earth.

Standing back from it all, high up on steps, we observed as respectful spectators while families brought their deceased loved ones down on stretchers, the corpses covered from head to toe in white cloth and decorated in garlands of flowers. The utter lack of emotion at the scene was in stark contrast to funerals back home, but it is said in the Hindu religion that to cry or grieve during the cremation holds back the deceased's soul and prevents it leaving this world.

And so, families drowning in heartbreak remained expressionless as they allowed their loved ones to depart both in spirit and in body, the fires consuming the physical evidence of their time on earth. It took a while to absorb the full impact of what I was seeing. A distinct 'pop' eventually told me that the skull of a body had cracked and when some cloth burned away to expose a human foot, looking grotesquely out of place amidst the flames, it began to sink in. My brain floated a little eerily in my head, the moment feeling surreal and strange, solemn and poignant.

By the time I'd come to some level of acceptance of the scene at hand, the sun had set and dusk was falling. In the fading light, only the bright flames of the fires could clearly be seen. It was time to go. Varanasi is a special place, the burning *ghats* filled with a potent, sacred energy. Life after death, death in order to create life, the one truth none of us can ever escape, the single equaliser among all of us: that one day we too will leave this planet, this body, this home and family, this life. My time in the holy city had affected me deeply. India was still working her magic.

Chapter 20

Dastardly Delhi

The journey from Varanasi to Delhi passed in the luxurious comfort of our upper-class tickets. I awoke next morning feeling snug and cosy in clean sheets and blankets, my head resting on a soft pillow. It reminded me of the train ride to Goa with the boys back in October as I hadn't indulged in such lavish travel since. I felt a small pang at the memory and wondered how they were doing, knowing from recent emails that Paul was still in Thailand and Rob had moved on to Laos. Then I thought of Alex and the boys and all my adventures these past couple of months and I smiled to myself. Who could have imagined how my trip would turn out after saying goodbye to my two original travel buddies?

Although the luxury was the same, there was one big difference on this train journey: our compartment was full of Indian travellers rather than fellow Western tourists. There is a noticeable difference between the kind of Indians you meet in the more expensive carriages and the cheaper second-class carriages. In fact, aside from everyone around us being Indian, the journey felt very similar to any train ride back home. The people in our carriage mostly wore smart, Western-style clothes, spoke fluent English and I felt less like entertainment and more like a regular fellow passenger.

That's not to say that travel in the second-class sleeper carriages isn't good. On the contrary, the people you meet there are infinitely generous, kind and curious and, for me, a little of India's raw authenticity gets polished off with each upper level of class. Ultimately, if you wanted to really dive into the heart of India, you could purchase a local ticket, which is incredibly cheap. However, unless you're willing to bulldoze your way through hundreds of fellow passengers for the five or so seats available, you may find yourself spending a twenty-hour journey lying on top of your backpack. It's not for everyone.

We arrived in Delhi late in the morning and, in our cluelessness, took a cab to the area called Paharganj, which was in fact only around the corner. But we knew no better, the taxi driver knew far better and so for 100 rupees (for a journey that should have cost no more than about 30 rupees) we were brought around on a little scenic drive of the city until he eventually looped back to Paharganj.

Our little excursion showed off one part of the capital and it seemed to be the scrappiest, most chaotic place I'd seen yet, which is really saying something. Paharganj was a mishmash of scraggly streets, crumbling hippie shops, dust and dirt, bloated cows, dingy makeshift food stalls, cycle rickshaws squished between auto-rickshaws, beggars and touts and an endless spider's web of tangled, knotted electric wires crossing the tops of buildings. The electrical system looked so bad that it held more resemblance to a clump of hair pulled off a comb. Not surprisingly, power outages were frequent in this part of the city. Unlike Colaba in Mumbai, however, Delhi's accommodation was much kinder on our wallets and we found a place less expensive than the Salvation Army and minus the cockroaches. Perhaps this city wasn't quite so bad.

Next morning Kiera and I visited Connaught Place, a name that harks back to colonial times. This area was posh and sophisticated: the roads and buildings were wide and clean and well maintained. It was like there were two sides to this city with one presenting a modern, respectable, advanced cosmopolitan image – Delhi the capital. The other, never too far from reach, was the chaotic, erratic Delhi, overcrowded land of poverty and struggle (though to be fair, I still think Agra was worse).

Before leaving Varanasi, Kiera had already booked flights to Goa for the day after we arrived in Delhi. She didn't have a lot of time left in India and fancied some chilled-out beach life for the remainder of her trip.

We hugged goodbye next day, an incredibly awkward thing to do when one person is wearing large rucksacks on their back *and* front.

'Take care of yourself and give the boys all a big hug from me. Especially Alex.'

'Ha! No worries there, girl, I'll be all over him for days once I get back to Varkala.'

'Oh Liz, what are you like? Look, I'd better go. Keep in touch, you have my email. See you!'

'Bye, sweetie!'

I was sorry to see her go. I would miss her easy company and our revelatory conversations. In fact I felt a little lonely now, all on my own. First Charlotte had left and now Kiera had too. I seemed to be constantly making new friends and then saying goodbye to them soon after. But that's the way of the traveller: you cross paths with wonderful, like-minded souls and then you move on and maybe you cross paths again one day in the future or maybe you don't. That's just the way it is.

I decided to figure out a plan of travel to take my mind off being all by myself. Logical, left-side brain said plan a few more stops and make my way gradually back down to Kerala, seeing more of India along the way. Passionate, heart-side brain said go straight back to Varkala and Alex right now, please and thank you. Two weeks away was proving more than enough. I decided to go to the train station to see what trains were available and make up my mind then.

Bearing in mind that I was still clueless about how close the station was to Paharganj, I naturally assumed I needed a taxi to get there. Walking up to a waiting rickshaw driver, I tried my luck with eighty rupees. A moment of the briefest surprise flitted across his face followed by a sudden yes. I stepped warily into the cab. You normally had to haggle hard with these guys: something was amiss here.

I was pretty put out when he drove me to the end of the street, turned a corner and stopped after about a thirty-second ride: there were no trains in sight.

'This isn't the train station,' I said pointedly, looking across at a travel agency.

'No ma'am, but here you get your tickets no problem,' he said confidently, with a dismissive head wobble.

'Well, OK, but that definitely wasn't worth eighty rupees,' I added. I could easily have walked the short distance. After a minute of some arguing, we settled on a fairer price of thirty rupees and I headed inside.

Ten minutes later I came back out, utterly disheartened. All the trains were fully booked up for the next week, meaning the only option to leave this city before then was to shell out 4,000 rupees for a flight – nearly eighty euros. I didn't know quite what to do. I couldn't permit myself to spend so much money, yet I had no desire to hang around Delhi that long either.

'Yes ma'am, you have your tickets?' The same driver was waiting outside for me.

'No, it was way too expensive,' I said, full of disappointment.

'I know a cheaper place, I can take you if you want?'

I looked at him in disbelief. 'Of *course* I want a cheaper place.'

'OK, let's go.'

Feeling more and more annoyed, I got back into the cab and he drove just a minute further on, pulling up outside yet another travel agency.

'Here you get the very best price. I wait for you no problem,' he assured me.

I entered the small premises and the man at the desk repeated what I'd heard in the previous one – no trains available, only expensive flights. Crap.

'I'm sorry,' I sighed, my hopes having plummeted down into my shoes. 'I really wanted to get the train, I can't afford to buy these expensive plane tickets.'

'Ma'am, why you are not going to the train station then?' he asked me, in a tone that suggested he clearly didn't find me too bright.

'Well, that's what I was trying to do but I don't know where it is and that rickshaw driver keeps bringing me to travel agencies.'

'It's very simple,' he told me, his tone softening. 'Leave here and turn right, continue straight down that road and take your first right again, there is the train station. It is about ten minutes walking.'

A straight answer at last.

I thanked him and left, spotting the tuk-tuk driver waiting outside; he was leaning against his cab, facing away from me. I decided I'd had enough of him trying to screw me over and made off rapidly in the direction I'd been told, praying for a ticket out of here as soon as possible. Delhi was becoming extremely tiresome. Just as promised, in about ten minutes I was at the station, waiting in line for the inquiries desk with a small form in my hands that I couldn't quite figure out. Glancing behind me, I inadvertently caught the eye of the man standing next in line. I had a moment of 'oh crap' when he and his friend smiled at me and started chatting, but it turned out they weren't the pesky bothersome type. Ajay and Kumar were in fact truly lovely.

'Where are you from?'

'Ireland.'

'Oh, very nice, very beautiful green country, no?'

Their energy was light and sincere and I found myself relaxing.

'So where are you going?' Ajay asked me.

'Kerala,' I answered. 'I'm not sure what train I'm supposed to get though.'

'No problem, the man at the counter will organise that for you, simply write on the form your destination, which class you prefer and the date you wish to travel.'

And it really was that easy. I put Varkala on the form (passionate heart side won out after all!), second-class sleeper and the following day's date then crossed my fingers. The bored looking man behind the counter duly looked up a suitable train for me and wrote down the details on my form before handing it back.

'You must go to this desk to purchase your ticket. Come, I will show you.'

Kumar walked over with me and gave my form to another member of staff who moments later asked for 750 rupees (not even fifteen euros) and then handed me my train ticket straight to Varkala, for the *very next morning*. It made me want to bounce up and down in happy relief, and then go punch that tuk-tuk driver in the face. I settled for a smile instead.

Grateful for their help, I waited for Ajay and Kumar to finish their own business then walked outside with them to the front of the bustling station.

'You are staying in Paharganj, yes?' Ajay inquired. I nodded.

'Then you just head straight down that road,' he told me, indicating a wide street going perpendicular to us. 'It is only about five minutes walking.'

Not 100 rupees in a cab then, I thought.

'Here, before you go, you take our numbers,' Kumar said, pulling out a small notebook and pen from his coat pocket. He started scribbling down his details and tore the sheet off. 'If you are having any problems while in Delhi, you please don't hesitate to call me or Ajay!'

And with that kind, genuine offer they waved me goodbye and I walked away from the two big-hearted angels back to my hotel and the chaos of Paharganj. My golden ticket to Varkala was snug in my pocket and I felt wrapped up in the warm reassurance that there were good, kind people in Delhi. I was about to phone Alex to let him know I was coming back in a few days when I thought how funny it would be to just show up in Varkala and surprise him. I put the phone away.

The afternoon was spent browsing shops, picking up some gifts for the boys and doing my daily one good deed. When a scruffy Tibetan man badgered me for money for a bus ticket to Dharamshala, I was so wary of being duped yet again that I decided no more money, I would offer food instead. He seemed OK with that. We went to one of the many little cafés along the ramshackle street and Tenzing noisily slurped his way through a chicken noodle soup. He didn't speak much and I was only too aware of the waiters all blatantly staring at us. I offered him my wet wipes to clean off some of the grime from his face and hands and he stuffed the entire pack in his coat pocket. Guess he needed them more than I did.

On leaving the café, he continued pestering me for some cash, seventy rupees to be precise, for a bus ticket to Dharamshala. If I'd had any inkling as to the actual cost of this ticket, I would have realised he was bullshitting me. But I didn't know and felt an inner turmoil of wanting to help in case he genuinely needed it and yet desperately wishing to avoid being scammed in India, yet *again*. I gave him thirty rupees and hoped I'd done the right thing.

Later on that evening, I was searching for a bookshop I'd been in earlier that was located in one of Delhi's maze of alleys. It became exceedingly tricky to find it when a sudden power cut plunged the smaller side streets into blackness, leaving even the main road incredibly gloomy, lit only by the few premises with generators.

Deciding not to venture into the dark and uninviting back streets, I turned around and headed back the way I'd come only to be accosted once more by Tenzing.

'Leeze, Leeze!'

I looked around reluctantly.

'Leeze, I got more money!' he told me excitedly. 'Now I just need thirty rupees more.'

'I'm sorry, man, I can't give you any more money,' I told him firmly. His jittery, wired manner was unsettling me, especially given the dim light.

'But Leeze, only thirty more rupees I need. Please, you give me thirty rupees,' he spoke insistently.

Feeling cornered, I wondered uncertainly what to do but in the end was saved from having to decide. 'Are you OK? What is happen here?'

A burly, fair-skinned bloke appeared next to us, looking from me to Tenzing with concern on his round face. I recognised him from just moments before, with his bulky physique and shaved head; he had been walking in the opposite direction to me and had obviously made a rapid detour back. I started to hope fervently that that was indeed a good thing.

'What is happen? You are OK?' he asked me in stilted English.

Feeling less and less sure of my current situation, I nodded a tentative yes. Tenzing had suddenly become mute in the man's presence, though as yet he wasn't budging.

'I think you leave her now, OK?'

Tenzing threw in one last pitiful attempt.

'Leeze, money,' he started to whine a little, seeing his chance – most likely for a bottle of whiskey – slipping away.

'Sorry, I already gave you some earlier. I can't give you any more.'

At that Mr Burly Skinhead became more insistent. 'You go now. You leave her,' he said in a tone that implied he would probably pick him up and lob him down the street if necessary.

Tenzing visibly sagged upon realising the game was up and as he skulked off, I turned to face his adversary. With an imposing muscled body and standing a good foot taller than me, I felt like I now either had a wonderful new bodyguard or, well, the other possible scenarios didn't seem so promising. I swallowed nervously.

'You want take some tea?' he inquired with a friendly smile while I pondered the question and his powerful frame. Did I really have a choice?

'OK,' I smiled back politely and we started walking.

Once again, life surprised me with its kindness. Omar from Iran was an absolute gentleman. He brought me to a quirky cosy café where we hung out with a Columbian girl that he already knew. We ate some snacks, drank chai, shared stories and finally, after paying for everything, my Persian hero walked me right back to my hotel door. He even insisted he carry my small shopping bag for me, the cutie. For such an intimidating facade, he was a true gem of a human being and I felt royally protected by him. His small role in my tale, much like that of Ajay and Kumar at the train station, is fully worthy of being included as testament to the profound effect such small, kind efforts can have on the people you meet in life. Omar, Ajay, Kumar: I salute you!

The following day my train was due to leave Delhi at 11 am. Feeling a little guilty for not really having seen anything of the capital, I decided to take a rickshaw tour of a few sights nearby including the sprawling Red Fort. The damp air was freezing; if only tuk-tuks had heating (and doors and windows). Delhi in January is damn cold and to make matters worse, my thick mop of hair was still wet from the hot shower I'd had that morning. I wrapped my shawl tight around my head but it made little difference in the bitter breeze and I was chilled to the bone by the time I collected my bags from the hotel. Strolling through Paharganj with all my gear I saw the station up ahead. 100 rupees for a taxi … would I ever live that down?

A rickshaw driver called out to me as I passed him.

'Yes, madam. You want taxi to station?'

'No, I *don't* want a fecking taxi, the station's right *there*!!'

The poor lad looked a little taken aback by my vehemence but I was sick of being tricked and cheated and charged outrageous prices. Enough already! Once at the station I found my train easily and, on reaching my carriage, noticed a printed sheet stuck to the door with all the passengers' names, including mine.

So long, Delhi, I thought, greatly relieved a while later when the train finally blasted its horn and started to leave the station. (Over the years, I've made numerous visits back to the city and it's grown on me a lot; in fact I'm quite fond of it now. Back in 2008, though, let's just say the great Indian capital didn't make a good first impression.)

Initially I shared my compartment with just a shy Indian lady called Meeny. She didn't speak much and I spent the first few hours gazing out of the window at the passing scenery as the train began its long journey south. There didn't seem to be much to do but read, daydream and of course drink chai. A few hours later, the train pulled into Agra and our peace and quiet was suddenly disrupted by the arrival of a bunch of rowdy Indian soldiers, six of them, all dressed in olive green uniforms and heavy black boots, making a lot of noise and clamour and leaving me feeling quite intimidated. The lengthy journey began to seem even longer.

As the day wore on, however, the men proved veritable gentlemen. They constantly offered to buy chai, coffee and snacks for me and Meeny, showed a genuine curiosity in where I was from and were delighted to look at the photos of India in my guidebook. Their intimidating presence soon switched 180 degrees to being comforting and protective.

It's a little ironic that when the soldiers disembarked the train next afternoon, uniforms packed away and dressed in civilian clothes, I felt a similar regret as to when they'd arrived. They smiled warmly and I waved, the carriage dull and empty in their absence.

Fifty-two hours on a train is a long time. It's a long time to travel if you've got company but it's even longer when you're on your own, sitting around staring out of the window watching scenery gradually morphing from dry, rugged terrain to the rich, tropical vegetation of Kerala while the cool temperature changes to the heat and humidity of the south.

Most of the journey passed easily enough but by the last morning I was ready to throw myself out of the door just to get off the damn train. To make matters worse, I had just come down with a bad case of the sniffles. Apparently, whizzing about Delhi in an open taxi with wet hair wasn't such a good idea; my nose started to dribble and, once the tissues ran out, I had no other option than to resort to using an old

T-shirt if I didn't want gooey snot dripping down my face. Meeny looked revolted but I could do nothing about it.

The final two hours felt longer than the previous fifty put together as I sat there in the sweltering heat, breathing through my mouth, a dull headache forming thanks to my now fully blocked sinuses. At long last the train started slowing and I spotted the massive yellow sign with large black lettering in Malayalam, Hindi and of course English: VARKALA. I was ridiculously excited and waved a happy goodbye to Meeny, all but leaping out of the carriage the moment the train had stopped. It was time to call Alex.

'Hi darling!' I said, hearing him pick up.

'Oh, hello! Where are you, *beta*?'

'I'm actually at Delhi train station trying to sort out a ticket.'

I grinned as the hustle and bustle of Varkala station around me created the perfect background noise.

'So where are you right now?' I asked casually. 'At home or at the shop?'

'I'm in the house. When are you coming back?' he asked, sounding disappointed.

'Soon, darling, I promise!' It was a huge effort to keep the excitement out of my voice. 'Look I'd better go and get my ticket, I'll talk to you again in a little while, OK?'

We said our goodbyes and I found a cab to take me to the house. Despite the long train journey, the intense heat and my full-on cold, the thrill of anticipation at finally seeing Alex kept me going. I leaned back on the seat, delighted as we passed familiar streets, my excitement reaching new levels as we neared the house. Pulling up outside, I paid the fare, grabbed my backpack out of the boot and hurried up to the main front door before the cab's running engine could attract too much attention.

I pressed the buzzer and held it down, the peal of the bell ringing for an obscenely long time, and giggled when I heard Sid shouting an insult in Hindi. His expression when he opened the door made me burst out laughing.

'Surprise!' I said with a grin.

'Leeze! But you're in Delhi,' he protested, confusion all over his face.

'Not anymore. Where is he?'

I entered the living room just as Alex was coming out of the kitchen and the expression on his face was priceless.

'Hello stranger!' I giggled as we threw our arms around each other.

'But you said you were getting a ticket,' he mumbled into my neck, laughing as he pulled me in closer. 'You said you were still in Delhi.'

'Gotcha!'

Sure, it might have been nice to be fresh and sweet-smelling for our big reunion (as opposed to exhausted, grimy and full of snot) but at the end of the day I was off the train, far away from Delhi and, most importantly, back with my sweet, still-shocked and delighted man. That was more than enough. Feeling utterly worn out now the excitement was over, I collapsed on the couch next to Alex while Ballu brought chai and the boys asked questions about my trip. Alex kept squeezing my hand every two minutes as if to confirm that I was indeed back, grinning at me each time he did it. I couldn't keep the smile off my own face as I leaned against him and sipped on my tea, finally starting to unwind. Damn, it was good to be back.

Chapter 21

Doubting Thomas

'Hi Charles!'

'Liz, how are you?'

I pulled out a chair for the English man to join me at my table where I was having brunch at the cliff. It was already over a week since I'd returned to Varkala.

'I'm good – much better, in fact,' I answered, thinking back to the nasty chest infection that had developed out of my simple cold. Note to self: do not sit in a windy café or fall asleep under a fan when you're ill. My chest had felt as though it were full of knives while my voice had temporarily faded to a painful raspy whisper. Not fun.

'Good to hear it. Excuse me!' he called loudly to a nearby waiter. 'One chai, please.'

Charles's eyes followed the young lad as he went into the restaurant's kitchen. 'He's a bit of alright that one.'

I shook my head. I'd first bumped into the rather eccentric chap outside the boys' jewellery shop a few days ago. He'd been hard to miss, given his unusual choice of hairstyle.

Imagine, if you will, a man with a shiny, pale, bald head, as smooth and hairless as a hen's egg. Then imagine on the very top, right in the centre, a bizarre smattering of stubby, black dreadlocks. It made me think of pineapples every time I saw him.

His somewhat unusual image was paired with a posh London accent and an insatiable urge to screw every male Indian that crossed his path. He could be pretty rude and obnoxious, especially to the locals, but he was friendly with me and I was intrigued with the kind of character that would intentionally choose such a hairstyle as his.

'So how come you're still hanging around Varkala?' he asked, finally dragging his eyes off the waiter.

'Because of Alex – oh wait, he wasn't at the shop the other day. He's one of the guys running the show and we kind of hooked up,' I said with a smile.

Charles looked at me, one eyebrow raised. 'So, you've got an Indian boyfriend then.'

I didn't like the tone that was colouring his words. It seemed to be suggesting 'there goes another one'.

'Yes, as do you,' I pointed out levelly.

Charles shook his head with a condescending smile. 'Not the same thing, I'm afraid, no. My boyfriend won't shag me and hop straight to the next tourist like I'm a piece of meat.' He paused to light up a long, slim cigarette and inhaled deeply, then crossed one arm and rested the other elbow on it, the cigarette poised in the air, the hand hanging backwards in that delightfully effeminate manner that only a gay man can truly accomplish.

'When it comes to straight Indian men and white girls, on the other hand,' he continued, adding little flicks of his raised hand to match his words, 'well, they just see you as easy sex.'

I frowned at him, disliking what he was implying about Alex. 'And what, all Indian men are like this?'

'Ninety-nine per cent for sure,' he replied, blowing smoke slowly out of his nose. He registered the expression on my face.

'Don't look at me like that, darlin', I'm just telling it like it is,' he said in an off-hand manner. 'Indian boys usually don't get to have any sex until they're grown up and married because the girls are practically locked up with chastity belts until the day they've got a husband. So the Indian boy never gets to let off some steam. Oh, thank you, that's great,' he said, pausing a moment to smile deeply into the waiter's eyes as he set the chai down on the table. The waiter smiled nervously back and left while Charles stared wistfully after him.

'A straight one, but they're the most fun when there's a challenge!' he murmured conspiratorially to me as he added some sugar to the tea, stirring it lazily.

'Where was I? Oh right, so the young Indian male is starved of any promiscuity by his own land and culture and then …' he paused, glancing my way before continuing '… hordes of easy white girls start to arrive in your town and they're pretty much all up for a good time. Before he can even get bored of one chick, she's gone already and there's another in her place. They don't see anything long term in it, since none of the girls hang around, and they all end up having an arranged marriage anyway and probably carry on doing much the same thing after it, sleeping around with girls like you while wifey minds the kids back in the village. Do you see what I'm getting at, love?'

'But you can't generalise like that! Not all Indian guys are the same,' I countered defensively.

Charles tapped his cigarette on the ashtray and leaned back in his chair. 'Perhaps not all. But most, believe me.'

'Well, Alex isn't like that,' I said crossing my arms resolutely. 'And it's not like I'm like that either, I don't sleep around.'

Charles didn't seem reassured by this. 'So then you're new to this, he'll run circles around you before you know it. He probably has another girl somewhere on the go as it is.'

'Alex isn't like that!' I repeated, somewhat exasperated now. The kind of person Charles was describing was worlds away from the sweet innocence of Alex. Without doubt, he was not the kind of girl-crazy sex-hungry animal who couldn't keep his pants on for two minutes.

'Honey, they all say that. But do you actually know? How well do you know him, how well do you trust him?'

'*Completely.*'

My 'that's enough' tone had its desired effect.

'OK, OK,' Charles held up his hands in surrender before sighing. 'But if you come back early some day and catch him in bed with another girl, don't say I didn't warn you.'

I inwardly scoffed at the very idea while our conversation turned to lighter topics and I finally decided it was time to get up and do something with my day. Despite my conviction while defending Alex, an uncomfortable little seed of doubt had in fact been planted by Charles's words and it niggled in the back of my mind.

It wasn't that I thought for one moment that Alex might cheat on me, he was far too kind and innocent to be that kind of playboy and my surprise arrival back from Delhi was more proof of that. What got me was what Charles had said about Indian boys who got together with white girls while still planning to marry a traditional Indian bride down the line. If our relationship were tested, where would Alex's loyalties lie, towards me or his family? Would he too decide to settle down one day with an Indian wife and was I just a passing bit of fun for him?

My naive little honeymoon dream of 'everything's possible' was starting to lose its faith. Because even if Alex saw me as more than a bit of fun, just what were the implications of us being together long term? Did it mean I had to move to India or that Alex would move to Ireland? Suddenly everything seemed far too complicated.

Unfortunately, Alex was away in Goa all that day and most of the following one too (he regularly travelled on business, usually to source gemstones). The time apart allowed my doubts and worries to spiral into a whirlpool of suspicion, which I might not have heeded so much but for one other factor.

In the time since I'd arrived back from the north, another pretty, fun and intelligent young woman had caught Sid's eye, and more besides. I really enjoyed Felicity's company and was glad when she came to stay in the house with us for a while, but I felt torn. It was barely a month since Sid had apparently declared abstinence from any more girls on the cliff to Charlotte and yet here he was, quite clearly *not* abstaining from the lovely Felicity. I unwittingly shared with her the tale of Sid's promise to Charlotte one evening, before realising the budding romance between them, leaving both of us in doubt about the deeper feelings of our respective boys.

'Having an Indian boyfriend is so complicated.'

It was the following day. Felicity and I had come to the cliff top for lunch and were at Clafouti restaurant, staring out at the horizon and relishing each sea breeze that provided some relief from the sticky midday heat.

'For sure,' she agreed, running a hand through her beautiful blonde locks, glistening in the sun. 'There are so many cultural things going on that I don't fully understand. I don't know how I feel anymore. Should I even be staying in the house? Should I continue this thing with Sid? I just don't know.'

I stared out at the magnificent view of the sea whose glorious beauty was somewhat lost on me at this stage.

'Do you think Charles was right? Do you think Sid and Alex are those kind of guys?' I had already shared with her the warnings Charles had given me the previous day.

Felicity was quiet for a moment.

'I guess I don't know them well enough yet to say,' she finally said. 'But I don't think you need to worry about Alex; he seems genuine and sincere and I don't think he would ever mess around with you.'

That's not really what I'm worried about, I thought to myself, but held back from voicing my real concern. I didn't imagine for a moment Alex would cheat on me. But at some point, he would have to make a long-term choice and which way would he go, loyalty to his family and his culture … or me?

By the time we left the café, the sky had become unusually grey and overcast, taking the sun's edge off the humid heat. I decided I needed a walk to try and clear my head and have a change of scene from constantly hanging out at the cliff. I strolled down beyond the smaller black beach, passing endless coconut forests and following bumpy paths and rocky tracks. It felt good to venture further afield and eventually I turned inland and found a main road to loop back home. But on arriving back at the house, with no Alex there to assuage my doubts, they returned full force and I found myself feeling worse and worse.

As you may recall from earlier in my travels (the bizarre massage during our camel safari and of course the whole Jack saga) I'm not too hot on dealing with unpleasant or confusing emotions and situations. That evening found me in Rock-and-Roll Café, hanging out with Felicity and a few other tourists and guzzling rather strong cocktails. By the third one I was well on the way to rum-induced escapism. Even when Felicity eventually left, I stayed on with the others, chatting and laughing, and ordered yet another mojito.

'Hey!' I said in surprise when Felicity returned a little later. 'How come you're back?'

She crouched next to my chair. 'I've been at the shop with the guys. Alex is there, he's waiting for you to come over. They've closed up for the night and he's ready to go home. He won't come here, apparently the local guys might cause problems for him, but he was wondering if you'd like to come back with us now? It's getting pretty late.'

I groaned inwardly. Could she not see that I was quite obviously trying to avoid dealing with reality? I hadn't spoken properly with Alex since the previous morning, before I'd let Charles's words carry me off into suspicion and doubt. He'd arrived back late in the evening after I'd gone to Rock-and-Roll Café, so I still hadn't had to confront the situation. Unfortunately, much as I would have loved to, I couldn't avoid it forever and I really didn't fancy walking home alone through the quiet back roads late at night.

'OK, I'll come with you,' I told her, draining the last of my drink and pulling out my purse to pay.

Most shops were already shut and the absence of their lights threw long shadows on the normally brightly-lit cliff top. When we reached Alex's shop, Ameer was already asleep inside, while Alex and Manju sat on the wall waiting for us. Alex grinned delightedly when he saw me, opening his arms to give me a big hug. My body must have felt like a stiff pole for he realised instantly something was up.

'What's wrong?' he asked pulling back, a worried smile on his face, his eyes searching. 'You like another boy?' he suddenly asked in a voice that suggested he'd known all along that this day would come but still it was breaking his heart.

'No, it's not that,' I replied honestly, shaking my head. It definitely wasn't that. 'Let's talk when we get home.' I tried smiling to reassure him. Seeing the upset and worry in his eyes was as bad as watching a puppy being kicked.

Incredibly, we managed to squish four of us onto a scooter and Manju skilfully manoeuvred the bike back to the house. Once there I said goodnight to everyone and went straight up to our room with Alex close behind.

'So what happened?' he asked the second we were in the room.

'I'm kind of drunk, maybe could we talk in the morning?' I yawned, crawling onto the bed without bothering to change. In my hippie clothes I was practically wearing pyjamas as it was.

'But why you weren't happy to see me?' Alex persisted. 'Why won't you tell me what's wrong?'

I thought for a moment of slipping easily and blissfully asleep and ignoring the whole situation. Instead I turned around with a sigh and recounted the conversation I'd had with Charles and the subsequent doubts it had sparked about our future.

'That's why I was weird with you,' I finished with another yawn as the lateness and alcohol started to take over.

'But *beta*–' Alex stopped when he heard Sid calling him from the hall. He sighed. 'I come back in two minutes,' he told me slipping out of the room. By the time he returned I was fast asleep.

Things seemed strange when I awoke next morning. My head felt sore, my eyes were heavy and my heart felt sad and droopy, like a wilted flower. Then I remembered. Alex stirred next to me. I rolled over and saw him lying on his back, his eyes staring at the ceiling, lost in thought.

'Good morning,' I greeted him tentatively. He didn't look at me, didn't even move in response. Now that I was lying next to him, things didn't seem the same as they had in my head for the past two days.

'Are you OK?' I asked. He always pulled me in for a hug first thing in the morning but he was acting as if I wasn't even there.

'I'm fine,' he said dismissively.

'You're obviously not fine,' I told him, rolling onto my front and leaning up on my elbows. He was still staring at the ceiling.

'I'm sorry I fell asleep last night before we could talk, I'd had too much to drink.'

No response. I tried again. 'We could talk now if you like?'

'Why to talk?' Alex asked finally. 'After two months to-gether you have no idea about me or how I feel, you believe some English guy you don't even know.' He paused and I

217

was silent as the truth in his words sank in. He seemed genuinely upset. I spotted a tear rolling down from the corner of his eye and caught it with my hand before it ran into his hair. But then there was another, and another.

'If you think like this, then you should go home to Ireland,' he told me resolutely as he lay there unmoving, little rivulets of tears rolling down the sides of his face.

I got a sudden tug of fear in my stomach as I thought the unthinkable. We'd been so loved up since we got together but was it possible that it could actually end? I tried to hug him and wipe away his tears but he remained totally unresponsive.

'I'm sorry, Alex,' I told him, full of remorse. 'I got so confused. Our cultures are so different, I started to worry that we were looking at different futures too. I mean, what happens when I go home in a month?'

'But you don't have to go home, you can change your flights and stay longer. If you want to,' he told me, finally lifting a hand to wipe his eyes and sniffing back his hurt.

'Do you still want me to do that?' I asked hesitantly.

My flight home was booked for 20 February and we were very nearly finished with the month of January. If I wanted to stay longer in India I would have to change the return date of my flights and also get a new Indian tourist visa, as my current one was nearly up. We'd talked about this before but never decided on a specific plan of action.

Alex turned to face me at last. His big brown eyes shone. 'Of course I want you to, *beta*,' he said. 'I told you before, I love you and I want to be with you. It's up to you, I'm not going anywhere.'

'So you're not going to leave me and marry a sweet Indian girl in a couple of years?' I asked, half joking and half serious.

'Darling, I can marry you tomorrow, no problem,' he told me with utter candour.

'Whoa there, slow down!' I laughed before instantly bursting into tears.

Alex frowned in puzzlement. 'What happened to you?' he demanded, finally pulling me in close and wrapping his arms around me while the worry and stress of the past few days poured out.

'I was so worried that maybe you would change your mind and swap me for an Indian girl and then I was thinking that I'd actually *made* you change your mind!'

'*Arrey*, Liz,' he laughed and kissed my forehead. 'You can't lose me, *beta*. I promise.'

I laughed with relief as we hugged and kissed and finally all was good between us again. When we finally got up to shower and dress, I realised something important: we'd just made it through our first argument as a couple. Heck, this was like a real, adult relationship. Could it be, was I *finally* growing up?

I never saw Charles again. Despite the fact that he'd caused me untold stress with his misinformed opinions of Alex, he'd also helped propel us out of the holiday romance stage of our relationship into something deeper and more meaningful. It was the first time I began to feel that we were really in it for the long haul. All thanks to a man with a pineapple hairdo, who seemed to change relationships as often as his clothes.

Chapter 22

Kanyakumari and a significant date

'Liz, do you wanna have papaya juice?'

'Oh, yes please. I swear this place is even hotter than Varkala.'

Alex handed me the refreshing juice a while later and I downed half of it there and then. We were on a minibreak, just the two of us, no entourage of boys all speaking in a language I didn't understand and stealing my man away from me. It was just me and Alex for the next few days in Kanyakumari, the southern-most tip of India. I made my way over to a table in the little café and Alex followed. I couldn't get over the taste of fresh fruit juices in India; they were impossibly delicious.

'What did you get?' I asked, trying to slow down and savour the rest of my drink.

'Orange. It's good.'

He reached across the table and took one of my hands in his, the straw still in his mouth, sucking every so often as he gazed at the street outside. He seemed totally relaxed. I stared down at our hands and realised something.

'Hey, how come you never do this in Varkala?'

'Do what?' He turned to look at me curiously.

'You never hold my hand or anything when we're out in public.'

I didn't like the slight accusatory tone that had entered my voice, but it was suddenly sinking in just how much Alex avoided any and all public displays of affection, however innocent, when we were on the cliff. Now that I thought about it, even just walking there together I often found myself trailing behind him, but since going away he had suddenly turned into the most doting boyfriend imaginable.

'It's the locals,' he answered simply. 'If they get jealous then maybe they cause problems for us and the business. This is our first time we have a shop in Varkala and I don't want to cause a fight. They have all the local connections and we don't speak their language.'

'Oh, I see,' I said, starting to understand. 'So I'm a problem for you?' I raised one eyebrow suggestively.

'Darling, you are my problem, but I am your solution.'

'Oh God, you're so cheesy'

'You don't like to hear the truth, *beta*, that's not my fault.'

I gave his leg a dig with my foot. At that moment an Indian family entered the café, the dad carrying a cute toddler in his arms, the mum following and looking effortlessly elegant as Indian women always do. Alex and I watched the little girl who was fascinated with us, staring intently our way as her parents ordered their drinks. Alex instantly started smiling and waving at her and, after frowning in concentration at us for a moment, a big grin spread across her face as she looked from Alex to her dad and back again. The smile disappeared, however, the moment I joined in the game.

'Well, you're clearly the favourite here,' I told Alex, nodding a hello to the parents who seemed happy to see me smiling at their little girl. I glanced over at Alex, still waving and grinning at the kid; he'd make a great dad one day. I sat up suddenly as I realised what I was thinking. A great dad to just whose kids exactly?

I cleared my throat. 'So, um Alex, how many kids would you like to have one day? You know, waaaay in the future?'

'Two,' he replied with certainty. 'One boy, one girl.'

'Right, are you going to put in a personal order for one of each?' I teased.

'Bah darling, two boys or two girls – is no problem as long as they have your blue eyes.'

Aww, how cute. Highly unlikely, but very cute.

'Alex, if we had kids together, they would arrive in the world with your gorgeous, big brown eyes.'

'No blue?' Alex looked disappointed.

'I'm afraid not. Anyway, let's not have kids right now or anything, yeah?' I added lightly. 'Considering both our parents would probably disown us if we did? Not to mention the fact that we only know each other about five minutes.'

'No problem, *beta*, we have plenty time. First we grow up together.'

I stared at him. 'I can't believe that after only eight weeks we're considering settling down and having a family.'

Alex shrugged, not at all as alarmed as I was. 'It's the Indian way, darling. Here we get married as strangers.'

'How can you marry someone you don't even know yet? What about falling in love?'

'We do. But you guys fall in love before the wedding. We do it later.'

'Really?'

Alex shrugged again and a thought crossed my mind. 'What about you? Aren't you supposed to have a traditional arranged marriage?'

'My family is waiting for me to say when,' Alex told me simply. 'My father asks me each year when I want to get married, I always tell him next year.'

I rolled my eyes.

'Seriously?'

'I love my family but I don't want to live in the home. Too much household politics.'

'And your family wouldn't mind if we wanted to get married someday?'

'Well, maybe,' he conceded. 'But I can convince them no problem.'

I thought about that for a moment. 'And if you couldn't?'

'I can convince them,' he said confidently, rubbing my hand tenderly and smiling at me. 'Don't worry, *beta*. It will all be OK in the end.'

It was hard to doubt him. I smiled warmly and squeezed his hand in mine. 'Love you, darling.'

'Love you too, *beta*.'

After a few days we finished our little slice of heaven and returned to Varkala, the rest of the boys and our daily life on the cliff. The trip away together, along with the Charles incident, had been a significant stepping stone in our relationship. I completely adored Alex and felt more comfortable in his easy loving presence than I had with nearly any other human in my life – so much so that I had reached the stage of farting in front of him without dying of embarrassment. Now that, let me tell you, really is love.

* * *

20 February 2008 was a significant date. It was a date I couldn't wait for before I left Ireland, a day I wished would hurry up and get here already because it seemed light years away when faced with the daunting prospect of surviving four and a half months in India. It was the day I was supposed to fly home from Mumbai.

But of course I didn't fly home to Ireland, I didn't even go anywhere near Mumbai, for I had recently contacted my airline and changed the date of my flights home to the beginning of August, over five months away. This meant though that I would have to get a new Indian tourist visa, as my current one was due to expire in ten days. In order to do that, I would have to first leave the country and then submit my application at an Indian embassy abroad. We were so far south in Kerala that Sri Lanka seemed the obvious choice and so, on 20 February, rather than board a plane to Ireland, I drove with Alex to Kerala's capital Trivandrum to visit the Sri Lankan Airlines office. We stopped at a cashpoint en route to take out cash, which is where I discovered a small problem.

'Damn it! I can't believe it, I forgot my credit card!'

I rummaged pointlessly around my bag again, but I could already see in my mind exactly where it was in our bedroom.

'I've left it in the house. How could I be so stupid?' I paused, running my hand over my face in frustration.

'*Arrey* no problem, *beta*, why you getting so upset? I pay for your flights,' Alex said without a second's thought, taking his bank card out of his wallet and slotting it into the ATM.

'Sorry, I'll pay you back, I promise.'

'I pay for your flights, *beta*, don't worry,' he said again, tapping at buttons. The machine began making a whirring sound and soon a wad of notes appeared below.

'Don't be silly, Alex.' I shook my head.

Alex collected the cash and his receipt, carefully tucking it all into his wallet, then started walking back to the car.

'*Arrey*, Liz, is only money. Why you making such a fuss? You're too Irish. My mum says, when in Rome be like Roman. You're in India now, be like Indian. Here, if we offer you a gift, you take. Otherwise people get offended.'

'But Alex–'

'*Beta*, when I come to Ireland, you pay for me there, OK?'

'Oh! Oh yes, of course I will.' I paused, looking at him with a heart full of soppy adoration. 'Thanks Alex!'

'Shut up, darling. Let's go!'

I grinned and sat into the car as we continued our way into the city centre. That's when the significance of the date struck me: I should have been saying goodbye to India today and here I was planning to stay on until August. Feeling as though this held profound meaning, I shared my thoughts with Alex.

'Very good. You want to go home instead? I bring you back to Varkala and you can pack?'

'God, you're so sarcastic.' I sighed, slightly exasperated. 'I just mean it's interesting, you know? I made sure when booking my trip that I could change the return dates in case I needed to come home sooner. Like if I got really ill or was miserable and hated India. I never once thought I'd be changing the tickets to stay longer or that I'd find myself a sweet Indian boyfriend.'

'So is that what you are telling all your friends at home? Showing off that you have a brown-skinned boy?' Alex made a funny face at me, looking for a reaction.

'Yes, darling. That's what I tell all my friends back home. Oooh, look at me, I have an Indian boyfriend. They're all really jealous.'

'Really?' He looked genuinely surprised. I stared at him.

'No. That was me being sarcastic.'

'But maybe they're a little bit jealous, no?' His eyes, fixed on the road, flicked back towards me for a split second.

I shook my head, unable to keep the smile off my face. 'Yes, darling, they probably are a bit jealous.'

He grinned then, with a smug nod of his head. 'You see, *beta*?' he said, lifting his hand to indicate his face. 'You see the effect of this?'

'Oh, for the love of God.'

I would fly to Sri Lanka just two days later. The big Indian adventure wasn't ending as planned but when had *anything* in India ever gone to plan in the entire five months that I'd been there? It was time for a mini adventure before recommencing my epic Indian tour. That meant leaving the great subcontinent and my darling cheeky pup for a short while to go it alone in a new country. Piece of cake, right?

Chapter 23

Sri Lanka: the pearl of the Indian Ocean

'Don't cry, *beta*!'

Very much *not* a piece of cake.

'Sorry,' I sniffed, pulling back from Alex and wiping my eyes.

We were outside Trivandrum airport early in the morning and it was the day of my flight to Colombo. I was bawling like a baby.

'I'm sorry, I just really don't want to leave you and I really don't want to get blown up!' I wailed into his chest.

Back then, in 2008, Sri Lanka was still in the midst of a civil war, with frequent bomb scares across the country, particularly in the capital, Colombo, right where I was headed. It was considered very low risk, obviously, or I wouldn't have been travelling there. Nonetheless it made the journey there on my own that bit more daunting which, on top of saying goodbye to Alex, meant I was an emotional wreck.

'Darling, nothing will happen, you're going to be fine. It's only a week until you come back.'

'OK,' I mumbled and clung to him again.

'Alright?' Alex asked a moment later.

I nodded, knowing if I tried to say anything I'd just start wailing again.

'Call me from Colombo when you find your guest house. Mind yourself, *beta*,' he told me gently and we hugged one last time.

In Indian airports, only people that are actually travelling are allowed to go inside so, as I handed my tickets and passport to the security guard for inspection, Alex had to wait by the barrier with a crowd of others waiting for loved ones. Following the guard's nod of approval, I walked in the doors, turning around one last time to wave. But although I scanned the throngs of bodies I couldn't find him anywhere and, beginning to feel weirdly self-conscious with so many faces all seemingly staring at me, I gave up and headed in with a heavy heart.

On top of the worries I had about the security problems in Sri Lanka and my sadness to leave Alex, I also felt a child-like yearning to stay in Varkala in a cosy bubble of comfort and security. Sri Lanka was the unknown and the unknown is always a little scary. Of course, a lot of these feelings were exactly what I'd had to deal with before coming to India (and look how *that* turned out) so I really should have known better. Instead I fretted and worried myself to tears, resisting what I had to do every step of the way like a petulant child, complete with pouting bottom lip and a blotchy tear-stained face.

* * *

The flight to Colombo was brief, just forty-five minutes, yet we were still served a three-course meal and I had to giggle in spite of my woes as I watched the beautiful Sri Lankan stewardesses scurrying up and down the aisles, desperately trying to clean up everything in time for landing. Their colourful, elegant saris were quite possibly the most amazing cabin-crew uniform I've ever seen. Arriving into Colombo's sleek modern airport felt comforting and reassuring until I spotted numerous soldiers standing guard in full uniform with terrifyingly large AK47s. Reassurance was replaced by pure terror. I think this was my first time coming across armed soldiers and I felt a similar sensation in my gut to that of the first plane ride to India: namely that I might just poop myself at any moment. Calm down, Liz. For god's sake, they're there to protect you!

My passport stamped with a thirty-day visa, I walked tensely over towards luggage collection, full of anxiety and wishing I was just about anywhere else. Things improved, however, when I got chatting to a few other tourists and caught a bus into the city centre with them. As we sped along the busy roads, it surprised me how similar everything was to southern India. The Sri Lankan women mostly wore brightly coloured saris; palm trees and many other tropical plants dotted the landscape; three-wheeled taxis sputtered along the chaotic streets and their drivers charged exorbitant prices to unsuspecting tourists. Just like India. It would take me a while to notice the subtle differences between the beautiful little island and Kerala but when I did, I couldn't believe I'd ever thought they were the same.

Once off the bus I said goodbye to the other travellers who were catching a train straight to the hill town of Kandy and hopped in a taxi to the Indian embassy so I could pick up a visa application form. Then I searched for a guest house. First one on my list, the Ottery Inn, didn't look too promising. With several windows boarded up and a general look of ruin and neglect, my heart sank. It must have closed down since the guidebook had been written. But seeing as how I was right outside it, I knocked on the door anyway and was surprised when a sweet Sinhalese woman named Anika answered it and informed me that she did have a room available.

Following her down a gloomy, dusty hall and up some bockety stairs she showed me into a little room with a bed, a fan and not much else. It was shabby and basic but also clean and cheap. Relieved, I dumped my backpack on the floor and sat on the incredibly soft bed. Moments later, with a sound like lifting a flat stone off the river bed, I finally managed to get my bottom back out of the mattress, leaving a groove inches deep. I stared at the sagging bed then shrugged. It would have to do.

From there on, the day passed in a flurry of activities, from filling out my application form to making passport copies, wandering around the city, eating lunch and even getting a spontaneous haircut. I got so caught up in all the hustle and bustle that it wasn't until late in the evening I finally realised I'd better call Alex and let him know that I'd arrived safe and sound.

'So how are you, *beta*?'

'Super tired. It's been a long day.' I yawned into the receiver as I spoke, remembering I'd been up since before 6 am. There was an unnatural pause.

'You looked very sad when you was leaving,' Alex finally said.

'I wanted to wave to you but I couldn't find you in the crowd.'

There was another weird pause before Alex answered. It finally clicked with me that there was a delay in the connection.

'I know, I was waving but you didn't see.' I could hear him yawning too. 'I been waiting all day for you to call.'

We chatted a while longer but when the yawns started taking over the conversation we said our goodbyes and I left the little internet café to go back to my guest house. It felt quite cosy sinking into my squishy mattress later on; a little strange, and I hoped it wasn't actually going to swallow me whole, but definitely cosy.

Next day, visa application submitted, I headed straight to the train station with my luggage. It was Wednesday and I had been told to come back to the embassy on Monday, so it was clearly time to travel. I had to giggle when I walked up to the dinky little local train with all of its, what, four carriages? After five months in India, where the trains were so long you literally couldn't see from one end to the other, Sri Lanka's train looked like a cute toy model. In fact, it was very comforting to an Irish lass like me who had just spent so long in the vast subcontinent. In some ways Sri Lanka reminded me of Ireland, albeit tropical style.

I passed the next three hours watching the Sri Lankan countryside whizz by, full of lush greenery and gorgeous unspoilt nature, cottages appearing here and there with pretty little gardens. It felt distinctly different to India and a lot less chaotic.

'Hello, madam! Can I sit?'

A man stood by the empty seat beside me. I nodded for him to take it and he struck up a conversation, but I was in full travelling-in-India mode, instantly suspicious he was trying to sell me something.

'My name's Rodney. Where are you from?'

'Ireland.'

'You have accommodation booked in Kandy? I have a guest house there.'

Bingo! I knew he wasn't just being friendly for the sake of it. That said, I actually didn't have any accommodation organised. I'd planned, well, nothing really past showing up in the popular hill town. Dubious at the convenience of Rodney's sudden appearance, I listened on.

'It's very nice guest house, not far from station, and I have car waiting to collect me.'

Whoa there Liz, what if he's some weirdo going to kidnap you? I thought.

Rodney was looking at me intently, apparently reading my mind. 'You don't worry, I'm a good man with simple business. Here,' he said, rummaging through his briefcase and pulling out a slightly worn notebook. 'You read this, all the many tourists who stay with me they say very nice things, so you don't worry. It's nice place and not expensive.'

Leafing through many pages full of various notes in all styles of handwriting and languages, I finally figured he was genuine. How did I know I could trust him? Well, I was relying on gut instinct to be honest, as I had done from day one with Paul and later with Alex and the boys. So far it had served me well and given I had no idea where to stay once I reached Kandy, it was hard to refuse.

'OK, thanks. I'd be happy to stay in your guest house.'

Boy did I mean those words when we arrived into the town in the evening, where the words 'pissing rain' were fully appropriate. In the crowds and chaos of leaving the train I lost track of Rodney and walked uncertainly up to the main exit, staring out at the bleak, darkening sky and the water pelting the ground. I shivered involuntarily. It was a lot cooler here than in Colombo and for an instant I suddenly felt quite lost and alone.

'Liz!'

Suddenly I spotted Rodney, shielding himself from the deluge with his briefcase and beckoning me to hurry up. I jogged after him, dumping my backpack into the boot and getting into the car where I found three more Westerners, wiping their wet faces and laughing and chatting together in a language I didn't recognise.

A girl smiled at me. 'Rodney found you too?' she asked in English.

'Yeah,' I smiled back feeling a lot better now I was in the warm dry vehicle and with fellow tourists. At least if we were being kidnapped I'd have company.

'OK, guys?' Rodney called to us from up front with a big smile and a thumbs up. 'Let's go!'

Green Guest House was a quaint, spacious hotel and serious value for money. My bedroom was enormous, with a high ceiling and a sprawling double bed. Rodney was a decent, likeable guy while clearly an astute businessman, having acquired four new guests on his trip back from the capital. He was also quick to sell me his package tour to Adam's Peak, a mini-mountain a few hours away, whose summit was the site of a sacred Buddhist temple and supposedly the number-one tourist activity in the area. Somehow, in spite of my frugal mindset, I went ahead and booked the package deal even though it cost about the same price as my flights to Sri Lanka.

You know, had I been the sort of traveller who actually made an effort to learn a little about the places they were going to – the intelligent kind of traveller, in other words – I might not have agreed to Adam's Peak. In fact, if I'd had an inkling of what it would entail, I probably would have gracefully bowed out with a 'thanks very much, Rodney, but no freaking way!'

However, as you may have gathered by now, I'm fairly rubbish at the planning and researching side of things. I'd love to say that it's because I'm a spontaneous explorer who leaps from one adventure to the next, and perhaps there is a small grain of truth in that, but it's probably more accurate to say that I'm an anxious home bird with a touch of wanderlust and when I get bored of the mundane routine, I set myself a challenge by flying off to foreign lands. The only way I can ever go through with these plans, as I mentioned earlier on, is to dive in head first before I talk myself out of it. So if I came to India mostly blind, then I came to Sri Lanka both blind and deaf.

And that is how I voluntarily booked myself in to climb a mountain – in my bright pink Crocs – after months of lying around on beaches. But of course.

The morning after arriving into Kandy, a taxi brought me four hours further up into the country's remote hills, dropping me off at a pre-booked hotel. My room was colourful and pretty and spotless. So far so good, I mused, unzipping my bag and grabbing a sweater. It was chilly up here. Stepping out onto my balcony and hugging my arms to myself, I stared out at the hilly landscape, noticing one point looming up higher than any of the others: Adam's Peak.

Hmmm, looks pretty big, I thought, then promptly forgot about it, heading to the restaurant upstairs for dinner.

The harsh beeping of my alarm woke me in the dark of the night at 2 am. It was time to get up and hike in order to reach the summit by sunrise, which apparently was what you were supposed to do. I pulled on my clothes, got my little rucksack and went up to the main entrance of the hotel to wait for my young guide, Moruly, a local lad who worked in the hotel and was going to accompany me on the walk (seeing as how I literally didn't even know where to start).

There was a heavy silence in the building and I questioned for the first time the sanity of what I was doing, although in that moment it was simply why on earth I wasn't still asleep in bed. Moruly finally appeared with his torch and a sleepy smile and we set off. I should have known when I first saw it from my balcony. Of course, ideally, I should have known before I ever even considered embarking on the hike and would have, indeed, had I bothered to do any research.

Five thousand steps to get to the top, that is Adam's Peak. Five. Thousand. Steps. By my third pit stop, sitting in one of the ubiquitous cafés provided to fuel spiritual (or in my case idiotic) pilgrims, I sipped a hot chai and stared up at the summit, which still seemed the same impossible distance away that it had been over an hour ago.

'Oh God, Moruly, I don't know if I can do this,' I moaned pathetically to the bouncy and ridiculously fit young guide. The sky was still pitch black, the steps only lit by the lights of the cafés.

He grinned at me, full of happy energy. 'No problem, Liz, of course you can. Come on, let's go!'

With a sigh, I finished my tea and continued on up the steps. There were many other people going both up and down the mountain, some of them genuine pilgrims, some of them tourists, and at one point a middle-aged local man overtook me, carrying a massive gas canister on his shoulders. I gazed in fascination at his legs that sported calf muscles the size of watermelons and shuddered to think of my own ones, currently in a serious amount of distress. Being a beach bum for the past few months had not prepared them for this. I carried on with a grim determination that lasted about five minutes before my lungs started to feel like they were going to explode and my legs began to cramp.

'Come on, Liz, you go so slowly,' Moruly shouted, cheerfully bounding on ahead of me.

'I. Fucking. Hate. You!' I muttered under my breath and continued to spew out silent insults while crawling along behind like an injured snail. I think it helped; the anger acted like fuel and kept me going, in spite of an intense urge to quit and roll back down the way we'd come. Near to the top, my leg muscles, fully disgusted with me, officially threw in the towel. I grabbed the steel railing and began quite literally trying to haul myself up with my arms, my calves screaming agony with each step.

There were a few tears of relief when incredibly and unbelievably, after three hours of solid, torturous climbing, we finally reached the sacred Sri Pada temple at the top. Feeling as though I was teetering around on wobbly stilts, I joined the many other people milling about, some praying, some sitting on benches chatting, some taking turns to ring a large, sonorous bell. The temple was a small, simple structure built on a concrete plateau and surrounded by prayer flags. While this may not have been very impressive, at least the views should have been, especially at sunrise, which we had managed to make despite my slow progress. I stared out at the valley way below that was completely obscured by heavy clouds while the sky gradually lightened to a dull, overcast grey. A delicate mist left a sheen of moisture on my sweater and I shivered in the damp chilly air: no view, no sunrise. I wondered if I dared ask myself was it worth it?

Unfortunately, what goes up must come down and so of course we had to make the descent. But that shouldn't be too hard, right?

Wrong. So very, *very* wrong. Walking down steps is *not* easier than walking up steps. Descending Adam's Peak may not have caused my lungs to burst into flames as it had during the ascent, but there is an important thing to note about descending a steep hill of several thousand steps: if you don't actually wish to cartwheel down the mountain then you need good strong legs to control your momentum.

Good strong legs. Right, because I obviously had that in abundance. My muscles at this stage were about as tough as jelly and it took many more pit stops and nearly an hour longer to get back down to the bottom than it had to reach the top. About halfway through, Moruly's chirpy personality dimmed noticeably.

'Come, Liz! You really want to stop again?'

'Yes, Moruly, I want to stop again because if I don't, I might just barrel down the last five hundred steps like a human snowball. OK?' I smiled grimly at him.

He instantly returned a full innocent smile and I felt bad for being snappy. Despite our chai and biscuit breaks, he was probably hungry for a proper breakfast and would have been home hours ago if it weren't for me.

With a bone-weary sigh and trembling legs, I hoisted myself back off the rock. 'OK, let's go.'

Nearly eight hours after leaving the hotel, at 10 am, I finally made it back and collapsed onto my bed, exhausted to my very core, my body as limp as a rag doll. But I couldn't stay there for long. My taxi back to Kandy would be arriving in an hour or so and I needed to shower and have breakfast.

Fresh and clean after washing I felt slightly better already and made my way up to the restaurant, groaning as I climbed up the four small steps from my room. There was a loaded, aching stiffness gradually filling my calves; it made taking a single step up or down feel as though someone was stabbing them with knives.

Uh-oh.

It took over a week for my poor legs to recover from Adam's 'Agonising' Peak. Until then, anything even vaguely resembling a step produced a sharp spasm of agony and caused my face to pucker as though I'd just bit into a lemon. Alex thought the whole thing was hilarious when I recounted my experience to him, but it took some time for my poor legs to forgive me; some time and a lot of hobbling.

The afternoon after the climb, my taxi dropped me back to Kandy and I remained mostly horizontal until the following day when I paid a visit to the Pinnewala Elephant Sanctuary. Given my penchant for all furry/feathery/leathery creatures, I was enthralled with these ungainly trumpeting giants and acted like a kid at a party, bouncing and squeaking delightedly at every little thing they did, all the while teetering around on my fragile legs.

Just a few days after arriving, it was time to return to Colombo and the cosy Ottery Inn and, funnily enough, I ended up in the same room as before. Sinking down into the soft, squishy mattress, I contemplated life. I was missing Alex a lot now, despite all my adventures, and it didn't help that on all our calls the delayed connection between our responses made natural conversation stilted and awkward. I felt a real loneliness as I thought about going to get dinner on my own yet again. While I was quite proud that I'd managed everything this past week completely by myself, boosting my self-confidence and proving my previous fears and worries wrong, I'd reached a point where some company would be really sweet. It was probably the first time in all my travels that I'd gone so long without meeting anyone to hook up with and I hoped that, once all my visa plans were sorted, I would find a friendly fellow traveller to hang out with for a while. With that thought, I headed out for dinner. Company could wait, my hungry belly couldn't.

Chapter 24

When the plumbing gets stuck

'Please, you wait in here. Yes please, you all wait in here!'

The official directed me and the other visa applicants into what appeared to be a kind of lecture room. I sat in the middle of a row of seats and glanced up as an English guy sat next to me.

'Hey! How you doing?' He had neat features and an open, friendly smile. I smiled back but before I could reply he was already chatting again.

'God, they make you wait ages, don't they? Are you here for another tourist visa?'

'Yeah, how'd you guess?'

'You've got the typical Indian hippie thing going on.'

I glanced down at my Ali Baba pants, tank top and the thin shawl draped over my shoulders. Now that I thought about it, he wasn't the first person to ask if I'd come from India.

'Is it that obvious?'

'Pretty standard. I'm Sam, by the way.'

'I'm Liz. You here for a tourist visa too?'

'Uh-huh.' He glanced around carefully before leaning closer and speaking in a hushed voice. 'I've been teaching English at call centres in Bangalore the past two years. This time when I switched companies, they didn't organise a proper contract in time so they told me to come back on a tourist visa and they'd pay me cash in hand for a while. I obviously didn't mention any of that on the form,' he added in a whisper.

Before I could say anything we were called to hand in our passports and then told to collect them at 4 pm.

'So, you got any plans for the day?' Sam asked as we strolled out of the embassy into the warm, sunny morning.

'Nope.'

'Want to grab some breakfast? I got up kinda late.'

'Sure.'

And just like that, I got some company.

'When are you going back to India then?' he asked later over lunch.

'Well, I'm supposed to go back in a couple of days but Alex won't be finished his business trip yet and I'm really enjoying it here. I wouldn't mind seeing more of the country before I leave.'

'I was actually planning to go to the airlines office and change my flights,' Sam said. 'You want to do it too?'

I grinned at him and nodded, feeling excited.

Taking a tuk-tuk to the city centre with Sam's no-nonsense bargaining, we reached the Sri Lankan Airlines office and went upstairs. I was reminded of the cabin crew on the flight over as I watched gorgeous, elegant young ladies gliding through the office with their fitted saris wrapped perfectly around their slender frames. I felt like a gauche, ugly duckling in their presence.

'Those are quite possibly some of the most beautiful creatures I have ever seen,' Sam whispered to me, awestruck, as yet another vision of graceful loveliness swept past us.

'Sam, you're drooling!'

That afternoon at the embassy, my return flight now booked for a week later, I was thrilled to open up my passport and find a brand new Indian tourist visa stuck to page seven. When Sam came outside after me though, he didn't seem happy.

'What's up? Did you get your visa?'

'Yeah but they only gave me a three-month one,' he complained, frowning. 'They were looking at all my previous stamps and work permits and they kept asking questions about why I wanted to go back as a tourist. Damn! It makes things so awkward, I'll probably have to head back to the UK for my next visa.'

'Sounds like you were lucky to get even three months.'

Sam sighed with a brief smile. 'Yeah, I know. Still annoying.' He jammed the passport into his small sack, settled the bag on his back and suddenly brightened up. 'So, you want to go get dinner?'

By the time we finished eating we'd organised to meet up next morning at the bus station and head to the town of Galle on Sri Lanka's beautiful southern coastline. I was delighted. Not only was I going to see more of this charming country but I now had the travel buddy I'd longed for as well; Sam was bright and intelligent and so easy to be around. I may have only met him several hours earlier but I felt as though I'd known him years already.

Lying in bed that night, I felt a funny sensation in my tummy and, a moment later, let out a squeaky fart. I started giggling automatically but then stopped as I suddenly realised this was the first sign of any movement from my bowels for quite some time. Being constipated wasn't exactly an issue I'd counted on before coming to this part of the world.

I tried to jog my memory – when exactly, was the last time I'd done a poop?

Oh dear God, today was day four. Four days! What on earth was going on down there? I'd never in my life gone that long without doing my number twos. I settled back on the bed, realising there was nothing I could do about it at 11 pm. Hopefully tomorrow things would start working again.

Next day, sitting on the small, clean bus, I shuddered as I pondered yet again the amount of food at various stages of decomposition in my gut. Day number five and my body was still bizarrely silent. Sam burst out laughing when I filled him in on the issue.

'Ha! You haven't gone for a dump for five days? That's hilarious.'

'Thanks for the moral support, man!' I snapped.

'You'll be fine, Liz. They have doctors here too, you know, you can go see one tomorrow. Relax and enjoy the trip.'

Have you ever been disgustingly, horrendously constipated? If not then let me assure you: patience and tolerance are two friends that get chased away by hair-pulling rage and frustration. As we travelled south, I contemplated the different ways I'd enjoy smacking poor Sam in the face if he made one more suggestion to chill out, relax or get over myself.

A few hours later, we arrived in the quirky little town of Galle. In March 2008 it was just over three years since the devastating tsunami that had battered the southern coastline of Sri Lanka and many other parts of south-east Asia. While the huge, ferocious waves pounded the shoreline repeatedly, the old part of Galle was saved from total destruction thanks to its seventeenth-century colonial fort walls, but the rest of Galle was one of the worst-hit areas in the country. By the time we visited, there was minimal evidence left but I imagine the locals must still have been reeling from the traumatic experience and probably would do for years to come.

We found a shabby but pleasant home-stay run by a sweet Galle family and spent the afternoon walking around the town. By evening, I was starving as well as cranky; I couldn't bear to add more food into my already overloaded system, making do with a fresh pineapple juice while Sam tucked into his dinner, my mouth watering at the tantalising smells wafting over from his plate.

Next morning I awoke thoroughly freaked out; day six and still nothing. Drastic action was now required. I spoke to the sweet grandfather running our little guest house and explained my embarrassing predicament. With a reassuring smile and kind words he instantly set about organising everything for me, calling his friend Mr Priyantha, a tuk-tuk driver, briefly explaining things and instructing him to take me to the local hospital. Within minutes of arriving I was already on a chair in the doctor's room, while Mr Priyantha presumably explained everything to him in Sinhalese. The doctor nodded and turned to me.

'You have a problem with constipation, madam?'

'Yes.' At which point I promptly burst into tears, mortified yet unable to stop myself. The whole experience of being ill so far away from home was absolutely terrifying.

Unperturbed, the doctor jotted down a few notes. 'Are you pregnant, madam?'

'No.'

'I see. Lie down over here, please,' he told me, indicating the examination table. I allowed my stomach be poked and prodded for a few moments.

'Any pain here?'

'No.'

'And here?'

'No.'

'Thank you. Come down now, please.'

Sitting across from his desk again, I waited anxiously as he scribbled something on a piece of paper. Finally he looked up.

'You must have an enema,' he informed me, handing the slip of paper to Mr Priyantha who'd been waiting patiently by the door the whole time. They exchanged words in Sinhalese again. Mr Priyantha then brought me out of the doctor's office to a small pharmacy within the hospital where he got the enema solution for me. I felt slightly better about things already just from being in the hospital; it was like any back home, clean and brightly lit with that unnatural but reassuringly familiar smell of disinfectant. Once we had the enema solution, Mr Priyantha then brought me to a little room down the hall where a nurse was waiting and he indicated I was to go inside. The brisk, tiny woman shut the door behind me and pointed at the examination table.

'Lie, please!'

With only the vaguest notion of what now awaited me, I duly lay down on my back, my earlier fear returning full force. I had no idea just what exactly an enema was.

'On side,' she instructed sternly as I caught sight of her snapping on tight latex gloves. With a feeling of impending doom, I turned away from her and onto my side. She pulled the top of my trousers down and grabbed hold of my bum cheek.

'One minute and it is finish.'

There followed the most bizarre sensation of a litre of liquid entering a part of the body where a litre of liquid had never before gone. It didn't hurt but it felt very, very strange and, in my highly strung state, tolerance for weirdness and the unfamiliar was at an all-time low.

'OK. Finish.'

My trousers were briskly pulled back up and I was able to sit up, wiping at my leaky eyes. An expression of great surprise filled the nurse's face.

'You feel pain?' She sounded incredulous.

'No. No pain,' I assured her with a sniff. No pain, just the terror of having a big tube shoved up my bum, I thought, before hopping off the table and wondering what was next.

The second my feet hit the floor, I knew. 'Oh my God! Where's the toilet?!'

The nurse grinned for the first time, opening the door and pointing down the hall. I have never run so fast in my entire life. Propelled by the sensation of an impending waterfall cascading out of my butthole, I took off like my feet were on fire, making it to the toilet in about two seconds flat. Without going into too much detail, let's just say that, after almost a week, the chocolate hostages were finally released …

A short while later, emerging from the cubicle, I spotted Mr Priyantha sitting in the hall, patiently waiting.

'OK,' I told him, smiling with relief. 'We can go now.'

Sam was sitting on one of the little garden chairs outside our room when the tuk-tuk rolled up a while later. I paid and thanked Mr Priyantha profusely (yet another kind angel sent to mind me on my travels) then went over to Sam.

'Success!' I declared in elation, before recounting the experience in all its gruesome detail.

'Enough, Liz, enough,' he begged, blocking his ears. 'I don't want to know.'

I laughed at his pained expression. 'So, what should we do today?'

What we did, in the end, was take a bus further south to a place called Unawatuna with picturesque beaches, relaxed coastal charm and a wonderful local restaurant that had organic, wholesome things like brown rice (something I have rarely found in India), fresh salads and the best homemade granola I have ever tasted. During the afternoon, we wandered around on our own for a couple hours, having arranged to meet in a specific café later. On the way there, I stopped short at a thunderous BANG. Holy crap! Was that a bomb?

No bomb, Liz, just thunder. I scurried along the path and reached the café's sheltered terrace just as the rain began, the soft trickle transforming into a massive downpour within seconds. A little later, a bedraggled Sam walked up to me.

'Got a bit wet there, did you?' I asked wryly.

'Not really,' he replied with a grin. Then he turned his face upwards, mouth opened wide and arms outstretched. I shook my head.

'What are you like? Come in and have a cup of tea!'

* * *

The next day Sam headed back to Colombo while I spent my last few days soaking up the beautiful beaches, chatting with the locals and revelling in a general vibe of utter relaxation. But I was missing Alex quite a lot by now and I looked forward to returning to India – until, that is, I discovered he wasn't going to be home when I got back.

'Oh, OK,' I said, but my heart had already collapsed in a heap, utterly deflated.

'I'm really sorry, *beta*, this business in Goa is going to take longer than I thought and both Sid and I have to stay until it's sorted. I'll make sure Ameer is at the airport to meet you.'

'That's OK,' I repeated mechanically, not wanting to show how disappointed I was. I'd been counting down the hours till we were back together again, but it seemed I was just going to have to wait a bit longer.

A couple of days later I said goodbye to the lovely people of Sri Lanka and flew back to mystical India. As promised, cuddly Ameer was waiting for me when I walked through arrivals in Trivandrum airport. We took a cab back to Varkala and the familiar sights and scenes of India were incredibly comforting, from the iconic Ambassador cab to the local men at chai stalls in their funny Keralan skirts (known as *dhotis*, they're essentially large cotton cloths that Keralan men wrap around their waist and they are as much a symbol of the local culture as, for example, the kilt is in Scotland).

It was three more days until both Alex and Sid were due back and to pass the time I busied myself with cleaning the house – a considerable task given it had only had boys living in it for the past two weeks. Luckily, I also found two new friends for company. The first was Dom, a tall, chilled-out Aussie surfer, who had been befriended by the boys and was staying in the house. His daily routine was to wake around midday, drink chai with Ballu and smoke his bong followed by hours spent on his guitar, which he played like a reincarnation of Jimi Hendrix. At 4 pm he usually ventured down to the sea and body surfed until after sunset, at which point he either got stoned while the boys cooked or whooped up a feast himself for all of us (one of the perks of having a chef stay in the house). I couldn't imagine someone more easy-going to live with.

My second companion was a sassy American gal from Vashon Island, Seattle. She, like me, had also switched from travelling around India to sinking into the sands of Varkala because, well, that's what often seemed to happen in this place. (Sweet Felicity, however, had managed to move on to Mysore, deciding her yoga studies were more important than a budding romance with Sid.) Hope – kind and funny Hope – walked like she meant it, knew literally everybody on the cliff by name and was the only long-term Western fe-male staying in Varkala. She was my saving grace. Over the course of the next two months in Varkala, we passed many hours drinking lemon sodas, playing card games and trying to figure out our lives together. I don't think I fully appreci-ated her at the time for it's quite possible I would have gone completely insane for lack of like-minded female friendship had she not been around.

But of course back then, I was rather distracted by my besotted heart, given up totally to the boy himself, speaking of whom, the day did finally dawn when both he and Sid returned home. In a swirl of delighted anticipation, I set about beautifying myself with pedicures, facials, perfumes and coconut oil. This time I would be fresh and gorgeous for our big reunion.

'Ooh, that smells good, Ballu.' I inhaled deeply as I walked into the kitchen that evening where the happy-go-lucky guy stood over his cauldron of curry, carefully stirring it. He shook his afro curls and flashed me his trademark grin.

'Yes, Leeze, it's good food tonight. Very good food!'

'Aw man, your food's always good,' Dom drawled, ducking his lanky frame as he strolled into the room. 'So, the guys are back tonight?'

'Yup. I'm ridiculously excited!' I said, practically bouncing on the spot. Dom nodded.

'Me too. I've been missing them so bad. God, I can't wait to get my hands on Alex's skinny bum and give him a big squeeze.'

'Ha ha, there's no need to mock.'

'There's every need, Liz. Every need,' he said with a lazy grin, starting to roll up a joint. 'So when are they coming?'

'Around 10 pm, I think.'

'Yes, Leeze, 10 pm.' Ballu nodded his head. 'Alex say to me on the phone.'

'Not long to wait so!' I said delightedly.

The excitement reached stupid levels as ten o'clock approached.

'Oh God, I think I'm gonna puke,' I moaned, clutching my stomach with the anticipation. It didn't help that I was starving (we were waiting for the boys to arrive so we could all eat together). It also didn't help that 10 pm became 10.30 pm and eventually 11 pm and still there was no sign of them.

'You hanging in there, Liz?' Dom asked as I sat on the couch, my foot tapping in agitation, a cushion clutched to my stomach.

'I'm so tired of waiting. It's nearly midnight. Where is he?'

The boys merely laughed at my angst.

'Alex coming, Leeze. No worries!' Ameer told me confidently.

A sound outside finally alerted us all. It was a car pulling up outside the house. Doors were opened and shut and two familiar voices could be heard. My face nearly split in two from grinning. Reaching the door just as it opened, there he was, slipping off his shoes, his big happy smile lighting up my world.

'Oh, hello!'

'Hi!' I grinned idiotically at him and then we wrapped our arms around each other and didn't let go as I soaked up the warmth and firmness of his body against mine at long, long last.

'I missed you,' I mumbled eventually into his neck.

'Me too, *beta*.'

We finally dragged ourselves away from each other so Alex could say hi to the rest of the guys and so that we could all eat at last.

'Happy now, are you?' Dom teased as we sat together around the food. Alex's arm was draped naturally over my crossed legs and my knee rested on his thigh; we were as close to each other as physically possible.

'Shut up!' I grinned at him, squeezing Alex's hand affectionately. All was right with the world again.

Chapter 25

Indian family life

The rest of March passed us by in a quiet lethargy of trips to the cliff and very little else. Just when it began to feel like my brain was turning to mush in the intense muggy heat, Alex sprang the following news on me: 'My niece is getting married next week in Jaipur.'

'Oh. Are you going to it?'

'Of course. My family will kill me if I don't.'

'Oh, that should be nice,' I replied, trying to be happy, but inwardly feeling a pang that he'd be leaving me.

'So do you want to come too?' A slow smile spread across my face. It seemed I was going to get my Rajasthani wedding after all.

* * *

Arriving late at night into Jaipur airport, the taxi drove us through the dark and quiet streets towards Alex's house. It had taken nearly twelve hours of travelling, including a five-hour taxi from Varkala to Cochin and a flight that stopped in both Bangalore and Hyderabad, to finally reach Jaipur.

'So, just explain to me one more time – your family definitely knows I'm coming, right?'

'My brother knows.' He sounded worryingly vague.

'You have three brothers and a mother and father,' I pointed out. 'Are they all expecting me?'

It felt like I was nagging him but then again, I was meeting my boyfriend's family for the first time. This would be nerve-wracking back in Ireland and here I was about to do it in a culture and language as foreign and incomprehensible to me as algebra equations had been back in school. I used to cry over them; I hoped the same wouldn't happen here.

'*Beta*, don't worry,' Alex told me confidently. 'In India, we always expect guests.'

'Yes, but are they expecting your girlfriend? Do they even know you have one?'

Alex didn't answer straight away. He'd said before that some of his family knew he had a girlfriend but I got the impression he'd kept pretty quiet about it and he definitely hadn't told his dad yet. This in itself was daunting but, on top of that, his family spoke pretty much no English, had very different customs and ideas of appropriate behaviour to what I was familiar with *and* there were around forty of them living in the one building. Small wonder I was feeling nervous.

'*Beta*, really, you worry too much. My family will be happy to see you. But call me Ali while you're there, they have no idea who is 'Alex'.'

I had discovered some time ago that Alex was more of a nickname while his real name was a traditional Muslim one, Akbar Ali. But by then the name Alex had already stuck with me and there was no going back; Alex he was and always would be.

The taxi turned off the main road down a narrower street and made a sharp turn into a pokey alley, stopping outside a house three levels high. We stepped out into the warm night air and collected our bags. Alex pulled open a narrow sliding gate and I followed him into a little courtyard packed full of scooters, surrounded on all sides by the tall house. He strode up to one of the several closed doors and tapped on it, while I peered up at the two extra floors that rose above us in the dark silence. A moment later there was the sound of a bolt sliding back and the door opened a crack. Alex exchanged a few hushed words with his brother Majid before the door closed again and, a second later, another door to our left was opened.

We entered the sparsely furnished space where a wooden double bed took up most of the small room with a 'mattress' that looked barely an inch thick. In the dim light, I also noticed a desk in the corner and blue shutters on the wall opposite us. It was all very simple and functional. Alex's brother, an older, portly man with a neat moustache, blinked sleepily, spoke a few words to Alex and then glanced curiously at me, returning my smile with a shy one of his own.

'He's asking if you want anything before you sleep?' Alex told me.

'Oh no, I don't want to bother them when it's so late. I'm fine.'

The men chatted for a moment in Hindi. Watching them I got the impression that Alex was the senior brother despite Majid looking at least ten years older, not to mention the fact that he was married with four kids. Yet as they spoke I could hear Majid asking questions with an innocent curiosity that was quite endearing, particularly given his manner had so far been a bit gruff and monosyllabic (though that could have had something to do with us waking him up in the middle of the night). At any rate, there were no hugs or delighted smiles upon seeing each other for the first time in over six months, just a brief conversation before Majid headed back to the main room to join his sleeping family, closing our door softly behind him. I wondered if it was a cultural thing, a male thing or simply that they weren't especially close.

'OK, *beta*? You know I can't stay here with you tonight.'

'I know,' I answered. Considering so many Indian couples don't even meet each other properly before getting married, sleeping in the same room in his family's home was out of the question. 'Where's the toilet?'

'Come, I show you.'

He led me back out to the courtyard and we went to a corner where there were two old wooden doors, one for the toilet and one for a shower room. Flicking on a weak bulb, Alex pulled open the door, glancing inside before letting me in.

I stepped in to use the typical Indian-style latrine. Aside from the fact that I had to squat, the whole thing reminded me of a house that used to belong to my nana in the remote Irish countryside of West Cork. That house was as old school as you could get, full of draughts and creaking floorboards, and its toilet was in a cobwebbed outhouse that made your bum freeze. This felt similar, just minus the damp and the cold. Once done I filled the little plastic jug from the tap, 'flushed' the toilet and went back to the bedroom.

'OK, darling, I go now,' Alex said, giving me a hug and a quick kiss before leaving.

I lay down on the hard bed, the fan whirring above, and pondered this house full of people who didn't know me. Feeling a little nervous of what tomorrow would bring, I rolled over, wincing as I did. Man, the bed was hard!

At 7 am I was roused by the sounds of the house and the city starting their day: kids shouting to each other, cars beeping, neighbours outside chatting, vendors passing by the house with their sing-song calls for onions or sweets or vegetables. I drifted back to sleep until a while later I was awoken again, this time by Bollywood dance tracks blasting out of a stereo upstairs.

Not knowing where Alex was and feeling too shy to face his family alone – some of whom might or might *not* have been expecting to see a random white girl in their midst – I stayed in bed, turning over onto my tummy to give my sore, stiff hips some relief.

Finally, at 9 am, I had no choice but to get up as I desperately needed to pee. Tentatively, I opened the inner door leading to the rest of Majid's home. A boy of about nine dressed in a cream and brown school uniform was sitting on a stool, a copybook on his lap. I'd barely got the word Ali out of my mouth before he was scampering off. He came back a second later and beckoned for me to follow. As I did, I passed his mum squatting next to a mound of wet clothes on the concrete floor. She was busy scrubbing a pair of jeans with a bar of soap, her shawl elegantly framing her face, which lit up the moment she smiled at me.

I followed Alex's nephew, Arshad, passing through the room his family had all been sleeping in the night before.

It was completely bare save for a fridge in the corner with a TV on top (they rolled out thick mats each night to sleep on and packed them away in the morning). Two of the walls had small shelves built in with a few trinkets on them, while the kitchenette was at the back in a little alcove; it consisted of a portable gas stove on a stone shelf to the right and a ground-level tap and drain to the left, their sink. There were some small, high shelves there too, where the plates, pots, dry goods and spices were stored, but so much of the food they ate was bought fresh each day that there was little need for more storage space. In the main room there was a big concrete shelf up near the high ceiling where larger items could be kept but the whole thing was incredibly minimal with no oven, no endless cupboards filled to bursting, no large table and chairs, no rug, no sofa … It was a little stark but I liked it.

Coming outside, I heard Alex calling me and looked up. He was leaning over the balustrade of the first floor, yawning.

'Jesus, you look wrecked.'

'I am, *beta*. Come upstairs.'

We went into one of the first-floor rooms, apparently the 'boys' room'. It was dark with a small glassless, mesh-covered window, a huge double bed taking up half the space, an old-fashioned couch and a small press with a TV on it.

'I didn't sleep yet. I went to my sister's house all night and when I come back, I thought you will get up soon.'

'I'm really glad of that because I desperately need the loo. Is there one I can use up here?'

We passed the entire day hanging around the house, surrounded at all times by kids (less in the morning when most of them were in school but around twelve of them later on in the afternoon). They were absolutely fascinated with me. I couldn't put on face cream or even write in my diary without several small faces staring up at me or peering over my shoulder. It was a little intense being surrounded by so many bodies enthralled with my every move, but it was also incredibly sweet, especially seeing how much they all loved their 'cha-cha' (uncle) Alex. He was clearly the novelty fun uncle, showing up out of the blue every few months and playing with them like a big child himself.

After lunch he gathered a group of his nephews in the small courtyard to play cricket. Like anything in India, it was raucous and rowdy with lots of arguing and laughter, but it got cut short. Irate at being disturbed from his nap upstairs, Alex's uncle came out and started shouting at the kids. Alex instantly scooted into the corner where he couldn't be seen, giggling like a naughty boy and with his finger to his lips, warning the kids not to give him away. On spotting me downstairs, his uncle stopped shouting, staring at me quizzically before smiling and nodding and quickly disappearing back inside his room. I still hadn't come across Alex's dad.

This might seem odd, but in fact it was simply a mix of the language barrier combined with very different customs and cultural norms. Alex's family was less a family in the standard Western sense and more like a tribe, his father being the chief of the extended clan. I had met some of the women in the home (it being a traditional Indian family, they were all stay-at-home wives) and they were very friendly and welcoming. But the fact that I spoke no Hindi and they no English meant that they couldn't do much more than pester Alex for information on who I was and what I was doing in India, on my own, so far away from my own family.

His father, retired from a government office job, was a strong, authoritative man, according to Alex, one not prone to sitting down for gossip or chit-chat, particularly not with a young white girl that spoke no Hindi. A well-respected figure in the local community, the whole idea of meeting him was now massively daunting, especially as we wouldn't even be able to communicate properly.

The kids, of course, didn't care if I understood them or not; they would chat away happily, throwing at me whatever random English phrases they had learned at school ('Favourite food? Favourite Bollywood actor? Favourite colour?') and they delightedly repeated back my responses to the adults later: *dhal fry* (it was pizza actually, but I went with the popular lentil curry to make life easier for all of us), Sharukh Khan (a mega superstar in India's movie industry and quite incredibly hot) and purple (in case you were wondering).

Any other kind of interaction, however, resulted in a fair bit of confusion. 'Food?' for example, a regular question during my time with the family, could mean any of the following: Would you like some food? Did you already have some food? What kind of food would you like? When would you like to eat?

This was of course all for my benefit as they were absolutely exquisite hosts, generous to the extreme and concerned for my well-being. As long as Alex was around he could of course translate for me, but whenever I had to manage on my own, it felt like I was swimming out of my depth and drifting farther and farther from the coastline.

It didn't get any better that first day when the kids brought me upstairs to show off their moves to the latest hip-shaking Bollywood songs. Before long they were insisting I join in. Now, I'm a self-conscious dancer at the best of times but the cringe factor in this scenario – right around the time they all decided to stop and watch me doing a complete solo, with several of the adults also looking on – well, mortified doesn't even begin to describe it.

Later in the evening Alex left me upstairs with one of his sisters-in-law who lived on the top floor while he did a few jobs. I sat there politely smiling and drinking chai while tall and elegant Firjana was full of grins and head wobbles, the chattiest and friendliest of all the adults. It didn't bother her in the slightest that I hadn't a clue what she was saying; she was enjoying every minute of my presence regardless.

'Hum market challo?' she asked later and finally I thought I recognised a few words. Market and *challo* = Let's go to the market? I nodded with a smile.

Firjana disappeared off into the other room for a few minutes. Their home was almost an exact copy of the other homes I'd already seen but with a thick mattress on the floor alongside a small worn desk that had an old-school computer and, of course, a TV on a shelf above that. This main room led off into a larger one with just one big armoire, a camp bed and a fridge. Again there was the small alcove with the little kitchenette (this one had a regular, waist-high sink).

Firjana reappeared a few minutes later, dressed head to toe in a flowing black burqa. I was a little taken aback; my limited experience of seeing women dressed in such a way had been while hanging around London Heathrow's Terminal Three, several months ago. But then the burqa will do that to us Westerners as it is such a foreign concept seeing a person completely swathed in black material with only their eyes visible. (I personally believe our reactions have something to do with the fact that a person's subtle body language – their stance, small facial expressions and so on – are entirely hidden by such attire, and subconsciously we rely on them to assure us of a person's true intentions. But that's just my own theory on it.) At any rate, while India is not a Muslim-only country, nor are the members of Alex's family strict orthodox Muslims, when the married women head out and about, they generally dress in the full burqa. For them it's completely the norm – in fact I often think they enjoy the ritual as it marks them out as women of a certain status. Wearing the burqa is like a badge of honour for them (but again, that's just me speculating).

Back to our little market trip, however, and Firjana, all in black, smiled and gestured for me to follow her downstairs where there was a tuk-tuk waiting outside. It turned out there were quite a few of us going to the market though I had no idea why and couldn't ask. We managed to squash four adults and five kids into the three-wheeler and proceeded to bounce and chug our way through Jaipur's dusty main streets.

It being my first time in Rajasthan's capital, I peered out at the sights as we whizzed past, the streets full of the same hectic buzz as Jodhpur and other cities I'd visited with Paul and Rob six months before. This time, though, I was viewing it all from a very different perspective, accompanied by my new Indian family. I couldn't wait to tell the boys all about it.

Known as the 'Pink City', the old section of Jaipur has the most beautiful architecture although it really is more of a rusty orange than pink. Whatever the colour, Rajasthan's large capital is utterly charming, with its high vaulted gateways into the old quarters and the uniform yet decorative Mughal details throughout its main bazaars, not to mention its impressive palaces and museums. The entire city is surrounded by distant hills and ancient sprawling forts. I couldn't believe that the boys and I had skipped this city on our travels around Rajasthan – it seemed that Shannu had been right when he'd said we were crazy not to have visited it. As with most Indian cities, Jaipur is a mixture of smooth wide roads, pot-holed streets and narrow, crumbling lanes and of course, everywhere you go, plenty of chaos. The area we arrived into, however, was a hotspot for disarray with narrow streets filled with goats and vehicles, piles of rubbish, mangy street dogs and coarsely haired pigs snuffling through the waste. Throngs of people wandered in and out of the scene and, well, it was rather messy. But the roads took the biscuit. It was as if someone had dug up random chunks of the street and we were bounced off our seats repeatedly by crater-sized pot holes.

What kind of market were we heading to, exactly?

My question was answered shortly after when we pulled up to a narrow alley with dirty grey water running through the gutters. As I followed the others up a residential path, I noticed a few local kids running around barefoot, only to stop in their tracks the second they spotted me.

Well, market she may or may not have said, but market definitely wasn't what Firjana meant. We had arrived at the home of Rasheeden, Alex's older sister, whose daughter was soon to be married. Despite the chaotic squalor on the streets outside, on entering big black, wrought-iron gates I found myself in a beautiful, spotless, marble-floored house. Like Alex's home, it was bare save for minimal furniture. But unlike Alex's, it was much smaller; two bedrooms downstairs, both with large double beds, and a spacious main hallway with a spotless toilet and shower cubicle; upstairs a tiny kitchen, a large living room (empty except, of course, for the TV) and another small toilet. The rest of the space upstairs was a large open terrace with steps leading up to yet another slightly smaller terrace on the rooftop.

Given the hot, dry climate of Jaipur, Rasheeden's small family spent 90 per cent of their time outside – and why wouldn't you, when your view included the magnificent Tiger Fort (Nahagarh Fort) that stretched across the nearby hilltop. Firjana introduced me to Alex's sister, a vast woman as wide and round as she was tall, robust and formidable and with a face of thunder even when she smiled. This woman should have been running a country, never mind a small family.

'*Salam alaikum*,' I said politely as Alex had taught, bringing a surprised smile of delight from Rasheeden who returned the peaceful Islamic greeting ('*Alaikum salam*') before promptly conversing in Hindi to which I shrugged my shoulders with an apologetic smile. Firjana seemed to explain for me then, because Rasheeden replied with a long, satisfying, '*Aaaaaachaaaa*' ('I see') glancing back at me and then asking a few questions of Firjana, clearly intrigued.

There were many more excited faces to greet and smile hello to before the kids ratted on me and, within minutes, a Bollywood track was blaring and the adults were requesting that I dance for them. Some of the kids had started bouncing around so, feeling it would be rude to refuse and trying to ignore the cringe that was already creeping up from my toes, I joined the couple of hyperactive youngsters in the middle of the floor and dutifully began to sway. Within seconds, I was completely alone once again, with an audience of over twenty people all watching as I self-consciously swung my hips, waved my arms and slowly but surely turned scarlet. I could hear a voice in my head groaning in despair: Oh crap, stop dancing, Liz, for the love of God, *stop*!

Desperate to escape, I gave an exaggerated wipe across my forehead and a gesture asking for water, only half pretending to be too hot and tired to continue. Jaipur in the month of April is always around 40°C and the air is as dry as sandpaper. I was gasping.

Released from my performance duties, I was allowed to sit down with the other women and nurse a cool bottle of water. But it didn't stop there. I was quite literally bombarded with questions as to whether I needed more water, if I was hungry, if I wanted some chai, if I wanted to lie down, if I wanted to sit on a chair, if I would dance again (NO!), if I was happy, if I was bored … and these were just the ones I understood. Many more were definitely lost on me, but one thing was quite clear: they were all, both kids and adults, incredibly concerned that I was OK, doting on me like twenty overprotective new mums.

The constant attention, however, along with my earnest attempts to understand and communicate, in a language I barely knew, were gradually frying my brain. It felt a bit like moving from a hermit's cave in the Himalayas straight to Tokyo during rush hour with zero Japanese. How on earth did I even end up here? Well, I knew the answer to that at least, speaking of whom, where was he and when was he going to rescue me from this clutch of mother hens and their noisy offspring?

In the middle of yet another moment of blushing embarrassment – moments that seemed to be trailing me like a pack of bumbling puppies all day long – my knight in shining armour did finally appear. I was sitting in the midst of all the women and one of the teenage girls was busy drawing some pretty henna designs on my hands (a temporary form of intricate tattooing done with wet clay that's popular all over India). Halfway through her work, she wanted to write my name and then asked if I had a boyfriend. I was momentarily stumped; there was no sign of Alex yet so I couldn't look to him for guidance. Would they be disapproving if I said yes? I still wasn't sure if Alex had even told anyone. At the same time, I didn't want to lie and say no.

It turned out I didn't need to actually *say* anything since my traitorous blushing face gave the game away, as it always does. Without my uttering a word, the girls and women around me started laughing and clapping because Liz very clearly did have a boyfriend. Grinning and looking up at me intently, the young girl asked another question. *'Nam?'*

Oh God, they wanted his name! Well, now I was in a pickle. Name and shame the boy? Keep quiet? What to do?

'Ali? You boyfriend, Ali?'

I turned neon pink, thinking feverishly, Oh man, what will they think of that?

It wasn't hard to understand just exactly what they thought of it: the delighted shrieking and raucous laughter would've been understood in parts of China or Africa and probably could be heard there too, while I gradually turned the darkest possible shade of puce. And that was the very moment Mr Alex Ali chose to arrive as we heard the door downstairs opening, followed by his familiar voice. My besotted heart swelled to bursting as he came into view at the top of the stairs, completely relaxed and confident. He was greeted by a chorus of near-hysterical females all teasing him mercilessly.

Not in the least bit perturbed, Alex leaned casually against the wall and replied to them with something evidently hilarious, setting them off into yet more high-pitched hysterics. It must be said that, in my experience, Indian women seem to be quite excitable, much like a flock of noisy hens – whether happy or anxious, there's an awful lot of commotion involved.

Alex's unruffled response, particularly compared with my lack of composure, had me so sick with love that if he'd asked me to marry him in that moment I would have sprinted down the aisle before he'd even finished the sentence. This was quite appropriate since apparently someone suggested that, after his niece Shammi's wedding, Alex and I should tie the knot next day. Cue even more shrill mirth.

'You OK with all these women?' Alex finally asked me, taking in the girls clustered around me drawing henna and some of the older women seated nearby who'd started singing, one of them playing a small drum, in typical pre-wedding fashion.

'Yup,' I answered with a grin, barely hearing what he'd said as I considered literally eating him, he looked so good.

'So I go join the men on the roof, OK?' And he left me to it.

A few hours later many people had gone home and there was a much smaller group of us relaxing together. Rasheed-en had whipped out a professional engagement album, her daughter Shammi's of course, full of photos and captions and bursting with colour. It was a very ornate affair, as I leafed through image after image of the bride-to-be. She was dressed up in a fabulously intricate outfit, a brightly coloured, bejewelled sari and enough costume jewellery to open up a small shop, including a golden nose ring half the size of her face with a chain running along from her nose to her ear. I thought she would have looked absolutely beautiful if not for her make-up, a combination of bright red lipstick and garish blue eye-shadow.

The most interesting thing to me, however, was the glum expression on Shammi's face throughout all the photos. None of the people photographed seemed to think it necessary to smile for the camera but while most faces remained simply flat or stern, Shammi looked truly depressed. I glanced across at her now, cuddling one of the family's toddlers and giggling and I couldn't get over the difference. Why wasn't she happy in the photos? Did she not want to get married? As I browsed through the album, Alex's sister and her family badgered him for information about me.

'They want to know if you miss your family?'

'Of course I do, but if you want to explore the world you can't exactly drag all of them along with you. Anyway, we don't have quite the same close bonds as you guys in India, at least not in my family.' I shook my head, imagining us all living together like Alex's family. Whoever survived would probably be guilty of mass murder.

'They want to know why you're travelling then, if you miss them.'

'I love coming to a country I've never before been to, exploring new places and experiencing a completely different way of life. It's fascinating.'

There was some discussion among Alex and his family then, before his sister said something incomprehensible to me.

'She's asking if you learn any Hindi in Ireland,' Alex told me.

'No, in school we study English and Irish and usually some European languages.'

From the expression of disbelief on their faces after Alex repeated this back to them in Hindi, I could figure out for myself what they were saying next:

'What? None? You don't know any Hindi?'

Alex started laughing at their reaction.

'They think you're crazy because you don't know any Hindi. It's too weird for them!'

It wasn't long before the over-stimulating events of the day had me yawning every couple of minutes. The family had already organised mats and blankets on the terrace, their bedroom for the night. I said good night to them as Alex brought me to one of the bedrooms downstairs where I would sleep by myself. After such an intense day, it was a relief to be on my own at last. I sank gratefully onto a bed that had a big thick mattress – hooray! – and lay my head down on the pillow only to groan involuntarily. It was about as soft as a rock.

Chapter 26

Wedding anticipation

Next morning I awoke early to several kids wandering curiously into my room. No rest for the wicked. Once I was up, Shammi and her sisters/cousins called me to join them in the next room, where they were all applying a paste of turmeric mixed with water to their faces and arms, another pre-wedding custom. Turmeric, or *haldi*, is used because it's believed to purify and cleanse the body; it's also thought to protect the bride and groom from any bad omen that might harm them before the big day and the ritual of applying the paste is an inherent part of every traditional wedding in northern India, be it Hindu or Muslim. I squatted down beside the girls and willingly rubbed the sloppy stuff up to my elbows but resisted when they suggested I put it on my face – while it was fine on them, I didn't really fancy looking like I had jaundice for a week. I was feeling pretty pleased with myself for joining in with them and slotting neatly into this vastly different culture, so when Alex came downstairs to check on me, I smiled up at him proudly – look at me, the world's best girlfriend, taking it all in my stride.

'*Beta*, this colour isn't suiting you, you should wash here in the sink,' he told me, looking dubiously at my yellow arms. Guess it's a good thing I hadn't smeared the stuff all over my face.

'When are we going home?' I asked, as I rinsed off the paste in the hall sink.

'We have chai and then we go, OK?'

I was glad to leave, thinking I might get some quiet time to myself back at his house, but once there it turned out I needed to go shopping for some wedding outfits (not surprisingly my Ali Baba pants and tank tops just would not do). Alex called on friendly Firjana to bring me shopping and he asked one of his cousin's older daughters, Jasmine, who spoke some English, if she would come too and translate for me.

We took a taxi to the centre of Jaipur's russet-coloured walls in the old part of the city. It was an area full of vibrant energy, hectic traffic, crowds of people and endless bazaars selling everything from textiles to food to electrics to stationery; we visited several clothes stores where a lot of aggressive shouting took place between Firjana and the shopkeepers. I glanced uncertainly at Jasmine as Firjana yelled at yet another exceptionally grumpy-looking salesman.

'Don't worry, bargaining!' Jasmine reassured me with an easy smile.

I wondered was it better or worse that I understood none of it.

By the time we were finished and ready to head back to the house, I'd settled on two *salwar kameez* outfits (consisting of pretty knee-length tunics, matching trousers and light shawls). One was lilac satin – according to Firjana and Jasmine, its tunic was *so* last year's fashion – while the other was deep sparkly pink and cream. I also purchased bangles, fancy shoes and some make-up since I had zero items in my hippie backpack that counted as dressy. Thanks to Alex insisting on paying for everything, I handed over great wads of cash with carefree abandon and it felt like I was on a crazy shopping spree. Yet the grand total worked out to be less than fifty euros. You just can't beat India for the bargains.

As soon as I was back home in my little bedroom, the women of the household flocked to my room to inspect my purchases. I giggled as they oohed and aahed over each piece, passing comment between themselves, and it seemed that, despite my dated fashion choice with the lilac suit, they approved. Or at least they were too polite to say otherwise.

* * *

Of the numerous little cultural differences I had to adjust to, the one I found most bizarre was that all of Alex's sisters-in-law pulled their shawls completely over their faces whenever his father or uncle were around. The material was so light and thin you could almost make out their faces and of course they could see perfectly through them, but why on earth did they do it?

Across Rajasthan and several other northern states, there is a prevailing custom that women cover their faces when in the presence of older male in-laws, such as their husband's father or elder brother, as a sign of respect. It's not a religious thing, Hindus and Muslims both adhere to it. In other less conservative states, such as Kerala, Tamil Nadu or Himachal Pradesh, it's pretty much non-existent. It seems oppressive to women and yet another example of India really being a man's world. In moments of outraged indignation, I've asked Alex why the men don't have to do anything like it around their mother-in-law or elder sisters-in-law, but he always just shrugs; having grown up with this tradition he doesn't get what the big deal is for me. Nor do the women for that matter, at least the ones in Alex's family. On the odd occasion that he has asked them about it on my behalf, they've always been completely accepting of it, even puzzled by my question – why should it matter? It is what it is.

But then, in my experience, that's the general Indian mentality in a nutshell; they're so damn good at accepting their fate, surrendering to the cards they've been dealt and making the best of it. Alex's female relatives are a prime example; they all seem so very content and yet the life of a woman in traditional India (which is still the majority of the country) is not easy.

Once married, the bride moves into her husband's house, leaving behind the home and family she's known all her life. It's a huge upheaval in the young woman's life as she moves away from her parents, siblings, cousins and childhood home, hence the reason brides are so often miserable and in tears in their wedding photos (and, I realised, why Shammi looked so depressed in her engagement pictures). On top of this, they arrive into a strange new home where they have to learn the new system fast because the young Indian wife must always be meek, obedient, respectful, hardworking and, if she lives in the north, must also hide her face when around her husband's elder male relatives.

As depressing as this may sound, there's actually a lot more to it. The Indian wedding, with its extravagant festivities and days and days of celebrations, is a wonderful rite of passage that most women eagerly anticipate. Becoming a wife and starting her own family gives the bride important new status, one that's clearly marked by the traditional newlywed 'uniform' of endless bangles, toe rings and henna tattoos. And while the young couple in an arranged marriage may not get to spend time together before the wedding, these days cousins and younger brothers and sisters help them to exchange numbers and they will often spend endless secretive hours talking to each other on the phone. They can develop quite the crush on each other and it's common for a budding romance to be there long before the big day. It's obviously a tough transition for the girl – the goodbyes between the young bride and her parents at the end of the wedding night are heartbreaking to watch – but she's prepared for it since childhood and it's the inevitable next step in growing up. Given how good Indians are at accepting the way of things and making the best of them, I think the majority of women in these traditional marriages really are happy and they grow to love both their husband and their new home.

But back to the tradition of face-covering: considering that I wasn't married or even Indian, I was thankfully exempt from the whole thing, yet it made me a source of uncertainty for the adults in the family. I fell outside of the rule book and they didn't know quite what to do with me. For the women, seeing me speak to Alex's uncle face to face on our second day there (with the help of Alex translating) was quite shocking. I wonder if, for them, the fact that I didn't cover my face, or even my hair, was the equivalent of being half-naked …

Nonetheless, Alex's uncle was extremely warm and friendly towards me; perhaps because he was the baby brother he didn't worry too much about maintaining a strict status quo. Alex's father, on the other hand, was the head of the house and definitely not so friendly. I met him on that second day as he passed by in the courtyard, his stern glance resting briefly on me before he carried on. In his late sixties, tall and proud, with a shock of white hair and piercing eyes, he was a respected, eminent figure within the home and local community, and he didn't seem to be into giving away smiles or carefree friendly greetings. Ultimately, I think the language barrier, together with our large cultural differences, were simply too much for us on that trip. I was terrified of saying or doing something wrong and far too timid to attempt breaking the ice, preferring to smile politely from a distance. It was fascinating to observe how everyone's energy changed instantly when Alex's father was around (the women's posture suddenly upright and alert, grown men temporarily turning into obedient kids) but he had a quiet, powerful presence that demanded respect and attention. Even Alex became a little bit child-like and awkward around his dad whenever he spoke to him.

In contrast, Alex's mum was the cutest little old lady; I wanted to scoop her up and give her a cuddle each time I saw her. Her silver hair was always hanging down her back in a long braid, though most of the time, like the other women, it was covered by the large shawl she wore over her head (even though, being married to the oldest man of the house, she was the one married female that never had to cover her face).

While Alex read the newspaper each morning, she would sit quietly nearby, chatting to him and giggling occasionally, rarely looking for much of a response. Squatting comfortably against the wall, she would fumble absentmindedly with her dentures while peering out at the world from behind incomprehensibly strong prescription lenses. She was perhaps the sweetest, kindest mother one could ever hope to have and clearly the source behind Alex's soft, gently loving nature. Alex introduced me to her on our first day and I always felt comfortable and relaxed in her presence, wishing I could actually chat normally with her and bridge our two very different worlds.

Unfortunately, as with everyone else, I had to settle for smiles and shrugs. Alex's family seemed to have readily accepted me and I was both delighted and relieved, but I literally had no clue what anyone said to me unless Alex was there. If you've never experienced being the centre of attention, surrounded by people all speaking a foreign language, let me assure you that it is intense. Add to that the pressure of them being my boyfriend's family and the boiling April heat … I'm surprised I didn't burst into flames.

* * *

The night before the wedding in India is almost as big as the actual day itself and everyone in the house spent the afternoon getting dressed up. I wore my lilac suit that had since been fitted by a tailor and Jasmine offered me some extra make-up and helped do something with my hair besides my usual messy bun. While she combed my thick mane, I fanned myself with a notebook. My suit's heavy synthetic material was smothering in the heat. Jaipur's pre-monsoon temperatures are wickedly high, and it is such a baking dry heat that my body felt as though she were shrivelling up like a prune from the inside out, no matter how much water I guzzled.

It didn't help that we had arrived by plane straight from tropical lush Kerala whose air was so laden with moisture you could almost cup your hands and drink from them. Our bodies had had no adjustment time while travelling to this zero-humidity region and my nose had become dried out like a dusty pressed flower. Jaipur in April necessitated bikinis, chilled white wine and large swimming pools and even then you'd probably give up after ten minutes and head into an air-conditioned building. Unfortunately, neither tiny swim suits nor alcohol would have gone down well with Alex's family (or most of the rest of northern India) and we simply didn't have time to visit one of Jaipur's pricey outdoor swimming pools. So instead I found myself sipping hot chai, dressed in heavy clothes and with an overhead fan that felt more like a hair dryer. Not a pool or wine bottle in sight. I had showered just ten minutes before, but I was already sticky with sweat.

When we left the house, we somehow succeeded in cramming fourteen bodies into a single tuk-tuk (truth be told I think a couple of the kids were hanging off the roof and possibly two more were clinging to the driver's legs). Once we arrived at Rasheeden's house, the bodies spilled out and, having untangled my limbs and clothes, I followed too with little Mouscan, Majid's sweet seven-year-old daughter, clasping my hand tightly in hers.

We had to wait a while outside the house since to enter we needed to bend the laws of physics and squeeze an excess of humans into an impossibly small space. All of a sudden there was a loud commotion at the front of the line and ladies started shrieking and throwing themselves out of the way like a line of synchronised swimmers. A split second later I was following suit as a lone Indian cow came charging towards us. The stampeding animal disappeared onto the main street and having smoothed our ruffled feathers we slowly but surely inched our way inside the building, joining the throngs of relatives already there. Good old India.

The house was so crowded and packed it was difficult to move anywhere; you could almost feel its walls heaving and groaning under the strain. When it was time to eat, we sat in long rows on the floor, both downstairs and upstairs. Alex and numerous other male cousins acted as waiters for the night, picking their way through the endless bodies with large pots and ladles out of which they served dhal and other dishes onto paper plates for us. I was squished in between Jasmine and her sweet sister Reshma and absolutely melting in the heat. But when Alex passed by offering us food, he had rivulets of perspiration running down his face and his shirt was soaked with sweat. Just to finish us all off completely, the food was so spicy it could have lit a fire on Pluto.

Sweet Reshma did her best to mind me for the night, truly she did, but there was no escaping the endless attention that trailed me like an unwanted spotlight everywhere I went. There was always someone pulling me to come over here, to eat this, to try that, to pose for a photo, asking me questions I could never understand and, of course, demanding that I dance. Alex popped his head up the stairs later on to check how I was.

'Help me, please! They keep making me dance on my own,' I whined, hoping maybe he could whisk me away from these clamorous ladies.

'Just take their hands and pull them up with you,' he told me airily before disappearing back downstairs.

With a sigh of resignation, I gave it a go. As they played more music and had me spinning self-consciously in their midst, I made a beeline for one of the aunts and grabbed her hands, trying to drag her up with me. She instantly started shrieking and giggling, shaking her head and desperately resisting. No matter who I tried, it was the same self-conscious hysterical reaction and refusal to participate. My patience for the whole debacle was rapidly wearing thin. It was fine for me to be the circus monkey but try getting them to join in and suddenly it was too embarrassing. What about me? Jesus, if I turned any more red in the face, my skin was going to blister.

I was tired of being bombarded with intrusive questions and demands that I rarely understood, despite concentrating so hard my brain felt ready to explode. I was tired of feeling like a freak attraction as people pointed at me and talked about me right under my nose. At the end of the day, I was actually just plain tired. It was nearly 1 am and I'd had enough stimulation that evening to send me cartwheeling into outer space, yet somehow I was *still* straining to be impeccable and 'make a good impression'. I needed to chill, in every sense.

When Alex called me downstairs a while later and told me he was going to drop me home, I could not have been more relieved. His cousin Sartaj was outside on a motorbike and the two of us piled on behind. Just as we were driving off, a street dog snarled aggressively before charging us and trying to eat my leg but thanks to Sartaj stepping on the accelerator we got away in the nick of time.

'OK, *beta*? I have to go back,' Alex spoke softly as he brought me into my bedroom. Majid and his family were already home and asleep.

'OK,' I whispered back, feeling very much not OK, but realising there was no point mentioning it when Alex was already walking back out of the door to Sartaj. Feeling utterly exhausted, I changed out of the dratted, stinky suit into my cotton pyjamas and then realised I had no bottle of water.

Uh-oh.

Here's a free bit of advice from me to you: if you stress and strain for too long and do nothing to ease the tension, then just like a pressure cooker, eventually steam of some kind will blow your friggin' lid off. That's what happened to me that night. As kind and welcoming as Alex's family had been to me so far, I had reached my limit of both the relentless attention and stress of not being able to communicate properly. And that's not even taking into account the horrendous heat, which was exhausting in itself. The lack of any water that night was the final straw and I let out all the pent-up pressure in the only effective way I know how, by bawling my eyes out until my pillow became soaked with tears and snot. It was such an emotional deluge that, if there were an Olympic event for crying, I reckon this particular performance would have been a contender for gold. After an impressive amount of time, the tears finally subsided and I dropped into an exhausted sleep, quite possibly snoring as loudly as Alex's brother Majid.

Chapter 27

Turning Indian

The sky was already dark when the tuk-tuk dropped us all at the wedding venue next evening, a pretty garden surrounded by high walls with a stage area and numerous chairs. There was also a small secluded room where the bride was sitting with her mum and several other female relatives. (Unlike at a Western wedding, in India the bride is always there first and the groom is the one to arrive in style.)

In the centre of the space was an area for drinks and food and off to one end was a DJ, with large speakers belting out the latest Bollywood tracks. This was a typical Indian wedding venue, costing the equivalent of roughly 800 euros to rent at the time, before any of the food, music or any other extras were considered. The first thing visible upon entering was the most incredible display of extravagance: the bride's dowry (though rarely openly admitted as such). It covered a huge space near the entrance and included dozens of new suits for the bride, shirts, shoes, pots and pans, a washing machine, a refrigerator and even a red shiny motorbike.

There is a thing in India about displaying your level of wealth in society and emphasising how far up the rungs of 'successful' you've made it. Weddings are the biggest and most important moment to showcase this and the amount of money spent on them relative to a family's income is hard to believe. Poorer families will take out huge loans, sinking themselves into a lifetime of debt just to provide a suitably impressive marriage for their daughter. Indian fathers quite possibly start saving for their child's wedding from the moment they discover their newborn is a girl. It's crazy and senseless to me, but it's just one of those Indian traditions that remains unquestioned.

It was hard not to enjoy the big event. As I wandered around the garden with Jasmine and Reshma I wished Paul and Rob could have been there to experience it too, marvelling yet again at how my trip had transformed since we parted ways. The large garden was brimming with people even though the groom and most of his (several hundred) relatives were not yet there. The women were brighter and more beautiful than a field of tulips – their brilliant suits sparkled, the lights dancing off all the sequins and jewels of both their clothes and their shimmering, tinkling bangles. The men were somewhat dull and plain by comparison. Times and styles have changed since but, back then, a lot of them were wearing shirts over jeans with a few even wearing regular sneakers. Except for Alex.

He had spent half the day sleeping (after staying up the entire night again at his sister's house) and had been helping to set up this venue all afternoon. The last I'd seen of him as I left the house earlier was a decidedly sweaty and smelly boy about to take a shower. So when he arrived at the venue in off-white linen trousers, a light shirt in pastel green and his hair tied back in a small ponytail, clean shaven and ridiculously handsome … it wouldn't be exaggerating to say I pretty much died and went straight to heaven. Several times over.

Unlike the previous evening where Alex had been tied up the entire time, for this night he was all mine. I felt a little guilty abandoning Jasmine and Reshma when they'd done their best to mind me, but it was a relief just to be with someone who spoke English.

Of course, this was all very un-Indian and unorthodox behaviour. Unless you were under the age of about ten, girls stayed with girls and boys with boys, while here I was spending the entire night surrounded by Alex and his buddies. For once, my lack of Hindi was an advantage as nobody knew what to do with me. I think they were glad to let Alex take over.

The differences between the traditional Western wedding and the Indian one are striking. In the typical Irish church ceremony, it's all hushed calm and an atmosphere of nervous anticipation as the groom anxiously awaits his bride to make her grand entrance. The ceremony is conducted in front of a silent congregation and it's all very formal, polite and, well, subtle. You may have gathered by now that in India *nothing* is subtle – it's all colour and joyful chaos and as much noise as possible.

This particular wedding was a Muslim ceremony (which obviously differs to a Hindu or Christian one) and the bride waited in hiding for most of the evening while the groom arrived on the back of a bejewelled, ornately decorated horse, surrounded by literally hundreds of extended family members. They were heralded by the noisiest, most raucous band of musicians I have ever heard. Dressed in their band garb of turbaned hats, tired white uniforms and glitzy leg-warmers and with their battered trumpets blasting, their clarinets wailing and warbling and their drums rolling and thumping, I reckon it was enough to wake the dead and make them get up and join in the festivities.

Despite the rude assault on my classically trained Western musician's ear, there was a joy and a bounce to the music, perhaps because of what it symbolised, as much as the musicians' valiant efforts to blast tunes from their ancient instruments.

While the groom and his horse entered the gates, streams of people poured in around him. I was in the welcome line of girls all waiting to toss confetti as he came in but despite his steed being a long-term, experienced Indian wedding horse (i.e. virtually bomb-proof) and despite tolerating the hordes of people jostling around him and the deafening, screeching musicians only feet away, the petals tossed over him were so terrifying that he started and shied violently. It required several strong men to grab his reins and calm him down before he turfed off his rider perched awkwardly on top (which is pretty ironic, but that's horses for you). The poor groom could only cling on for dear life, relying on blind faith and his relatives to get him safely to the little stage where the ceremony would be conducted, quite literally blind for he wore a *sehra*, a headdress with a long veil of stringed jasmine flowers that completely obscured his vision. (The significance behind the *sehra* is firstly, to ward off the evil eye and secondly, to ensure that the bride and groom don't see each other until after the ceremony. It's used predominantly in northern India.)

'Now what happens?' I asked Alex, once the groom was safely ensconced on his seat up on the stage.

'The holy man must ask the bride if she is agree to marry and then the groom. Once they both are agree, then that's it.'

'What if one of them says no to the wedding?'

'Then they cannot marry. They both must say yes.'

I pondered this a moment as I watched some of the groom's relatives crouched beside him on the stage, chatting to him while he waited.

'So, does anyone ever actually say no?'

'What do you think, *beta*?' Alex asked me, gesturing around at the lavish affair, as if to say, could anyone refuse at this stage?

'So, what's going on right now?' I asked him, as an old, wizened man wearing a typical Islamic cap approached the groom, sat cross-legged on the floor in front of him and started talking.

'Now he's asking him – this is the ceremony where they pray and then the couple is married. They always ask the girl first.'

I frowned. 'What, this is it? The all-important ceremony? But nobody's paying any attention,' I said in confusion, indicating all the people milling around the large garden, chatting amongst themselves, few of them even slightly interested in what was going on with the cluster of men around the groom.

'That's the Indian way, *beta* – only the close relatives participate in the prayers. You expect this many Indians to sit quietly?' he teased.

I shook my head, unable to wrap my mind around it all. 'It's just so different to back home. I mean the ceremony is the whole point of the event, so how come people are kind of ignoring it?'

'*Arrey* Liz, people are too busy catching up with friends and family they haven't seen in long time. They're here for good gossip and good food! Come on, let's go eat.'

We went to the large tables where staff served food onto our plates and then sat ourselves down on the grass to eat. Barely had I finished the meal when the great and formidable Rasheeden arrived and commanded my presence for photos with Shammi; she all but dragged me along by the *dupatta* around my neck. Since I hadn't even finished chewing, I had to wave my oily, food-covered hands at her to be able to wash them first.

It was thankfully brief: a few snaps of the morose bride, her vast warrior mother and the awkward white girl. Then I was all but shoved out of the room to make space for the next people to be photographed.

'Do you have to go back again?' I asked Alex as we arrived home sometime later. Despite the late hour, the house was a hive of activity with people returning from the wedding and getting ready for bed, all in high spirits.

'Yes, darling, I must help with cleaning and packing things. Tomorrow they all go to Jodhpur.'

'Jodhpur?'

'That's where the groom is from,' he said, as he got ready to leave. 'Alright? You have water, no?'

'Yup, won't be making that mistake again. See you in the morning. Oh, and try and sleep a little tonight, yeah?'

We hugged and stole a few sneaky kisses, despite the open door only being partially covered by a fluttering curtain.

'Ooh, I've missed that,' I laughed, pulling away from him. Given the strict rules of zero promiscuity in the household and the fact that we slept in separate rooms each night, we were on a kind of fast from each other.

Alex half-laughed, half-moaned. 'Three more days to Varkala, three more days to Varkala.'

And with one last kiss, he left.

* * *

'That was such an intense experience,' I declared as we entered Jaipur airport. 'When I get to Varkala I swear I'm just going to lie on the beach for a week and talk to no one.'

'Did I give you the tickets?' Alex asked, checking his pockets.

'Yes!' I took them back out of my bag and waved them at him for the second time that morning. 'You're such a tense traveller, relax.'

As I put them back, the large *dupatta* of my new Indian suit got tangled up and I fumbled awkwardly, realising it had caught in the zip of my bag.

Alex and his cousin Sartaj, a man with a keen eye for style, had taken me shopping a few days after the wedding, kitting me out with some pretty day-to-day Indian suits. Together with the henna on my hands and my sparkly bangles, I got approving looks wherever I went. The only slight issue was that I was constantly getting myself tangled up in all the extra material and, instead of the elegant grace with which Indian women carried themselves, I must have looked as clumsy as a toddler in her mum's high heels. I had to wonder: how did Indian women manage to do normal stuff like housework and cooking without either strangling themselves or setting their clothes on fire?

We went through security and the uniformed woman had a delighted smile on her face as she scanned the metal detector up and down my body.

'Very nice suit, madam! You are looking very nice!'

I smiled and thanked her and then tripped over my scarf going round to collect my hand luggage.

As we sat by our gate waiting to board, the week's events ran through my head, a whirlwind of colour and chaos. Intense didn't even begin to cover it. On the day before we left, sitting in a cousin's home with Alex and several of his female relatives (including his other older sister, Majeeden), they grilled Alex with questions about me, finally able to satisfy some of their curiosity.

'Does she live with her parents? *No?* Why?' This was the first shocker for them as the whole independent, solitary, Western theme baffled them. Why would you want to be alone when you could have company? (Not that you have much choice in India.)

'Does she have any brothers or sisters? Ah, two older brothers. They are married, yes? NO?'

This was even more confusing. Given I should have already been married by now (at the ripe old age of twenty-four), my brothers' bachelorhood stunned them.

'So, what is her religion? What do you mean she doesn't have one? Of course she does!'

They didn't seem to care that I wasn't Muslim, but the idea that I didn't follow some particular faith – *anything* – was one of the hardest concepts for them to accept. Eventually I conceded that I'd been born a Catholic, just to ease their minds. Explaining why I no longer followed dogmatic religions and their imperious ideals was for another day.

As I reflected on his family and being in Jaipur, there was one thing about the whole experience that caught my attention: despite the fact that I was the weird white girl who wore ugly Western clothes, spoke no Hindi and worse still was some kind of faithless heathen, they seemed to have accepted me, warts and all. I couldn't help a grin of delight upon realising I had not only survived meeting the in-laws, I had been welcomed into the entire clan with open arms, including even Alex's father. Well, I guess I can't say that for certain; I never actually sat down with him and had a heart-to-heart over chai or anything. But Alex had informed me that his dad had told him off on two occasions, once for leaving me in my room without switching on the AC, the second time for dragging me around the city all day in the boiling heat. It seemed there was rather a soft heart beneath the outer veneer and that maybe I'd made an OK first impression after all.

Meet the parents (or rather, the entire extended family) had been quite the success.

Chapter 28

Road trips

We spent just two more weeks in Varkala. The season was really drawing to a close now. The boys' shop had recently shut and all along the cliff were the skeletal remains of closed-up premises, many of them covered in battened-down tarpaulins for protection against the approaching monsoon season. The normally lively and boisterous cliff was nearly deserted, with only a smattering of tourists braving the formidable April and May heat. To be perfectly honest, I couldn't wait to leave.

For five months I had been based here and, while it was very beautiful, a mere ten-minute walk anywhere was exhausting in the heavy heat; the sea wasn't fun given its swirling waves and, besides Hope, I had found no one else to hang out with. I was so ready for a change of scene.

As we loaded up the car to bursting point on our last day, there was excitement in my tummy of the kind a kid feels just before Christmas. We were heading some 2,500 km north to Jaipur. After that, once the boys had all spent sufficient time back with their families (whom they hadn't seen in around five months), we would probably all travel up to the mountains. I couldn't wait. After so long by the sea, the thought of being high up in the fresh air of the

Himalayas sounded wonderful. Sid started the engine and moments later we were on the road. It was all I could do not to whoop out loud with delight as we zipped past familiar streets and places for the last time. No offence or anything, Varkala, I silently intoned. But I'm sick of the sight of you!

And with that, I settled back in my seat for the long drive north to Goa, which would be our first stop along the way. Alex and Ameer had caught a train the previous day, stopping off at Mangalore for business. They would join us in Goa the next day. Manju sat up front, leaving Ballu and me in the back and, with a few large bags between us, I was able to curl up and sleep most of the night while Sid drove us toward Goa.

There were numerous chai stops of course, but aside from a thirty-minute snooze late the next morning, Sid more or less just kept driving until we finally pulled up near Palolem beach around 5 pm that day … twenty-four hours after we had left Varkala.

Given it was now off-season in Goa, cheap accommodation was plentiful and we quickly found two cute beach huts, one for me and Alex (who had not yet arrived) and one for all the lads. After a delicious dinner in the nearby restaurant we were all asleep early, worn out from the long journey, though none of us could claim quite the same level of exhaustion as poor Sid.

A sound awoke me in the middle of the night. Disoriented, I sat up, wondering what was going on, till I heard a knock at the door and a lovely, familiar voice. I got out of bed and walked over.

'You're here! I thought you wouldn't make it till tomorrow?'

'We caught an earlier train,' Alex spoke softly, coming in and closing the door behind him. 'Sorry to wake you, *beta*.'

'No problem.'

I yawned, throwing my arms around him for a hug. Then we both climbed into bed and fell fast asleep, snuggled up to each other. Now the Goa holiday could really begin.

* * *

After so long in Varkala where the boys were never fully at ease (partly because of unfriendly territorial locals, partly because of the complex language of Malayalam), they seemed to totally relax in Goa, chatting and joking with the hotel staff and playing cricket with them each evening. It helped that the guys from the hotel spoke Hindi, the boys' own language, and it also helped that the boys were now officially on holiday themselves and not thinking about business anymore. Alex, a new man since leaving Varkala, took to holding my hand every chance he got. I swam each day, delighting in a sea that wasn't quite as violently terrifying as the waters of Kerala, and I willingly put up with the inevitable bikini malfunctions for the chance to cool off in the intense pre-monsoon heat.

By the end of the week my skin had turned a deep golden brown, my sensual pleasures had been indulged and pampered and it was quite possible that my belly expanded several sizes. (What is it about Goa and me eating to excess?) The day came too soon when we had to pack up and continue the gruelling drive up to Rajasthan. This time Ballu caught a train on ahead of us and in his place were both Alex and Ameer, which meant that, just like when I was a kid on family trips, Liz spent most of the journey squished in the middle of the back seat, making the long arduous road trip all the more challenging. The mid-May heat was horrendous. We had air-conditioning in the car but there were a few occasions when, low on fuel and still miles away from a gas station, we were obliged to switch it off and make do with opened windows – it felt like being roasted in a fan oven.

We left Palolem at dusk, driving through the night until around lunchtime next day when, unsurprisingly, Sid completely ran out of steam. At that point, my sweet, slightly anxious man took over the wheel and let Sid pass out in the back for a couple hours. Anyone taking on India's wild traffic needs a steely resolve but for Alex, not the most confident of drivers, it was particularly nerve-wracking: he sat bolt upright, as tense and vigilant at the wheel as a wound-up squirrel. But thanks to him we managed to cover more ground while Sid recharged his batteries. The landscape changed bit by bit, lush vegetation being replaced by dusty fields, tropical plants dwindling before disappearing almost completely.

On and on and on – the high sun started descending towards the horizon and still we kept on driving. She set completely and the sky became black as coal and we were still going until, finally, I dozed off. Vaguely registering that the car had stopped and the boys were getting out, I took full advantage of the empty back seat and sprawled across it. A little later, I awoke to an irritating burning sensation in my arms and legs. I scratched at it for a while until the infuriating high-pitched whirring made me realise what was going on. Somebody had left the windows open and a cloud of mosquitoes was now feasting on my exposed limbs. Sitting up, I swatted vainly at the little critters circling around me like tiny buzzing birds of prey, all trying to find a juicy patch of skin to land on.

'Gotcha! Eeeww.'

The mashed up little insect was mixed up with a trickle of blood – my blood. Without thinking, I wiped my hand on the car seat before slapping at another one, and another. My tree-hugging ideals of non-violence had vanished; the little buggers had to go. Eventually I realised that I needed to quit my rather futile mosquito blitzkrieg before I started smashing the car along with them. I got out of the vehicle and wandered wearily over to Alex and Manju, who were up drinking chai.

We had pulled over at one of India's many highway pit stops, open through the night and offering food, drinks and free camp beds to sleep on. Travellers on overnight buses, heavy-goods truck drivers and of course people like us could stop at these points to eat or rest during long journeys. Alex handed me his little chai cup and I took a sip, spotting Sid and Ameer across from us, fast asleep on two of the camp beds and wrapped up in bedsheets from head to toe like mummies. Unfortunately, mosquitoes are clever as well as infuriating. The sneaky buggers were flying up in the gaps between the slatted canvas underneath, munching greedily on the boys' backs. Poor Sid eventually gave up, much as I had, tiredly pulling himself up from the bed and joining us. He lifted up his T-shirt revealing around fifteen large red welts on his back. It wasn't a pretty sight.

By 8 am next morning, after a spicy Indian breakfast, we were on the road again. Several hours of driving brought us to Palanpur, a city in the state of Gujarat, after nearly two full days on the road. There was some difficulty in finding a suitable hotel that had the required C-forms for tourists since Palanpur wasn't exactly on India's tourist trail. The C-form is a piece of paper that foreign tourists must fill in with their passport details and other relevant information. All hotels are obliged by law to have them if they have non-nationals as guests and it provides a degree of security for foreign travellers in India, as the forms are always sent on to the local police office. We finally found a hotel that had them and were able to shower and freshen up, which, believe me, was much needed after forty-five hours in a car.

Then the bomb blasts in Jaipur happened. Around eight detonations in the space of fifteen minutes, right in the crowded main bazaar of the old part of the city. The boys were blessed that none of their family or friends were hurt and, despite the exhaustion from our travels, they remained glued to the television screen till late that night, poring over the news images of their beloved city. We were supposed to spend two nights in Palanpur before heading on to Jaipur. But at 10 pm the following night, when I was already in bed watching TV and just about ready to go to sleep, Alex entered the room full of business.

'Darling, pack your stuff. We go!'

'Now?' I stared at him, my heart sinking.

'We need to go, *beta*. I'm sorry, but we can't stay in Gujarat.' He seemed worried. 'Maybe this bomb blast cause problems or riots; I want to be with my family just in case.'

With a weary sigh, I hauled myself out of the bed and got ready to leave. Thirty minutes later we were driving through the night once again. India is a country of so many differing religions and customs and, despite being such a huge melting pot of diverse faiths and beliefs, it does work for the most part. But violence and riots have happened several times in India's recent past, sometimes sparked by an incident similar to the bombings in Jaipur; it was only natural that the boys were anxious to get home as soon as possible.

So we left.

Our mammoth drive from Varkala to Jaipur lasted another fourteen hours until we finally pulled up outside Alex's home. We grabbed our bags from the boot and said our goodbyes to the rest of the crew, then Alex knocked on a door to the house that opened onto the street, peering inside the mesh upper half into Majid's home. A moment later, his niece Anjum let us in with a shy smile and we went into the same room I'd stayed in on the previous visit. We were finally there. I hoped I wouldn't have to sit in a car again for a long, long time.

* * *

Being back with the family once more was challenging, Alex's young nieces and nephews clustering around me like bees to a flower, but it was also kind of sweet. Indian family life is so full of energy, there's never a dull moment. There were constantly kids running in and out of the rooms and there was nearly always some upbeat Bollywood music pulsing out of the speakers upstairs. The adults in the family seemed delighted that the funny white girl who didn't speak Hindi was walking in their midst once again. Many hours were whiled away sitting with various sisters-in-law, all of them enjoying the novelty of my presence while Alex headed out and ran errands or met up with friends.

But, just like my previous visit back in April, it wasn't easy spending so much time being the centre of attention and not knowing what was going on around me; any time relatives came to visit I was asked to pose for endless photographs as they chatted and giggled and pointed at me. I often felt as if I should be in the zoo with a tag explaining my name and origins. The thing was, I couldn't get mad at his family, since every time I tried they would do something sweet like offering me a gift or some food or asking if I needed water or wanted to rest, treating me like a precious gem. They were incredibly kind and generous people and it wasn't their fault I had landed in their home and spoke no Hindi. No, I couldn't get mad at them. But I could get mad at Alex.

While I sat around the house each day, the skin melting off my face in the heat, Alex kept promising we'd do this or that: visit the famous Monkey Temple, go to the cinema, shop for Indian outfits or go out for coffee. I could easily have headed out by myself if I'd known that was really what I should be doing but instead, I sat around waiting for a boy who had so many things going on he'd completely forgotten all of our plans. The pressure cooker was turned up full again and getting very close to exploding. On one particular afternoon, after sitting around for hours yet again waiting for him, the steam was practically coming out of my ears by the time Alex arrived home.

'What's wrong, *beta*?' His tentative question. You could almost hear his heart sinking as he took in my foul mood, knowing what this might entail.

'Nothing!' Translation: everything, and if you don't realise that by now, then get down on your knees and start praying.

'OK.' Nervous reply. Like most men, he was bewildered by my 'all is well' answer versus the vibes of hot angry flames radiating off my body. 'So, we go to my sister's house then?'

'I thought we were going to the cinema tonight?' This through gritted teeth, flames licking the floor by his feet. I could see it in his eyes before he said anything; he'd forgotten all about our movie plans for this evening.

'Shit! Sorry, *beta*, I forgot–'

'You promised!' I berated him vehemently.

'I know, but I completely forgot. I told my sister we will call to her tonight,' he implored, still standing in the doorway, almost as though ready to flee at any moment. '*Beta*? We can go to cinema tomorrow, no?'

And then his phone started ringing, that awful, hateful, despicable piece of technology that seemed to go off every ten minutes since we had reached Jaipur. He automatically reached for it and I had a flashback to the previous day in the car: I had been mid-sentence when it started blaring and he picked it up and spoke in Hindi, like I wasn't even there. The shrill ringtone was like a red flag to my bull.

'Don't. You. Dare. Answer. That!' He recognised the murderous tone to my words and quickly silenced the machine before tossing it aside.

'I'm so sorry, *beta*, really. I completely forgot. We can go to the cinema tomorrow, I promise.' He was really trying now, coming over to me and throwing an arm around my shoulders, kissing me gently on the cheek.

'Is that just another wild promise?' I questioned sourly. 'You've been making a lot of them recently, I'm starting to think you never mean what you say.'

'*Arrey*, no, *beta*, I just been distracted. I'm really sorry I forgot our plans tonight. Tomorrow we go to the cinema – real promise.' He smiled as I finally softened and no longer wished to throttle his neck. 'Oh, my angry baby,' he laughed gently, pulling me in close for a hug.

'Sorry.' I sighed. 'I think it's the heat, it's so exhausting.'

'Then let's go to the mountains with the boys,' Alex suddenly suggested. 'Jaipur's too hot for us too. Let's go to Kasol or Shimla where it's cooler.'

'I think that's the best thing you've said all day.'

'OK, tomorrow I call the others and book the tickets. Sorry, *beta*, to leave you in the house by yourself.'

'Do it again and you *will* be sorry. Kidding, darling, I'm just kidding!'

In the end it was just us two and Ameer who caught an overnight bus to the hill town of Shimla a couple days later. As we pulled out of the centre of Jaipur, our vehicle was held up by an extravagant wedding procession and when we were finally able to overtake the huge group it was astounding: it seemed to go on for miles, with dozens of musicians blaring their instruments and pounding their drums amid the crowds of elegant, colourful humans. Midway, we passed a large fancy carriage filled mostly with kids and both surrounded and pulled by six lavishly decorated white horses, preceded by four oxen, also in fancy dress.

Ahead of this great display of noisy extravagance came the swinging rumps of four camels in sparkling costumes. But the *pièce de résistance*, the phenomenal (and enormous) cherry on top, was the creature leading the parade in all his towering glory: a giant, lumbering bejewelled elephant. It was the most incredible wedding procession I had ever seen.

Where the groom had been within the extravaganza, who could tell! The wild, warbling music faded into the distance and finally the bus picked up speed and carried us on our way. Only in India, my friend, only in India.

Chapter 29

Delhi belly

As the sky lightened next morning, the roads started ascending in earnest, our bus swerving around narrow, twisting bends, slowly but surely taking us higher and higher towards Shimla. This was my first time venturing so far north into India's mountains and with the damp grey and the abundance of greenery, it felt almost like home (aside from the fact that some of the region's valleys looked to be about the size of Ireland itself).

High up in the mountains, Shimla provided breathtaking views of lush green valleys below while the small town had a strong colonial influence. It had always been one of the more popular hill towns for the British when they wished to escape the intense heat of the low-lying cities and I could understand why: in late May it was a good twenty-ty-five degrees cooler than Jaipur. Shimla's preponderance of Indian tourists – specifically wealthy young honeymoon-ers – meant that cheap and cheerful accommodation was in short supply. It took us over an hour of trekking up and down the town's steep, winding streets to find a reasonably priced hotel and, despite the cooler weather, we were sweating by the time we eventually found a place to stay.

There didn't seem to be a lot to do in the pretty hill station (I could be very wrong about this but, as I've pointed out before, I'm not exactly big on travel research). Alex and Ameer, having already been there before, weren't interested in doing much beyond drinking chai and wandering through the town and I was too lazy to explore any of it myself, preferring to hang out in Café Coffee Day and drink sweet iced lattes. As a result, just a few days after arriving we were on the move again, travelling across the most nauseating, twisty, hilly roads that made me feel like I might spew vomit out of the bus window, much like the poor woman behind me was doing. It was a relief when we finally reached Kasol, another hill town, this time in a region called the Parvatti Valley.

Kasol, nestled deep into the hills with just a sprinkling of shops, restaurants and hotels, was not a very happening place and it may just have had something to do with the vast quantities of a certain plant that grew freely along the side of the road. Half the Israeli population seemed to reside in the little town, spending their days lounging in cafés and restaurants, obscured by thick white clouds of weed. Despite the huge numbers of this infamously raucous and noisy nationality, they were all notably calm and chilled out. Funny that.

While there, Alex and Ameer dabbled in the soft stuff too. Well, Alex dabbled while Ameer indulged like an alcoholic propelled off the wagon by rocket fuel. He didn't really talk much the entire time we were in Kasol and I don't know how much of it he remembers to this day. I, on the other hand, wasn't keen on a repeat experience of the disturbing paranoia it had instilled in me back in Pushkar, so I just hung out in the hotel with my stoned companions, frequently falling into a TV-induced stupor. There didn't seem to be a lot else to do; in fact there was even less to do than in Shimla, given there were no fancy coffee shops to go to. I could have got off my lazy bum and gone hiking, taking advantage of the incredible hill walks and beautiful views, but I think Adam's Peak may have killed all urges for such an activity (possibly ever again). So instead I lay on our bed staring at mindless Indian soap operas and the odd bit of cricket when the boys were awake enough to suggest it.

Just when I reached my limit of brain-numbing Indian television and started to feel like it was time for a change, it happened. On 1 June, exactly eight months to the very day that I arrived in India, in the middle of the night and in the depth of sleep, I was officially struck by the dreaded Delhi belly. Waking up and realising that my weird dreams had actually been my stomach yelling at me that it needed to hurl its contents, I scrambled into the bathroom and let it do just that. Sweet Alex roused himself and dutifully rubbed my back and held my hair out of the way.

The second time I made a nauseous dash for the bathroom, he stayed fast asleep and I couldn't blame him. What a thing to wake up to in the middle of the night, your girlfriend puking her guts up. Crawling weakly back into bed afterward, I thanked my lucky stars we had an en-suite. I was repeating these prayers throughout the following morning as I sprinted to the loo numerous times to do what I can only describe as a re-enactment of the post-enema incident in Sri Lanka; it took all my energy just to remain seated while praying fervently that my bum wasn't actually going to explode.

I spent the rest of the day in bed, dozing fitfully with a fever while my immune system waged war against the un-welcome occupants in my gut. During a couple of my more conscious moments, I mentally scanned the different meals

I'd had the day before. It was puzzling because I'd eaten much the same as the boys, other than breakfast which had been in the hotel as usual. OH! The second I recalled the *aloo paratha* I'd had for breakfast – a simple, spiced flatbread – my stomach reacted with a sharp, lurching cramp. It was as though my brain had brought along the previous day's meals for a police line-up and, upon inspecting the possible suspects, my gut started jumping up and down in agitation, pointing at the *aloo paratha* and shouting, 'That one! It was him, the bastard!'

It made no sense as we regularly ate meals in this hotel and seriously, how could you go wrong with fried bread and spices? But there was no ignoring the gut-wrenching discomfort I experienced each time I brought it to mind; rational explanation or not, the *aloo paratha* was definitely the cause of my illness. Alex minded me throughout the day and thankfully, in the late evening, things started improving and I was even able to eat some plain rice for dinner, my first meal in twenty-four hours. By the next day my fever had gone completely and my bathroom visits were solely for innocent pee-pee. My battle-scarred digestive system, still reeling from the events, took a little longer to recover.

Almost a week later I was a little concerned as things still weren't 100 per cent. I decided it might be time to get some professional help and sought out an Ayurvedic doctor who was close to our hotel. After a cursory inspection, he gave me some red little 'candy' pills that would help clear up what he considered to be a simple bacterial infection. I hoped he was right. Being sick would suck anywhere, but being sick while so far away from home was actually making me miss it the most I ever had on this trip, more even than when I'd had to say goodbye to Rob and Paul. I think I'd have been on the first plane back to Ireland if Alex hadn't been there with me.

It was a big relief when, on the eighth day after I first got sick, there was no movement down below whatsoever. On the second day of zero activity I reasoned this was a natural response to balance out the previous week's events. By the morning of the fifth day, with events in Sri Lanka still fresh in my mind, I was running back to the same Ayurvedic doctor and begging for something – anything – to get things going again. The pills this time were blue.

'Take two this evening with warm water,' he advised me. 'If there is no change, then tomorrow morning take two more.'

Feeling anxious about what on earth was happening with my body these days, I duly followed his instructions. Alex, Ameer and I were in a café, the boys playing pool with a couple of tourists, when I remembered to take the two bright blue little pills at around 5 pm. Hoping against hope to get my body back to normal, I washed them down with a glass of warm water. Thirty minutes later we left the café to go to a restaurant for dinner and as we walked outside, a very bizarre sensation in the depths of my body caught my attention; it was as though something large were stirring in there and it was accompanied by the feeling that I was having a kind of hot flush.

'Um, Alex, I don't feel too great.'

Alex glanced at me in concern. 'What's wrong, *beta*?'

'I don't really know but I think I might skip dinner.'

'Do you want me to come with you?'

'No, no, you guys go on ahead, I'll just go lie down for

a while in the room. Honestly,' I assured him with a smile. 'It's probably nothing but I'd feel better if I was back at our hotel room, near to a toilet.'

Alex frowned. 'Are you sure, *beta*? We can come back to the hotel if you like?'

'No – you and Ameer go have dinner and I'll see you later on.'

I gave him a quick kiss on the cheek and hurried back to our room where I flicked on the TV, grabbed the pillows and curled myself up in the foetal position. Waves of heat continued to roll through me along with sensations decidedly akin to an elephant lumbering around in my intestines. It wasn't painful but it certainly wasn't reassuring. Alex came back later and found me hugging a pillow, watching a random soccer game.

'How are you, *beta*?'

'Um, I don't know,' I replied, as the elephant continued to romp around my insides.

'What do you mean?'

I stared at him a moment, my mind somewhere else completely. 'Just give me a minute,' I finally said, getting off the bed and heading into the bathroom.

I wasn't even fully sure if this was what my body required, but, well you know, gut feelings and all that. After about fifteen minutes, Alex was knocking on the door.

'*Beta*? Are you OK in there?'

'Yup!' I answered cheerfully, understanding now what exactly had been in those blue pills and pleasantly surprised at how well they were working. It seemed at last that with the help of some Ayurvedic medicine, my bowels were back to optimum functioning levels.

The entire saga had lasted nearly two weeks, but the main thing was that I'd finally survived the dreaded Delhi belly, one of my biggest worries before embarking on my trip. It was a delightfully gruesome tale to add to my collection, which I made sure to share with Sid, Manju and Hazeen (another good friend from Jaipur) who all arrived next day. They were suitably disgusted.

* * *

I wasn't sorry to get in a taxi and leave Kasol several days later: I would always associate it with being ill and it was time for something different to clear the senses and bring me back to my old self. A better place I couldn't imagine than further on in the Himalayas, in a region that was the base for the Dalai Lama and his Tibetan government in exile. We were heading to Dharamshala.

The sky was dark grey and the air saturated when I woke next morning in Pine Tree Lodge guest house. We had arrived late the previous night, hiking downhill from the main road to reach a particular guest house where Rej, an old friend of Alex's, worked, and we'd bunked in his spacious room for the night. Leaving the boys still asleep, I pulled on my one warm hoodie and stepped outside to the large terrace to view the surrounding area for the first time. Enormous steep hills veered up behind and either side of us, giving me the feeling we were nestled in a gigantic Himalayan bosom. On my right was a sprawling forest of huge, glistening conifer trees. Behind us and all along the other hill was a smattering of trees with many hotels, restaurants and local homes dotting the natural landscape. As I breathed in the cool wet air, I realised how peacefully quiet – and very 'un-Indian' – it was.

There was one road close by, which led from the central town of MacLeod Ganj below (home base for the Tibetan community and the Dalai Lama's Tibetan government) right up to Dharamkot, a small area with restaurants and hotels further uphill from us. To get to that road wasn't easy (especially when lugging heavy bags in the dark of night, I might add). The only other route to MacLeod Ganj was to walk ten minutes down the steep hill to Bhagsu and follow the main road from there. But Bhagsu collected beeping, fume-pumping vehicles the way spilled honey collects ants; it was a full-force assault on the senses and a quick reminder that you were most definitely still in India. Where we were staying was far away from any of the pollution or chaos and exquisitely tranquil. For a girl who'd grown up in the empty Irish countryside and had been starved of anything even vaguely resembling it for the past eight months, it was deeply comforting to be in this damp, woody landscape again.

'Good morning, ma'am,' Rej greeted me with a big smile as he came outside from the small kitchen. 'You want chai?'

'Yes, Rej-*bhai*! She wants chai.' I turned around to see Alex standing in the doorway, gazing around blearily and yawning. He caught my eye and saluted me before pulling his blanket tighter around him. 'Morning, *beta*.'

'Good morning, sleepyhead.' I laughed as he swayed back and forth, trying to wake up. Rej and he chatted in Hindi a few moments before Rej headed back to the kitchen to make us tea. Alex came over to where I was standing under the roof's eave.

'This is so lovely, I feel like I'm back home,' I told him, linking his arm with mine and snuggling up to him for warmth. There was a background hum from the light drizzle, decorated here and there with sweet sing-song from little birds and that delightful scent of damp earth.

'Does it rain a lot in Ireland?' Alex asked, rubbing sleep from the corner of his eye.

'That is a ridiculous question,' I told him sternly. 'Have you learned nothing from me these past six months?'

'My mom says, 'a bad teacher blames her students'.'

I gave him a small shove. 'Yes, it rains in Ireland, my god does it rain in Ireland. As you'll find out when you come back with me.'

'Then I need a visa,' Alex reminded me.

'So, let's get that process started today. I go home in only two months and we've no idea how long it takes.'

'This afternoon we can go to the town and apply online.'

'How exciting!' I grinned, squeezing his arm at the thought of bringing him home to Ireland.

As we sat there quietly, I noticed several hens roaming around in the neighbour's garden below us. One robust, white-feathered mama had two little yellow chicks at her side who were cutely imitating her, scratching at the earth, foraging for worms and gradually venturing away from her. A movement in a bush caught my eye and a second later, I realised what it was. A mongoose was stealthily stalking the babies. Sure enough, it suddenly darted forwards, snatching one of the chicks in its mouth then racing away from the squawking, distressed mother hen who was in rapid, hot pursuit. She made such a ruckus, the mother of the house hurried outside to see what was going on, but there was nothing anyone could do; the mongoose was gone already.

'Wow! It's like *Animal Planet* up here,' I commented to Alex, feeling a pang as the mother hen returned to her one chick with mournful clucks and cries. Nature can be cruel.

'Good morning.' Sid had just come out to join us. We shuffled over on the dry step to make room for him as he called to Rej for extra chai.

'It's bloody wet,' he said, gazing out at the misty land-scape.

'I was telling Alex, it feels like home for me,' I said.

'So, it's raining a lot in Ireland?' he asked curiously.

'A *lot*.'

Sid looked at me a moment. 'Leeze, you are not looking good these days,' he said bluntly. 'You look weak, very pale.'

One of the most notable things about Sid was how honest he was; he always said it like he saw it, never sugar-coating the truth to save people's feelings. It was good on the one hand, since you never had to second-guess him, but at moments like this his candour could sting a little.

'We're not in Kerala anymore; you're just used to seeing me with a tan.'

'I don't think so. Are you sure you're in full health?'

'Yes. Jeez, you really know how to make a girl feel good about herself!' I snapped.

'Leeze, don't get mad,' Sid said in an infuriating, old-er-brother way. 'I think you are looking a little sick. Tell her, Alex-*bhai*.'

Alex turned his gaze on me a moment and pondered. 'Maybe he's right, I think you looks kind of weak too.'

Before I could respond, Rej arrived with small steaming glasses of chai and the three boys began chatting in Hindi, leaving me to consider their words. In fact this wasn't the first time one of the boys had commented on my appearance; Ameer had mentioned something similar recently. It was probably nothing, I decided. After all, as I'd told Sid, they were so used to seeing me with a tropical, golden tan which had faded this past month, it was hardly surprising if I didn't look quite so glowing anymore. I thought little more of it until later on that day, when I was coming out of the shower.

Putting on my cotton trousers, I pulled the drawstring belt around and noticed for the first time the excess of material at the front. They'd always been a little loose on me but now they appeared to have grown three sizes too big. As I stared down at the suddenly enormous pants, I remembered how my new Mumbai jeans had lost their shape recently too. I'd initially put that down to normal stretching but in fact, no jeans I'd had before had ever stretched to the point that my bum disappeared. The realisation dawned that my body must have recently shrunk several sizes; had I just lost a ton of weight from being sick? I guessed so, as I stared down at the baggy trousers. Come to think of it, I'd had a few dizzy spells too, especially when getting out of bed. It must have been from being ill in Kasol, there was no other explanation for it. With a shrug, I decided there wasn't much to do about it. I felt fine, hopefully it was simply a case of needing new clothes.

The next few weeks in Dharamshala – or the little towns of Bhagsu and MacLeod Ganj to be precise – were in sharp contrast to the previous eight months of my trip. Days were spent in cool green nature, hiking up and down hills, carrying rainbow-coloured umbrellas and purchasing decent runners to keep my chilled feet dry. Yes, that's right, chilled feet in India. How times had changed.

That's not all that had changed either; with such a predominance of Tibetans and Buddhist monks in the area, there was a very different vibe in the air. The Tibetans had a softer, quieter energy and their music sang of mighty mountains and untamed wilderness. It was a delightful mix of Indian and Tibetan culture, though of course some things remained the same: the chai and curries were still delicious and the traffic, by the main town square, was utterly chaotic. It was still very much India.

Chapter 30

Visa runs and skin and bones

June 24 dawned sunny and bright for the first time since we'd arrived, over a week before. It was a novelty to see the hills bathed in warm sunshine and a sky as blue as the ocean. I turned over in bed and Alex pulled me in for a cuddle.

'Happy birthday, *beta*!' he said sleepily, punching the air in victory then wrapping his arm back around me.

'Twenty-five today, what a momentous occasion,' I said, snuggling up to him.

'Come on, *beta*, we can have vitamin D for breakfast,' Alex said as he stretched. He paused, frowning as he rummaged under the sleeping bag and came up with a handful of my underwear.

'Ooh, they're finally dry,' I said delightedly, holding them against my face to be sure. Alex was staring at me quizzically.

'I washed them about five days ago,' I explained. 'With the non-stop rain they just wouldn't dry properly so I stuffed them under the sleeping bag last night. And it worked!'

'Very good, Miss Laundry Expert. Now, time for chai.'

It truly was a fabulous birthday morning up in the fresh, rain-washed mountains, the sun streaming light and warmth down on us from a perfectly blue sky. We charged up on solar energy, soon joined by the rest of the guys, and finally we all strolled into MacLeod Ganj for a late breakfast and some shopping. Deciding to have lunch up in Dharamkot, the tiny town uphill from our hotel, we caught two tuk-tuks up from MacLeod Ganj and happened to be dropped off outside the Vipassana meditation centre. I stared at the iconic gates with the symbol of the wheel of *Dharma* (truth) on it as Alex paid the fare. I had completed two Vipassana ten-day retreats before in Ireland (and of course I met Jack on the second one, when we were both part of the team of voluntary servers). I had always wanted to sit one while in India, given this was the country it originated in and, with barely two months until I returned home, it seemed like it was now or never.

'Alex, I'll follow you guys on. I'm going to run up and see if there are any spaces on the next course.' Before I could change my mind, I headed into the centre's grounds and within ten minutes I was registered for the ten-day retreat starting on 15 July, just three weeks away. I felt a mixture of relief and dread now that it was definitely happening.

A Vipassana meditation course is no blissful pampering retreat, you see. On the contrary, it is one of the most demanding (and effective) meditation techniques I've ever tried. It's a bit like waxing your legs – a bitch at the time but with fantastic results for ages after (though Vipassana meditation is possibly a more valuable use of your time). At any rate, challenging or not, a silent meditation retreat in the mountains seemed a fitting way to round off my epic trip to India, a land of such tangible spiritual energy.

I joined Alex in a café with amazing views of the valley below and shared my news. Asking where the boys were, he told me they had gone back to Pine Tree Lodge to cook up a feast for the evening and, when we finally went back to join them, it turned out they'd also decorated the little makeshift lounge next to the kitchen with streamers and balloons, while Hazeen had created one of the most delicious curries of all time.

This was followed by a rather massive chocolate cake with numbered candles marking my quarter-of-a-century milestone. I soaked up the love and companionship of my dear Indian brothers and my ever-loving, ever-devoted, cheeky sweetheart and decided it was probably one of my better birthdays. Then I scoffed half the cake, hoping to add some fat to my scrawny little body.

* * *

Over a week later, Sid, Alex and I were sitting on a bus heading back to Jaipur. In the intervening time we had begun the complicated process of applying for an Irish tourist visa for Alex. After many mistakes and phone calls to embassies, our online application was finally correctly submitted and we received a date on which to go to the VSF office in Delhi to apply in person. While Alex and I tackled the Irish one, Sid also applied for a French visa, hoping to visit a woman he'd met several times in Goa. My parents were thrilled when we asked them if they'd write a letter of sponsorship for Alex as part of his application process; I guessed they were pretty keen to meet this man who'd kept me away from Ireland for so long.

So it was that the three of us travelled down from the mountains to Rajasthan and set about the complex task of sorting out both visa applications, in a city that was hot enough to make your internal organs spontaneously combust.

We didn't spend much time with the family and so proper interaction with Alex's father was postponed yet again, although I did get a few stern nods in response to my polite greetings whenever I saw him. But our days in the pink city were a whirlwind of non-stop errands, printing off bank statements and sponsor letters from my parents and organising travel insurance, flight tickets, pages of detailed information about Alex's relationship to me and postal order fees. At 9 pm on the day before the boys had their appointments in New Delhi, we were still typing and printing documents in an internet café. After an entire day spent running around, we finally headed to the capital, once again driving through the night. We were all worn out from the day's stressful activities, yet still Sid managed to drive the entire way. When we arrived into Delhi early next morning, he had enormous black circles under his drooping eyes and a grey pallor to his caramel skin.

'Well done, my friend,' I teased. 'Today you can sleep.'

He smiled in spite of his exhaustion. We found a cheap hotel where the boys were able to freshen up and then caught a rickshaw to the French embassy, located conveniently close to the Irish VSF office. Just to add more stress to the whole thing, traffic was rush-hour busy and Sid's 9 am appointment ticked closer and closer as we made snail-like progress. But I needn't have worried; we made it on time and a short while later Alex submitted his application form in person at the nearby Irish office. It seemed it was all over.

'What an ordeal!' I exclaimed, flopping back onto the couch of the cool, clean Café Coffee Day.

'How long did they say until you find out?' I asked Alex, who looked almost as tired as Sid.

'Just one week.'

'Oh.' I paused as I realised something. 'That means I'll have just started Vipassana. Damn it, I'll have to wait till the end of the course to find out.'

Alex shrugged. 'It's only a few days, *beta*.'

'But I want to know *now*! You have to get your visa and come home with me,' I told him fervently. 'I couldn't imagine going back to Ireland without you.'

'So let's hope I get it,' Alex replied calmly, taking a sip of his coffee.

I gave his arm a squeeze, taking a slurp of my own drink and gradually calming down. I glanced over at Sid sitting across from us.

'Maybe we should get him back to the hotel before he falls off the couch,' I pointed out, noticing our tired friend's eyes had closed as he slumped down on the sofa.

We spent two full days in the centre of Delhi, doing a spot of shopping and sightseeing. Most of the visa-run day I spent by myself while the boys slept off their tiredness. On the second day, as we strolled around the city, we passed through a bus station and saw a funny machine that made me stop. It was a large, electronic weighing scales.

'Hey guys, hang on a second,' I told them, walking up to the huge piece of technology. It looked like some kind of juke-box or arcade games machine, with flashing lights and a little screen that gave instructions. I stood up on the pedals and slotted in my coin. After some funny bleeping noises, a tiny card popped out below. I picked it up and saw a printed drawing of Salman Khan – one of Bollywood's superstars – followed by the amount I supposedly weighed. Now I say supposedly because the number was so bizarre it had to be wrong. A little disappointed, I pocketed the card while Sid tried it out.

'I've gained two kilos,' he declared, stepping off the machine as he read his own little card.

A little put out that it worked for him and not me, I shrugged it off and we strolled on. What did we come upon next but a middle-aged man, sitting cross-legged on the pavement next to a typical bathroom weighing scales, charging two rupees (about three cents) for people to weigh themselves! My curiosity piqued after the incident with the Salman Khan card, I stepped onto the scales and watched the needle swing around and then stared and stared as it settled on the exact same number Salman Khan had given me: fifty kilos. I had apparently lost a whopping eight kilos in about four weeks.

'Shi-eeeet,' I breathed as I glanced down at my waist, imagining (much as I would have longed for back in the days of Agonda) that I could literally see it shrinking before my eyes. Only now I was slightly freaked. It's not like I'd been that big to start with and yet I seemed to have turned from a sturdy horse into an anorexic gazelle. How sick had I been? Had I pooped out half my insides?

'Oh my God, I'm wasting away,' I exclaimed as I got down off the scales and then stood up on it again to double check. 'Look!' I pointed at the needle, as Alex and Sid peered down beside me. 'No wonder none of my clothes fit me anymore.'

'*Beta*, you don't listen to us,' Alex told me reprovingly.

'*Arrey*, Leeze, I told you that you were looking weak,' Sid chimed in smugly.

'I'm not weak, I'm skin and bones! Apparently, a chunk of me disappeared down the toilets of Kasol.'

'*Arrey*, Liz, that's disgusting!'

'Sure but it's also true, darling.'

'Enough. Stop talking, Liz. You want to see Lotus Temple today or no?'

'OK, sure. I want to eat a bucket of ice cream too.'

Lotus Temple is a stunning work of art. The outer structure of the building is designed and built literally in the shape of a giant white lotus flower, sort of like the Sydney Opera house on a smaller scale. Lotus Temple, however, is a special house of worship, its doors open to each and every creed, its quiet, simple interior a soothing meditative retreat from India's frantic buzz and chaos.

I sat cross-legged on a shiny wooden pew, sunlight streaming in through the expansive windows, the soft patter of many bare feet and hushed voices resonating throughout the large hall, reminiscent of any church or cathedral I've ever visited. With a contented smile, I breathed in the peace and calm of the atmosphere. Uninterested in tranquil meditation, the boys chatted behind me until a cross official glared over at them, uttering a whispered yet forceful 'Quiet!' It shut them up for a second until they started sniggering together like naughty schoolboys. I sighed as the woman looked daggers at them, realising it was perhaps time to leave before we got kicked out.

Dinner that night was in the jam-packed quarters of Old Delhi, right alongside the capital's incredible sprawling mosque, Jamma Masjid. This was a section of Delhi new to my eyes. Literally crammed with humans, the streets, the pavements and the shops were all abuzz with constant movement and activity. We headed down a narrow alley heaving with bodies then turned left into a busy restaurant, joining a line of customers waiting to be seated.

'This is the best place in Delhi for meat,' Alex told me, raising his voice above the din. 'It's always completely packed. You will not get food this good anywhere else.'

A burly, sweaty waiter gestured to the family at the top of the line to follow him to a free table. Returning a moment later he looked us over, asking the boys how many, with barely a glance at me. It was refreshing to be somewhat ignored.

'They definitely have vegetarian food here, right?' I asked Alex later, as we were shown to our own table.

'Yes, of course. But this place is better for meat,' he added truthfully.

Yay, I thought to myself, hoping they wouldn't cook my lentils in halal goat fat.

Given that, in India, it's often better not to think too much about just how your food's been prepared, I blocked out any imaginings of what might have made its way into my curry and enjoyed the meal, fascinated at how the restaurant just never seemed to stop filling up. There was a constant line of people waiting to be seated and as soon as a table became free, less than a minute later there were new customers seated at it. Leaving the still-packed and bustling restaurant a couple hours later, we negotiated the manic streets to catch a tuk-tuk back to our hotel. As we walked, a young boy around fourteen or fifteen years old, with a dirty shaved head and filthy ragged clothes, started badgering us for money. His eyes had a distant glaze to them while his repetitive mantra 'Money, you give me money' sounded vacant and dull.

He motioned towards his mouth in the familiar begging gesture for food, but it was pretty obvious that if he got any money it would not be spent on a nourishing meal. As he doggedly trailed us, he collided with some smartly dressed Indian men. One of them grabbed the boy roughly by his shirt and shouted at him before angrily tossing him aside on the path. I stared at the scene in front of me, disturbed and shocked. The men simply carried on walking while the boy shook his head like a confused dog before scrambling clumsily to his feet and persisting in his single-minded attempts to wrangle money out of us. We got into a tuk-tuk that started to slowly pull out of the crowds and yet still the kid wouldn't quit.

'Moneee – give me moneeeeee,' he whined dully, his voice vibrating as he jogged alongside the taxi, his bare feet slapping the tarmac. The wretchedness of the situation made me feel sick. Sid took a coin from his pocket and handed it to the boy and finally the drug-destroyed young human stopped and fell behind the three-wheeler, returning to his soulless treadmill of poverty and addiction. The loss of his future weighed heavily on me as we went to bed that night and knowing that his life was a reality also for so many other humans left a hopeless, hollow space inside me. Sleep was a long time coming.

The following morning, we left Delhi, and Sid drove us up into the mighty Himalayas. My Vipassana retreat began in a few days, and the boys planned to stay near MacLeod Ganj again with Ameer and a few more friends. As the scenery flashed by, I daydreamed and wondered how on earth I was going to manage the next ten days.

Vipassana courses are hard. There are no distractions from whatever is going on inside your head, and my thoughts were currently being fuelled by high-level anxiety after discovering how much weight I'd lost. On the one hand, I reminded myself that I felt fine and I probably was, so why worry? On the other hand, I could be about to go into organ failure and require emergency treatment while stuck in a remote meditation centre in the Himalayas. Added to this (slightly unrealistic) fear was the knowledge that I wasn't exactly going to be floating through the course like a dreamy sixties hippie; this was hard-core Vipassana, a kind of boot camp for meditation. You didn't exactly have a guy yelling 'drop and give me twenty!', but it could be just as brutal. I'd done two courses before in Ireland so I was well aware of what lay ahead of me: hard work and long days spent in nothing but my own company. I swallowed a lump in my throat as I, once again, prepared to dive into the unknown. For what is more daunting and unfamiliar than spending ten days in total silence, with nothing to distract you … from you?

Chapter 31

Vipassana

A gong sounded outside my room. It was pitch black. I climbed out of my sleeping bag, fumbled around for the light switch, grabbed my toothbrush and went to the bathrooms. Some early risers were already showering, but I figured I'd do it after breakfast or during the lunch break when I had more time. A few girls stood around me and we brushed our teeth together in silence apart from the soft drumming of rain, the splatter of the showers and the odd hawking noise as people spat out their toothpaste. I kept my gaze down, despite wanting to take a peek at the others. After all, I was here to work with focus and concentration.

Wow, I love her leg-warmers, I must get a pair like that once the course is over. Hey, I could bring home a few as gifts. Ooh, but they'd take up a lot of space and my backpack is already quite full. Maybe I should just get a pair for me, then ...

Catching myself, I shook my head slightly. Damn it, Liz, it's 4 am! There was a lot of work to be done.

The word Vipassana literally means insight, or clear-seeing, and that was what I was going to be working on during my retreat: learning to see and accept things just as they are. Hopefully. (Let's just say, the ten-day retreat is a mere starting point in a practice that requires many years of hard work to bring about real, lasting change.) Vipassana meditation has nothing to do with any organised religion: it is a method of deep, concentrated introspection. The courses are run by volunteers and rely solely on donations from students that have already completed at least one ten-day course. All participants must abide by five precepts for the duration of the retreat: no killing, no stealing, no lying, no sexual misconduct and no intoxicants. They must also observe Noble Silence – this doesn't just mean no talking, it means no communication whatsoever with those around you. You can speak with the teacher during the lunch break if you are struggling with the technique and there are course organisers that you can approach if you're having any practical issues, but the goal is to cultivate a sense of working in isolation. The fewer outer distractions, the quieter the mind gets, and the deeper and more powerful your meditation becomes.

The man responsible for creating these particular meditation courses, the venerable S.N. Goenka, was a Burmese businessman, grandfather, and a big character, full of love and humour. He passed away in 2013, but even in 2008 when I sat my course in the Himalayas, there was a different teacher present, just as there had been on the two courses I did in Ireland. Goenka's method of self-inquiry grew so popular over the years that, in order to reach more people but still preserve the purity of the practice, his instructions were recorded throughout one course. These same recordings are now used on each Vipassana retreat and the teacher (a trained assistant and long-time Vipassana practitioner) is there, in place of Goenka, to offer help and guidance to students. On my course, we had a sweet little Indian man who always dressed in white and who emanated graceful stillness like a meditative monk. Which, I guess, he was.

Goenka's Vipassana retreats are gruelling, there's no other word for it. Each day you rise at 4 am, meditating for approximately eleven hours until 9 pm. Lights are out by 9.30 pm and, besides eating and resting, there are no other activities: you don't read, you don't journal, you don't do yoga or any strenuous exercise, and you don't interact in any way with your fellow course-participators. The one slight reprieve each day is the evening discourse, an hour-long video of Goenka discussing the meditation process. His explanations and funny anecdotes help to clarify what you've learned that day and they always bring a touch of light-heartedness to what is otherwise a very intense experience.

For the first three days, you spend each meditation observing your breath as you inhale and exhale. That is literally all you do, all day, for eleven hours. It might sound straightforward, if a little boring, but it's practically impossible. What actually happens is that you catch the odd breath here and there, amid dreams of saving the world, the occasional snooze, scrutinising your fellow meditators and frequently singing random songs in your head over and over again. This, by the way, is normal – slightly crazy and erratic, yes, but totally normal. Each time you catch your mind wandering off like a little toddler, you gently bring it back to the breath. If you're really in the zone, you might catch it over a hundred times in one hour. Other times, you might hear the recording of Goenka, signalling the end of the meditation, and realise you literally didn't notice your breath once during the entire sixty minutes. Whether you succeed at keeping the mind consistently trained on the breath or not, the first three days help you to cultivate deeper focus and concentration and prepare you for the most important element of Vipassana: the body scan.

On the afternoon of the fourth day, Goenka talks you through your entire body, from the top of the head to the tips of the toes, then back up in reverse, instructing you to pause at each spot and observe what sensations are present. The point is to become aware of your current experience in the deepest layers of the body without reacting to whatever arises. You may experience numbness, tingling, discomfort or pain but instead of craving relief, or getting frustrated, you try to notice these sensations without any judgement. This is the fundamental practice of Vipassana: to undo your reactionary habits and train the mind to remain calm and clear at all times, no matter what is going on.

None of this is easy, you understand. I mean, it's hard enough just staying silent for ten days and sitting for hours working on the same thing over and over, all while being driven demented by a mind that's as rational and co-operative as a rabid monkey. But good old Goenka didn't stop there. He realised that the most powerful way to develop equanimity is to delve deep into unpleasant physical sensations, staying with them even when the one thing the mind wants is to run as far away from them as possible. So he decided that, after learning the body scan, there would be three one-hour group sittings each day during which students would be instructed to pick a comfortable position at the beginning of the meditation and to then stay completely still, right until the end. That, my friends, is what makes Vipassana so challenging.

Sixty minutes is a looooong time for the body to remain in one position. It's nearly guaranteed that you will get aching stiffness in your back or pins and needles in your feet or a pain in your knees; something in the body will become uncomfortable and your instinct will be to seek relief. Yet whatever arises, the aim is to not move a muscle; instead, you try to observe the discomfort with a calm mind, and then continue the body scan, diligently tuning into each area of the physical body. By consciously choosing to sit with the discomfort rather than react to it, you are providing yourself with a rare opportunity to see your pain for what it actually is, a bubble of constantly shifting and changing sensations. The universal nature of all things is that *this too shall pass*. Everything is in a state of impermanence, even pain, and the premise of Vipassana is that it is our powerful negative reactions that cause the most suffering, not the actual sensations themselves. Once we learn to calmly observe all physical sensations, without grasping on to the pleasant ones or desperately wishing the unpleasant ones away, then we can also learn to stop clinging fearfully to our desires; we can learn to stop getting stressed or furious when life's not going our way. With consistent, dedicated practice, we can reach the goal of Vipassana, which is to be truly happy and at home in ourselves, no matter what is going on.

However, it's not about sitting still no matter what: the one-hour group sitting is meant to be hard work, not torture. The point of it is to help develop a deep and powerful inner calm. I bring this up because, while I managed to sit through all of the one-hour sessions without moving, I relied on an immense amount of grit and determination to do it and spent a few of the sessions feeling about as calm and equanimous as a psychopath. Which I don't think is quite what Goenka intended.

One meditation in particular, on the sixth day at 6 pm, brought me to my knees both metaphorically and literally. It started off like any other: I was doing the body scan and had already completed a few rounds, which I now knew to mean we were nearing the end of the hour. Then, suddenly, I lost my concentration. My foolish mind wandered out of safe waters and, with a growing panic, I realised I couldn't get back into the flow of the body scan. Sharks had been prowling in the distance, kept at bay by my deep absorption in the process, but that barrier between us was now gone and they were making straight towards me with a speed and focus that was pee-in-your-pants terrifying.

These 'sharks' were the physical complaints coming from my body. Thanks to my distracted mind, all I could now see, hear or feel, was the most excruciating, most intensely horrific pain in both my knees. It was as though hell's inferno had suddenly been ignited in these joints and I was consumed in flames of agony. But there was no question about it, I simply could not move. I was an old student, sitting in the front row, and the hour wasn't over yet. I *had* to stay still.

I really wish I could go back to that girl, give her a cuddle, and say, 'Liz, sweetheart, stretch out your damn legs!' Because if keeping still results in such untold physical and mental distress then you absolutely should move, otherwise you are just fighting the pain and testing the limits of your willpower … and that's not Vipassana. You need a deep and powerful concentration to be able to observe the physical discomforts in your body with a calm, clear mind and I had completely lost mine. In this situation, the only way to regain some peace of mind is to move the body and get relief. Alas, I stayed rooted to my cushion in agony because I couldn't bear the thought of 'failing' at the task at hand, of not being the perfect model old student to all the new students behind me. I may have managed to hold on till the end but I was a shaking hot mess afterwards and I reckon I smashed world records with my cry-athon that night in bed.

So yes, these courses are gruelling. But the more work you put in, the more you get out of them and, while I may have gone overboard (or even slightly off course) at times, my efforts brought me to a new level of inner strength, determination and humility. When we learned the last part of the technique on the ninth day, 'metta' (loving kindness), it felt exactly like the balm to my soul that Goenka intended it to be. We sat as a large group and silently wished ourselves and the rest of the world happiness and freedom from suffering. With a gentle smile, I felt the energy of the room scoop me up and hold me like a mother lovingly embracing her small child. It was truly beautiful.

After the morning meditation on the tenth day, we were finally allowed to emerge from our inner caves and chat with the other participants as preparation for our return back to normal life the next day. I stayed rooted to my cushion, eyes clamped shut, as I listened to people around me quietly leaving the hall and heard the outside chatter of human voices for the first time in ten days. The thought of emerging from my little meditation bubble seemed impossibly terrifying.

Transitioning back to human interaction is always a bit jarring after so many days in silence, hence it took me nearly an hour to feel brave enough to mingle and chat with the other students, but by the end of the day I felt ready to return to the outside world again. I went to bed that night with indescribable happiness and satisfaction seeping through every cell of my body. I'd done it, I'd survived yet another ten-day Vipassana course (and without organ failure, hooray). I felt like a new woman, and tomorrow, at last, I would see Alex. The excitement in my stomach was monumental.

The next morning we had our final meditation, ate breakfast and then commenced a group clean-up of all the facilities. Once everything was done, I strolled past the large hall with its green corrugated-iron roof, along the winding path bordered by tall conifers with the odd resident monkey, past the slope leading down to the long building with individual bedrooms for females only (the men's accommodation was on the other side of the meditation hall) and finally, past the dining hall where we ate our meals and where we had registered at the beginning of the course. I said a silent goodbye to the beautiful, forested centre, filled with gratitude for the ten days I'd spent there, and then went to collect my bags. It was time to go.

It felt a little surreal stepping outside of the centre's gates at last, knowing I was now free to come and go as I pleased with no set timetable to adhere to. I waved at several other participants standing together chatting and headed straight towards the little café nearby where I'd planned to meet Alex at the end of the course. My heart nearly tripped over itself when I spotted him sitting at a table wearing a red shirt and navy jeans, one leg resting on the other, absentmindedly scratching his forehead.

'Hello, handsome!'

He looked over at me and a smile lit up his face. 'Oh, hello!'

I grinned and went over to hug him, pulling him in tight, delighting in the firm warmth of his body once more and the familiar, sweet scent of coconut oil in his hair. He wrapped his arms around me before eventually pulling back with a weary smile as we both sat down.

'Alex, you look wrecked!'

'I been travelling entire night, *beta*. I left here just after you start the course, then I had to go to Bangalore, I was still there yesterday and my flight to Delhi got delay. So I miss my bus from Delhi and was worrying I make it to you on time. The boys went back to Jaipur a few days ago.' He paused, sitting back down on the chair. 'Finally I got later bus and came straight here.'

I placed my palm gently on his cheek. 'No wonder you're so tired.'

He said nothing for a moment, then looked straight at me. '*Beta*, you are still looking a bit weak.'

'Having only two healthy meals a day was never going to fatten me up, despite the fact that I just spent the last ten days sitting on my ass. Anyway, I may look weak, but I feel amazing!'

And I really did. The worries and stresses from before the course had just melted away and I felt calm, positive and ready to tackle anything.

'I think you should see the doctor in Ireland.'

'OK, I will, I promise.' And then suddenly, I remembered. 'Alex – your visa! Did you get it?'

'Ah, no,' he said, but he was still smiling.

I frowned in confusion.

'They said I can appeal the decision no problem. They ask me for more documents.'

'Oh, so you should still get it?' I asked cautiously.

'I'm not totally sure. Let's have chai,' he said, signalling to the café owner. He clearly needed tea, and probably a long nap, before we could discuss matters further.

'We'll get it sorted,' I said firmly.

'So how was your Vipassana?' Alex asked me, taking my hand in his and rubbing it.

I paused, considering the question. How to answer it?

'It was incredible,' I said finally. 'But it was pretty brutal. I mean, it probably didn't help that I aimed for absolute perfection throughout but then again, it showed me how strong I am when I really put my mind to something.'

We were both silent a moment, watching the clusters of students nearby, chatting and laughing before they headed off.

'Everyone seems so happy,' Alex commented, as our little cups of chai were served.

'Emerging in one piece, after ten days of Vipassana, is definitely something to smile about!' I told him with a wry grin.

'*Aachhaa*,' Alex replied a little absent-mindedly, yawning and leaning back to stretch his arms up over his head. His shirt rose up, revealing his flat, toffee-coloured tummy.

'Darling, you really do look exhausted.'

'I am, *beta*. Sorry.' He smiled apologetically.

'That's OK, we should head to Pine Tree Lodge soon and then you can sleep all you want.'

'*Beta*, maybe I sleep all day, you don't mind?'

'Course not. It's just so good to be back together.'

We shared a grin and then he leaned over and kissed me gently on the cheek. It was wonderful to be back together.

We spent the next two days like a honeymooning couple, relishing the joy of it being just us, without the rest of the boys for once. Then, with only a week left before I was to fly home from Mumbai, we finally caught an overnight bus back to Jaipur. There was a pang in my heart as we left the majestic mountains, descending the steep and windy roads in the haze of dusk. This particular region of the Himalayas had settled itself in a cosy corner of my heart (somewhere I would come back to again and again over the coming years) and leaving the mountains brought home the sad fact that I was soon going to be leaving India herself.

The pang, however, was quickly overshadowed by a large bubble of excitement. After so long away, returning to the West and my old life was a whole adventure in itself, combined with an immense satisfaction and pride in knowing I'd done it: *I'd survived India.*

My meditation practice disappeared completely in the chaos of that last week. Outside of the courses you are advised to practise the body scan for an hour in the morning and evening, although you don't have to follow the rule of sitting completely still. Fitting two hours of meditation into our hectic and busy lives is extremely challenging and certainly, amid all the frenzy and high emotions of preparing for my big return to Ireland, I felt as though I couldn't sit quietly for ten minutes, never mind an hour. It was exactly the kind of situation that called for a daily practice of quiet introspection, but instead, I decided to spend my time drinking chai and going shopping. Priorities, you know?

Curry, Chaos and Love

The few days we spent in Jaipur remain a hazy blur in the prelude to my departure. The daily monsoon rain transformed the dusty, arid city into a mucky, grey one full of puddles, Alex's family kept giving me little gifts to take home and there were frequent outings with Alex and the rest of the boys to the countryside, where they would cook up a feast, drink chai and smoke to their hearts' content. Meanwhile, Alex and I made sure to put together the necessary documents for him to appeal his visa decision. But throughout it all, my entire being was focused like a laser beam in just one direction: homeward.

Chapter 32

Time to say goodbye

'Sid's not coming?' I looked at Alex in dismay, feeling my eyes well up and a lump form in my throat. Conscious of the stares from people nearby, I willed myself not to cry. We were standing on the platform next to our overnight train to Mumbai, just minutes away from departure. Ballu and Ameer had come with us to help us stow our luggage on board and I'd assumed Sid – who had dropped us all at the station – would be there too, but apparently not. Handsome, funny Sid, such an important part of my epic trip, was gone already without even a goodbye.

'Do NOT cry, Liz. Please do not – oh, Liz!'

Despite my inner sergeant's commands, the tears started spilling out and I covered my eyes, mortified to be crying in front of the boys and (what felt like) the hundreds of other people all avidly watching me.

'It's OK, *beta*.' Alex tried to console me, pulling me in for a hug. 'You can talk to him on the phone.' I wiped my eyes and took a deep breath as Alex dialled Sid's number then handed me the phone. That pang of sadness I'd felt on leaving the mountains was now competing valiantly with my excitement to be finally going home, making for a frenzied emotional rollercoaster which soared and dipped randomly and without warning. In other words, I was liable to cry at the drop of a hat (so much for my Vipassana practice).

'Hello?'

'Sid! I thought you were coming to the platform with us. We never got to say goodbye.'

'Sorry Leeze, it's impossible to park there but don't worry *yaar*, we'll see each other again soon. You are coming back to India, isn't it?'

'Of course I am.' I sniffed, unable to hide the fact that I was still in tears.

'*Arrey* why you are crying, Leeze? You must be happy, you're finally going home to your family.'

'I know, I know. Sid, thank you for everything. You guys looked after me like a proper family this whole time. I'll miss you.'

'No thank-yous, Leeze. We will miss you too. Have a good journey home, tell your mum and dad we say hi!'

I laughed at that and finally handed the phone back to Alex just as the train let out a warning blast of its horn. We quickly said goodbye to Ballu and Ameer.

'Bye, Liz. You come back soon,' Ballu told me with his massive smile.

'Come on, *beta*, the train is going!' Alex said, ushering me onto the carriage.

With a smile and a wave, I hopped up the steps of the already moving train, Alex following behind me. Once safely on, we turned around to wave again at the two boys walking alongside.

'*Theek hai bhaiya?*' Alex called out in Hindi.

The boys waggled their heads, grinning and waving as the train picked up speed.

'See you, Leeze!' Ameer called as they finally fell behind us. I glanced at Alex, feeling on the verge of tears yet again.

'This is it, my last train ride in India.'

'Yay!' Alex teased before seeing my face and pulling me in for another hug.

'Don't be sad, *beta*, we still have all day tomorrow together before you leave.'

And that was the main reason my emotional world was so unstable at that moment. Against all my wishes, I was going to be leaving India without Alex. We were still waiting to find out about our appeal on Alex's visa application, so for now, we didn't know if or when he would come to Ireland. This meant that in two days' time I would be arriving at the conclusion of my incredible journey minus the most important part of the entire trip. I simply couldn't imagine leaving Alex behind me with such uncertainty hanging over us as to when we'd next see each other, but my money was pretty much gone. I had to go home, for every reason.

'Come on, darling, have some chai,' Alex told me firmly, stopping a passing chai vendor while I tried to pull myself together. Nothing better for easing the tears than a hot, sweet, milky tea.

On my last full day in India, I awoke on the trundling train, a few hours away from Mumbai, thinking back to my first ever Indian train journey with Paul and Rob. Ten whole months … where had the time gone? I leaned over my bunk to see if Alex was awake below.

'Morning, *beta*!' he smiled up at me with sleepy eyes.

'Morning. I've been in India almost a whole year, can you believe it? Nearly an entire year of my life in India.'

'Very good. Darling, I spent my whole life in India.'

Rolling my eyes at his sarcasm, I grinned at him none-theless. Everything becomes more precious when you realise it will soon be gone.

We finally arrived into Mumbai, found a hotel on the outskirts that would let us stay together – not an easy feat in this city – and headed into the huge metropolis to do the last bit of my souvenir shopping. I had begun my trip wandering the streets of Colaba with a fellow Irishman at my side, but I was ending it on those same streets with an Indian sweetheart. I had to smile every time I considered how this trip had turned out.

* * *

'How do I look?'

Alex tore his gaze away from the TV.

'Oh, you looks good, *beta*,' he said honestly, before turn-ing his attention back to the screen.

'Well, I'm ready,' I told him pointedly. It was a moment before he glanced back over.

'*Aachhaa*, so we go,' he said with a smile, switching off the TV and coming over to envelop me in a big hug.

'I'll miss you, *beta*,' he mumbled a moment later.

'Shut up, darling, or I'm going to start crying again.'

Sniffing back tears that had been flowing on and off all day, I gave him a peck on the cheek and we went out to catch a taxi.

'Just wait until you try the food,' I said for about the third time that day as we drove through the evening traffic. 'And how fitting is it that I had my first dinner in India in Khyber restaurant and now I'll have my last one there with you?'

Alex nodded an absentminded 'yes dear', singing a song he'd been mindlessly humming all day and tapping his hand on my leg to the words *'I love you'*, our hands clasped firmly in each others'. It was so cute it made me want to cry. Pulling up outside Khyber at last, we entered the plush, high-ceilinged building and a well-groomed waiter approached us.

'Good evening sir, evening ma'am, welcome. Table for two?'

'Yes please,' I answered as Alex glanced around him a little uncertainly.

The waiter showed us to a small table in the corner, elegantly laid out with cloth serviettes and heavy, shiny cutlery. As we sat down, he placed thick leather menus in front of us. Classical Indian music hummed softly in the background, accompanied by the murmur of customers and the gentle tapping of shoes against the marble floor. It was exquisite and just as I remembered it.

'Isn't this place gorgeous?'

'It's very fancy.'

Alex opened the menu but continued to look around him warily, still humming the same song under his breath.

'Are you OK, darling? You don't seem very relaxed.'

I leaned over, placing my hand on his knee, and he smiled nervously as if he'd been caught out.

'To be true, *beta*, I don't really like eating in such a posh restaurant because I'm not good with knife and fork,' he admitted, picking up a utensil and inspecting it apprehensively.

My heart sank. For our last meal together, I'd inadvertently brought him somewhere that made him uncomfortable.

'Crap, I didn't realise. Look, we'll just order *naan* bread, you don't even need to use the cutlery. I'm so sorry!'

'No problem, *beta*, we can enjoy, no?' He smiled and, trying to reassure me, took my hand.

I grinned at him as we interlinked fingers. 'Come on, what should we order?' I asked finally, turning my gaze back to the menu as I realised how hungry I was.

Once the food arrived, Alex visibly relaxed.

'What do you reckon? Is it up to your high standards?' I teased, licking my fingers.

'Hmm, is good!' came his slightly surprised reply.

A while later, stirring sugar cubes into our tea, we were both silent.

'You won't forget me when you go back to Ireland, *beta*?' Alex suddenly blurted out. I stared at him.

'How could you even ask?' I swallowed a gulp of hot chai to distract myself from crying yet again.

'Sorry, *beta*, I know you won't forget. Please don't cry here, just wait till we get back to the hotel.'

I had to giggle. In private he would hug and console me while I cried for Ireland, but he just couldn't handle me getting upset in public.

'Sorry, you're right.'

Alex looked at me carefully, studying me almost, and I wondered what he was thinking. 'Oh, Miss Blue Eyes!' he exclaimed happily. I found it both sweet and ironic because, while he was so enthralled with my grey-blue eyes, I just couldn't imagine eyes more perfectly beautiful than his own rich, chocolatey brown ones.

'When you go in Ireland, can you do me one favour?'

'What's that?'

'Can you bring back my chubby Liz?'

I grinned at his earnest expression. Only in India would this be considered a compliment. 'OK.'

'Good, *beta*. But please, you don't come back an elephant!'

I burst out laughing.

'*Arrey*, what's so funny?'

'You, Alex. Just you.'

In the taxi on the way home, he started humming again, tapping our clasped hands on my knee and nodding to the beat of his song, smiling at me each time he sang the words '*I love you.*'

I squeezed his warm hand in mine, wishing the moment would never end.

* * *

'Here *beta*, take this,' Alex insisted, stuffing a large sum of Indian rupees into my hands as the tuk-tuk jigged and bounced its way through a light monsoon shower. 'Airports are expensive, maybe you need it.'

'No, darling, it's fine–'

'Take it, that's an order! *Arrey*, I'm joking, Liz, don't cry please.'

'I'm sorry, I can't help it. I don't want to say goodbye.'

Alex put his arm around my shoulders and squeezed me close. 'I know, *beta*, I don't want you to leave too. But hopefully in a couple weeks I come to Ireland.'

He consoled me with a gentle kiss on my cheek as we rounded a bend and the airport came into sight. Moments later, my heart sinking, we pulled up outside the departures entrance. Alex got a trolley for my crammed backpack while I triple-checked I had my passport and ticket.

'Alright, *beta*?'

As Alex gave me a huge bear hug I dissolved into sobs, totally heartbroken. After so long away, I had to leave India without him, which wasn't how it was meant to end, surely? It felt like being split down the middle and yet it was time to go, of that I was certain. India was gently but firmly sending me home.

Alex held me tight as I wept like a baby. At last, he pulled back, wiping away my tears and smiling at me gently. 'You should go, *beta*, no? You don't want to miss your plane.'

'I know, I know. I'll miss you, darling!'

'I'll miss you too, *beta*. So much!'

We hugged one last time and I wrapped my arms around him fiercely, wanting to hold on forever. This goodbye stuff sucked.

'Darling!' Alex mumbled into my neck.

I sighed.

'I know. I should go.'

We pulled apart.

'Alex, I just can't thank you enough for everything you've done for me.'

'It was my duty, *beta*,' he replied simply. 'When I come to Ireland you'll do the same, no?'

'Absolutely, darling, and I'll pay for everything!'

I didn't like to think about how much more expensive Ireland was compared to India but at any rate, in that moment, I would have bought him the sun, the moon and the stars if that's what he'd wanted. And then we couldn't delay it any longer. It was time to go.

One final hug, one more kiss goodbye and at last, with a teary, drooping heart, I tore myself away and pushed my trolley up to the entrance. As the security guard handed me back my ticket and passport, I turned to wave and this time, unlike in Trivandrum, Alex stood out plain and clear.

'Oh, *beta*? Bring back my chubby Liz, OK?'

I blew him a kiss, smiling through watery eyes.

'Bye, darling.'

'Goodbye, *beta*.'

* * *

After ten life-changing months I was going home a new person – quite literally, given I was now almost two dress sizes smaller than when I'd left (my weight-loss remains to this day an inexplicable, lasting influence of my travels, with no ill-effects). The magic of this unique country had blown open my mind and radically altered my entire inner world from day one. Everything about those first few days in Mumbai had felt completely alien to me, as though I were no longer even on planet Earth. Throughout the subsequent ten months India had continued to work on me, toppling old, conditioned beliefs and expectations and pushing me so far outside my comfort zone that the only thing I could possibly do was surrender, just to survive.

On reflection, as I walked slowly away from my Rajasthani sweetheart and the most amazing adventure of my young life, I realised I had not only survived India, I had absolutely thrived on the whole experience. From food spicy enough to blow my head off to the milkiest sweetest chai; weed and alcohol to spiritual inquiry; scamming opportunists to kindness and warmth from total strangers; overwhelming poverty to outrageous wealth and luxury; tropical beaches to arid deserts to mighty mountains; epic train journeys; even more epic road trips; monkeys, camels and magnificent elephants; the boiling southern tip and the majestic snow-peaked Himalayas; the infinite generosity of Alex's family; my sweet adoptive Indian brothers; my two dear 'bodyguards', Paul and Rob; Alex and his deep, unconditional love for me ...

I never knew before going why I felt so compelled to visit India but given the above, how could I ever not have gone? As I waited to check in, I thought back to those first two months and how my efforts to meet up with Jack had backfired repeatedly after that fateful decision to travel up north with Paul and Rob. What if I had never shared the taxi with Paul into Colaba? What if I had chosen to go south to Goa, instead of Rajasthan with the boys, and had succeeded in meeting Jack? Where might I have ended up and would I ever have crossed paths with Alex?

I would never know the answer to those questions. The only thing I could be sure of was that travelling to India was the best thing I had ever done. Over the course of nearly a year, the subcontinent had expanded my mind and taken root deep in my heart. She was part of my life now and it felt as strange to be heading back west as it had felt arriving into Mumbai all those months ago. But just as she had first called me and persuaded me to come to her, this time India was gently insisting I leave. My incredible adventure had finally come to an end. It was time to go home.

For now ...

Acknowledgements

I have to thank my Mum and Dad for their ongoing support, in more ways than just this book; if not for them, the story would probably still just be on my laptop. My Mum, especially, has championed this project from the beginning.

Thanks to Úna, for sharing some brilliant insights and suggestions, and to Liz Keyes and my brother Rob for taking the time to read and advise.

Conor Reidy and Anne Cunningham, two great editors, helped enormously with their professional services. Thanks to them, the story and characters actually make sense. And because I kept on tweaking and perfecting the manuscript for another year afterwards, I had to get it proof-read a second time and Carrowmore Publishing helped me to polish the manuscript until it sparkled.

Meanwhile, Orla Kelly Publishing transformed the simple manuscript into this wonderful book! Not an easy feat and not one I could have done without her excellent services.

The magnificent cover design and map were created by Aisling Griffin of Treetop Studio; I never imagined a graphic designer could so perfectly capture the feeling of my story. Thank you so much Aisling! Find her here: www.treetopstudio.ie

The people who crossed paths with me throughout my travels are the essence of this book. Travel connects you to such an array of fascinating and diverse humans, however brief the encounter. I want to say thank you to each and every person that added their own touch of magic to my story. It's impossible to mention you all but I do have to acknowledge my dear travel buddies, Rob and Paul, who radically altered my entire trip for the better. Big love to you both!

It's no exaggeration to say that my life was utterly transformed by my journey to the mystical subcontinent. India has her problems, like everywhere else, but she is still a magnificent and deeply spiritual land, as are her people. Thank you to all the incredible humans there that looked after me (and also to those that challenged me!) throughout my travels.

Finally, though, this story belongs to one very special human: Alex, my absolute favourite person, who still has my back to this day. Back in 2007, I could never adequately answer the question, 'why India?' But I can now.

For you darling. It was always for you.

About the Author

Liz spent her childhood horse riding, playing piano and writing stories. In her twenties she replaced it all with travel and a mission to 'find herself'. (She's still looking.) Her most powerful spiritual teacher so far has been motherhood and she currently juggles being a Mum with both waitressing and helping her husband run his award-winning, ethical jewellery business, Caraliza Designs.

Born out of 'Curry, Chaos and Love', the name Caraliza contains both 'Cara' (the Gaelic word for friend or 'dear one') and 'Aliza' which combines Liz and Ali's names. They create unique, elegant jewellery designs, ethically handcrafted in sterling silver by their skilled goldsmith Ashis in Alex's hometown of Jaipur. They also sell responsibly sourced, luxurious merino wool shawls. Based in Cork, Ireland, they sell at events around the country as well as online (www.caralizadesigns.com). You can follow them on social media: @caralizadesigns.

In the little spare time Liz has left, she reads up on astrology, takes her little boy for nature walks, dreams of returning to the gym when their baby girl finally allows it and tries to squeeze in some writing. Liz lives in Cork with Alex and their two children, Bowie and Summer. For updates follow her blog www.coffeeandscribbles.com or check out her IG page @coffeeandscribbles.

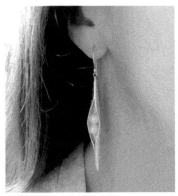

White Pearl Seedpod Earrings

Liz wearing a cosy Caraliza merino wool shawl

Please consider leaving a review!

If you enjoyed this book (and I really hope that you did) then it would mean a lot to me if you could spread the word, leave a review online or share it on social media. Positive reviews really help people in their decision to purchase books. Thank you so much!

Liz